DIALECTIC AND NARRATIVE

REVISIONS
A Series of Books on Ethics
General Editors
Stanley Hauerwas and Alasdair MacIntyre

DIALECTIC
AND NARRATIVE
IN AQUINAS

An Interpretation of the Summa contra gentiles

THOMAS S. HIBBS

UNIVERSITY OF NOTRE DAME PRESS

Notre Dame and London

Manufactured in the United States of America

Library of Congress Cataloging-in-Publication Data

Hibbs, Thomas S.
  Dialectic and narrative in Aquinas : an interpretation of the Summa contra
gentiles / Thomas S. Hibbs.
     p.   cm. — (Revisions)
  Includes bibliographical references.
  ISBN 0–268–00878–7 (alk. paper)
    1. Thomas, Aquinas, Saint, 1225?–1274. Summa contra gentiles.   2. Apolo-
getics.   3. Theology, Doctrinal.   4. Catholic Church—Doctrines.   I. Title.
II. Series.
BX1749.T45H53   1995
239—dc20   94–42615
                                                                          CIP

⊚ *The paper used in this publication meets the minimum requirements*
of the American National Standard for Information Sciences—Permanence of Paper
for Printed Library Materials, ANSI Z39.48-1984

FOR

MY PARENTS, MY BROTHER, AND MY SISTER

CONTENTS

ACKNOWLEDGMENTS

The remote origin of this study was a paper written for a graduate seminar on the *Summa Contra Gentiles* taught by Mark Jordan at the University of Dallas in the spring of 1982. Both his teaching of Aquinas and his essay on "The Protreptic Structure of the Summa Contra Gentiles" (*Thomist* 50 [1986], pp. 173–209) have been seminal influences on my thinking about the *Contra Gentiles*.

A number of grants made possible the writing of the book. A Research Incentive Grant from Boston College supported my work during the summer of 1991. As director of the program in Medieval Philosophy and Theology at Boston College, Steven Brown was instrumental in securing a grant from the Bradley Foundation, from which I received funding for research during the summer of 1992; for the years 1992–1994, the Bradley Foundation also supplied funds for a teaching assistant.

Steven Brown, Thomas D'Andrea, Mark Jordan, Fred Lawrence, and Norman Wells read portions of the manuscript and made helpful suggestions. Stanley Hauerwas and Alasdair MacIntyre, the editors of the Revisions series, made valuable suggestions, as did Jim Langford of the University of Notre Dame Press. John McCudden, a free-lance editor, made numerous helpful corrections.

Many authors of scholarly works express gratitude to their spouses for support during the period of composition. I used to regard such remarks as gratuitous. Having observed the multiplication and swelling of my own obsessions during the writing of this book, I repent my earlier thoughts. My wife, Stacey, deserves much credit, and not just for her patience and encouragement. She is the only person (other than the editors) to have been subjected to reading the whole manuscript; she has proven an indispensable editor, casting a critical eye on cumbersome, academic prose. What clarity there is in the writing is greatly attributable to her.

Some of my debts precede the support given to me by many generous individuals during the writing of the book. My parents, William and Shirley Hibbs, my brother, Michael, and my sister, Elizabeth, who were alternately exasperated and entertained by the far from intellectual obsessions of my youth, provided my first and enduring glimpse of the narrative of divine providence. My parents especially attempted to inspire in me the love of learning and the desire for God. For the arguments and the love, the sorrow and the laughter, we have shared over the years, I am deeply grateful. To them the book is dedicated.

1

PEDAGOGY AND THE ART OF WRITING

I. THE PRACTICE OF VIRTUE AND THE ART OF WRITING

Questions of style and rhetoric are not usually seen as relevant to the texts of Aquinas. In an effort to reach and present the truth as lucidly as possible, Thomas prefers to speak and write formally (*formaliter*). Among the arts concerned with speaking and writing, rhetoric receives less attention than grammar, and both of these much less than logic. Thomas calls poetry the lowest of doctrines.[1] He does defend the scriptural use of metaphor, but this is an exception that proves the rule, since scripture alone is able to raise the mind from sensible images to intelligible truth.[2] The pejorative assessments of poetry and rhetoric should not, however, be taken as the final word on the question of writing in Aquinas. For Thomas, matters of style are subordinate to pedagogical concerns.[3] In his many writings, Thomas avails himself of different genres of philosophic and theological composition. Some have suggested that he was searching for a way to present Christian theology in its integrity and amplitude. Evidence for his interest in the shape of Christian teaching can be had from the opening of the *Summa Theologiae*, where he describes the state of disarray of contemporary Christian teaching. The *Summa* attempts to reform the method and style of theology in order to improve theological teaching.

Tradition honors the *Summa Theologiae* as Thomas's most polished presentation of his own teaching. The impressive achievement of that text has led to a certain neglect of the other *Summa*, the *Summa Contra Gentiles*.[4] The purported missionary intent of the latter text has also had something to do with its neglect; a long tradition holds that Thomas composed the work at the request of Raymond of Penafort, onetime master general of the Dominicans, to be used as a missionary manual in Spain. A comparison of the titles of the two works seems to support the view that the *Contra Gentiles* has a more parochial end in view than does the *Summa Theologiae*. The received view of the *Contra Gentiles* is open to question, however.[5] Even the title is somewhat suspect, as the manuscripts favor the title *Book on the Truth of the Catholic Faith against the Errors of the Infidels* (*Liber de veritate catholice fidei contra errores infidelium*).[6] The difference between a *summa* and a *liber* is significant; the former contains both a complete and a summary treatment of topics, while the latter may focus on specific issues in greater detail and need not be limited to a mode of presentation tailored to a beginning audience.[7]

The importance and distinctiveness of the *Contra Gentiles* among Thomas's writings have not been completely unnoticed. Written between 1259 and 1264—after the commentaries on the *Sentences* and Boethius, and the disputed questions *De Veritate*, but before the commentaries on Aristotle and the *Summa Theologiae*—the *Contra Gentiles* has been called Thomas's "personal synthesis."[8] Chenu remarks that the structure and content of the work are determined by a "personal initiative" of the author.[9] Among Thomas's writings, the *Contra Gentiles* is the least determined by the form of public debate in the universities or by the tradition of commenting on authoritative texts, even if the work includes both of these approaches. Gilson notes that the work draws "arguments from many and diverse philosophies" and confirms "conclusions by means of all sorts of reasons whose very multiplicity is liable to embarrass beginners."[10]

The "personal initiative" of the work and its complex argumentative structure set the *Contra Gentiles* apart from all of Thomas's other works. The intention, method, and structure of the work remain subjects of debate. The assertion of a missionary intent is, as we shall see, unfounded, while the vague and somewhat anachronistic description of the work as apologetic raises more questions than it answers. The very title of the work, especially the phrase *contra gentiles*, has been supposed to support both the missionary and the apologetic reading. Yet, as Mark Jordan has shown, the term *gentiles* refers to "pre- or extra-Christian man," especially to the Greek philosophers, who represent the peak achievement of reason "under the tutelage of nature."[11] The title thus suggests the importance of pagan philosophy. The opening chapters of the prologue, which focus on wisdom, reinforce the emphasis on philosophy. Since wisdom is common to both philosophy and Christian theology, the work promises to do more than fulfill the ephemeral needs of the Spanish mission. It promises an explicit and sustained consideration of the relationship between pagan and Christian wisdom. The plethora of references to the wisdom literature of the Old Testatment in the first three books further illustrates the centrality of wisdom. No other work of Thomas focuses on the great debates of antiquity over the best way of life and over who teaches authoritatively concerning the highest good.

The prominence of wisdom in the prologue reveals the mode in which the text must be received by its audience. The first chapter, on the office of the wise, describes the wise person as one who orders parts in relation to the whole and who teaches the authoritative truth about the ultimate end of the universe. Thomas offers a sustained comparison between the practice of wisdom and the practices of crafts and sciences. In so doing, Thomas emphasizes the pursuit of goods internal and proper to an art, goods which are identified, ranked, and achieved only by master artisans. As he puts it,

> Of all things ordered to an end, the rule of their governance and order is taken from the end. A thing is best disposed when it is suitably ordered to its end, for the end is the good of the thing. Thus we see in the arts that the one, to whom the securing of the end pertains, is governor and ruler of another. . . . Arts that rule other arts are called architectonic. . . . The artisans . . . of these arts claim for themselves the name of the wise. (I, 1)[12]

Of the capacities possessed by artisans, Thomas focuses upon the political virtues of ordering and governing, which bring to the fore notions of hierarchy and pedagogy. Hierarchy is germane both to the ordering of goods within a particular craft and to the arrangement of various crafts in relation to one another. Wisdom orders subordinate practices or inquiries to the proper end of the art. Among a number of arts, moreover, the one that orders the rest to some unified end is said to be architectonic. Wisdom properly belongs to the one who considers the end of the entire universe, for, as Aristotle states, "it is for the wise to consider the highest causes."

The *Contra Gentiles* is an exercise in wisdom. The text presupposes some measure of intellectual virtue in its readers and provides ample opportunity for further exercise of those virtues.[13] Thomas's comparison of wisdom to a craft indicates that only those who are practitioners of intellectual virtue will profit from the text. Progress in any discipline requires submission to an authoritative practitioner, who aids the student in the gradual appropriation of the relevant virtues. Wisdom is an intellectual virtue, whose inculcation occurs through education and habituation.

While the text addresses issues that have been discussed in various cultures and at different times, Thomas dilutes neither his philosophical nor his theological sources in an effort to address an untrained interlocutor. Instead, he embraces an Aristotelian conception of wisdom and of the contemplative life, with its hierarchical understanding of the order of learning. Progress in philosophy presupposes knowledge of logic and mathematics; the student is to proceed in an orderly manner from natural philosophy through the investigation of the soul, ethics, and politics, and on to metaphysics.[14] In the opening of the *Contra Gentiles*, Thomas has little to say about the disciplines ancillary to metaphysics. The text is replete, furthermore, with references to authorities from various traditions. Thus, the text presupposes both erudition and intellectual virtue in its audience. A successful reader will be one who is situated appropriately with respect to the pertinent authorities and arguments. Appreciation of Aquinas's teaching entails apprehending its arguments from the vantage point afforded by the possession of the virtues.

The prominence of Aristotle in the prologue and throughout the text reveals that Thomas is working within a received tradition, with its set of authoritative texts. In many sections, he shows that support for a position can be found both in reason and in the words of Aristotle. Indeed, Thomas practices an art of reading in his interpretation of Aristotle's texts and in his dialectical encounters with Aristotle's commentators. He employs a host of dialectical strategies, which are the textual embodiment of the intellectual virtue of the author. Progress in the reading of the text, conversely, is possible only on the condition of docility to its pedagogy, that is, on the condition of the exercise of the relevant virtues. Jacob Klein's observation about the reading of Plato's dialogues is germane: without the active participation of the reader, "all that is before us is indeed nothing but a book."[15]

Many commentators have observed the complex, argumentative structure of the work. The method is largely dialectical. It reflects Aristotle's conception of dialectical inquiry, which is itself a continuation of the Platonic dialogue. The text has many extended dialectical encounters with received opinions. Thomas even uses versions of the phrase "to save the appearances," which is central to Aristotle's conception of dialectical inquiry.[16] As Aristotle puts it in *Nichomachean Ethics* VII, 1 (1145b2–7),

> As in other things, so too here it is necessary to set out the phenomena and, after having examined the problems, display the truth of all the reputable opinions . . . or at least, of the greater number and the most authoritative; if the difficulties are resolved and the opinions are left standing, the matter will have been adequately explained.

Dialectic serves to save the "reputable opinions," which include "observed facts" and received interpretations of the facts, and to resolve difficulties. It also provides, as Aristotle states in the *Topics*, a means of discovering first principles. Given the prominence of dialectic in the *Contra Gentiles*, the work might well be understood as a field for the pedagogical induction of principles, for the practice of what Aristotle called *epagogue*. Since a mark of wisdom is the ability to teach, Thomas's role is to present the phenomena and set up the conflict of received opinions in a way that facilitates the induction of principles, the elucidation of their import, scope, and application. In the *Contra Gentiles*, Thomas has this to say about teaching:

> The one teaching begins to teach in the same way that the one discovering begins to discover. . . . The external action of the teacher would be ineffective without the internal principle of knowledge. . . . As the physician is called a minister of nature in the practice of healing, so too the master engenders knowledge in the student, by way . . . of art. (II, 75)[17]

Like every art, teaching succeeds by producing; its goal is to produce dispositions or habits in the soul of the learner. But there is a crucial difference between the ways in which various productive arts reach their respective ends. In some, the matter to be formed is merely passive with respect to the agent, while in others, such as medicine, there is an active principle in the matter tending toward the end that the art helps to engender. Teaching is the latter sort of art; it cooperates with, and depends upon, the active powers of the student. The fixity of written words is, as Plato warns, an impediment to pedagogy. The danger is that the reading of mere words will render the student inert. To read a Platonic dialogue successfully is, as John Sallis puts it, "to seek to gain access to philosophy as such, to seek to begin philosophizing, through a response to the provocation which the dialogues are capable of exercising."[18] Like the dialogue, the dialectical structure of the *Contra Gentiles* seeks to provoke the reader to inquiry, to an appropriation of the virtue of wisdom.

Wisdom is an architectonic virtue; it understands the part in relation to the whole and thus supplies the only satisfactory justification of
the foundations and purpose of particular fields of inquiry. Wisdom is,
moreover, the goal of all inquiry. It orders all disciplines in relation to
the transcendent end of the entire universe. Aristotle's first philosophy
culminates in a treatment of the unmoved mover of the entire universe,
a being whose life is identical with contemplation, the activity in which
rational creatures find their fullest actuality and their greatest delight. For
Aristotle, metaphysics is in one sense a continuation of the inquiries of
the subordinate sciences, while in another sense it involves a reversal of
those inquiries. The tension is evident in the ambiguous reference to
metaphysics as *first* philosophy. Its priority is not temporal; instead, its
priority consists in its investigation of the starting points that subordinate
sciences take on trust. First philosophy, then, marks a shift from that
which is first in our experience to what is first in the order of nature
or being. The structure of the *Contra Gentiles*, which is sometimes said
to mirror the neo-Platonic vision of the cosmos as a going forth (*exitus*)
followed by a return (*reditus*), can also be described as continuing the
reversal of discourse begun in Aristotle's metaphysics. Still, the reference
to Platonism is not without merit.

Certain Platonic themes are prominent in the structure of the work.
One useful way of reading the work is in terms of an alternating series
of ascending and descending motions. The first book ascends from sense
experience to God as first cause; the second book considers the coming
forth of creatures from God; the third studies the imitation of, and return
to, God in the natural operations of creatures; and the fourth discusses
God's descent in the Incarnation and the ascent of rational creatures to
the direct vision of God. The theme of ascent and descent is allied to
the distinctively Platonic teaching on the relationship between image
and exemplar. The prominence of the Platonic language of artist and
artwork, exemplar and image, and of ascent and descent has implications
for how the *Contra Gentiles* ought to be read. The ascent begins from
an encounter with things in the world and leads to their transcendent
ground. Having made the ascent, one now sees differently the things
of this world. They are manifestations of their exemplar; or, as Thomas
puts it, "small streams of goodness" flowing from the fount (*fons*) of all
goodness (II, 2). Sensible forms are reflections of the divine wisdom;
human nature is an image of God; and the relationship of God to the
world is that of an artist to his artwork. The consequence for the reader

is that a rectilinear and one-directional reading of the text or of things will not do; instead, lower must be reunderstood in terms of higher, part in light of whole. The text thus requires the reader to double back and rethink earlier statements in light of later assertions. Is this not the hermeneutic correlate of Platonic recollection?[19]

The presence of these Platonic themes places further burdens upon a reader, who must attend to the dialectical or demonstrative features of the *Contra Gentiles* and also to its dialogical or narrative aspects. Although the notion of narrative is, I think, quite appropriate to the *Contra Gentiles*, it is apt to mislead. Narrative theories enjoy a certain currency now in ethics, hermeneutics, and theology. But the notion of narrative is so fluid that it risks vacuity. In Thomas's texts, dialectic finds explicit endorsement, while narrative seems to be a postmodern accretion. Indeed, the turn to narrative is sometimes understood to be a reaction against Kant, but it too often allows Kant to set the terms of the debate, that is, narrative is frequently allied to an antirealist, antimetaphysical epistemology. How can such a notion be compatible with Aquinas's *Contra Gentiles*, especially given the prominence of metaphysics in the text?

What makes the notion of narrative legitimate, indeed inescapable, is not a diminished appreciation or deconstruction of the metaphysics of the *Contra Gentiles*, but a proper understanding of it. Thomas's peculiar appropriation of the neo-Platonic motif of the *exitus-reditus* highlights the contingency of creation, in its origin and its endurance. The neo-Platonic tradition tends to view the motion of descent and return as a necessary, inevitable process. For Thomas, however, God is perfect and free; creation need not have been at all. Once creation exists, moreover, it remains dependent upon God, who may intervene in the natural order at his discretion. The openness of creation to divine initiative accentuates the importance of a nonlinear reading of things. What is available to us at our own level and by means of our own ability can never be the final word on the narrative of creation. What comes to light at a certain point in a narrative may well engender a revision of previous events or statements.

A nonlinear reading accords well with Thomas's distinction between the way the believer, in contrast to the philosopher, considers natural things. While the philosopher examines things as they are in themselves, the believer considers them as effects and signs of God (II, 4). The relationship of God to creation is that of an artist to an artifact. As an unfolding of divine providence, creation is a sort of narration (*narratio*), "a setting forth, an exposition, a telling or relating." In addition to creation, revelation, especially scripture, provides further access to divine providence. Thomas reads scripture as an authoritative narration. His treatment of the several senses of scriptural speech is instructive.[20] The polysemous character of scriptural speech is rooted in the peculiar capacity of its author, who can make not only words but also things signify. The historical or literal sense includes the narration of events. Thomas's illustrations of two of the spiritual senses, the allegorical and the anagogical, indicate the scope of the scriptural narrative. The allegorical sense of the Old Law, as of many parts of the Old Testament, is its figurative anticipation of the New Law. But not even the New Law is an end in itself. The New Law can be understood anagogically as a figural anticipation of future glory. Thus, scripture is a narrative not just in the ordinary sense of the term, as containing stories of various events. More profoundly, scripture is a narrative that divides and organizes the whole of time in relation to its transcendent beginning and end.

The structure of the *Contra Gentiles* is informed by precisely such an understanding of scriptural narrative. The chief objection to this reading comes from Thomas's division of the work in terms of the twofold mode of truth. The first three books treat of the first mode, of what is accessible to reason, while the fourth book treats of the second mode, of what transcends reason (I, 3). The influence of scripture, then, might seem to be appropriate only in the last book. Although it is not until the fourth book that scripture becomes a subject of inquiry in its own right, scriptural passages figure prominently in crucial sections of the first three books. I do not mean that they provide premises for arguments, but rather that they confirm and buttress certain arguments. They are, as Gauthier puts it, the "end and the reason for the proof."[21] Perhaps what is more important, scriptural themes and teachings inform the structure of particular sections and of the whole. Principles for the exclusion and inclusion of topics are often scriptural. Thomas devotes most attention to those philosophic debates that touch upon scriptural teachings concerning the nature of God, his relationship to the universe, and his providential orchestration of human salvation. Scriptural narrative thus has a certain primacy even in the first three books.

The common objection that the segregation of the first three books from the fourth risks presenting the properly theological teaching of the last book as an addendum to the so-called philosophical portion of the work is unwarranted. What is accessible to natural reason is subordinate to, and incorporated within, the comprehensive narrative of divine providence. Far from being an anachronistic imposition, the emphasis on narrative is thoroughly Augustinian. Consider Augustine's comment about human history: "Although the past institutions of human beings are set forth in historical narratives, history itself is not numbered among human institutions; for things that have transpired and cannot be undone belong to the order of time, whose author and administrator is God."[22]

The apprehension of nature from the vantage point of divine providence is not of course available to the *gentiles*. Just as those who lack the intellectual virtue of wisdom cannot but see the philosophic life as absurd, so too those who have not the dispositions requisite for Christian wisdom are likely to see the teaching of scripture as "foolishness." Thomas does indeed argue for the convergence of philosophy with a portion of what is revealed. He also argues that under the tutelage of grace the natural operation of reason is healed and perfected. Nonetheless, the dramatic narrative of scripture, which is prominent at the end of the third and throughout the fourth book of the *Contra Gentiles*, brings to the fore the radical shift in perspective involved in moving from philosophical to theological wisdom.

II. ORDER OF PROCEEDING

Much of what I have suggested about Thomas's art of writing in the *Contra Gentiles* is controversial. Indeed, what might appear to be a neutral use of passages can be defended only in light of a reading of the whole text. In what follows, I will do just that, by offering a reading of the method and structure of each book of the *Contra Gentiles* and, where appropriate, of the relationships among the books. Before turning to an exposition of the body of the text, it is important to attend to the prologue, which has provided the point of departure for most discussions of the work. A consideration of the prologue will enable us to have before us the various contending positions on the intent, method, and structure of the *Summa Contra Gentiles*. Against some of these positions and in partial agreement with others, I will outline my own reading of the work.

III. THE PROBLEMS OF THE PROLOGUE

In the third chapter of the prologue to the *Summa Contra Gentiles*, Thomas introduces the twofold mode of truth (*duplex veritatis modus*) concerning divine things. The distinction has been the source of many controversies;

it has figured prominently in accounts of Aquinas's understanding of the relationship between faith and reason, theology and philosophy. The very structure of the work evinces the importance of the distinction, as Thomas devotes the first three books to the first mode and the fourth book to the second mode (I, 9). Consequently, debates over the intent and structure of the *Contra Gentiles* have focused on the third chapter of the first book. The first mode, the purported mode of reason or philosophy, concerns what "faith professes and reason investigates" (*fides profitetur et ratio investigat*), while the second mode treats of that portion of revelation wholly inaccessible to reason. The distinction raises numerous questions. First, what motivates the distinction? A missionary goal or some other apologetic intent? The desire to establish a Christian philosophy? Or to accommodate Aristotle? Second, does the distinction correspond to that between philosophy and theology, reason and faith? Does the first mode allow reason to operate autonomously? Does it require that faith be held in abeyance? Or does faith provide the overarching context within which even reason operates? Third, how is the unity of the two modes established? Does reason perform this function? Or is unity assumed from the outset? Even if the unity of the two modes is not problematic, how is one to avoid seeing the matters of the fourth book as anything more than an addendum to earlier teachings? A final set of questions concerns the appropriateness of the contents of the first three books, which comprise those teachings amenable to rational proof; these books include not only the topics of the existence and nature of God and of human nature, but also creation in time, the angelic hierarchy, the question of natural desire for the beatific vision, divine law, the theological virtues, and the counsels. Are not at least some of the topics properly theological? What justifies their inclusion in the first mode?

Adequate answers to these queries can be had only from a reading of the whole of the *Contra Gentiles*. Nonetheless, the prologue provides some assistance, even as it raises difficulties. The answer to the question of what motivates the distinction has historically been tied to a tradition of regarding the work as a Dominican missionary manual. Chenu summarizes the traditional reading:

> A long tradition holds that Saint Thomas composed his work at the request of Raymond de Peñafort . . . , master general of the order of preachers, who, haunted by the presence of the Moors in the land of Spain and by the new hope of converting Islam, commanded his young colleague to equip missionaries with necessary intellectual arms.[23]

A modified version of the missionary thesis is defended by Gorce, according to whom the *Contra Gentiles* aims not at converting Muslims but at refuting the nascent Averroism in the universities.[24] Gauthier comments that, for Gorce, the work "remains thus a missionary instrument, but of an interior mission," an instrument of "university apologetic."[25] Gorce's thesis rests on feebly established premises, especially since the Latin Averroists he identifies as the targets of the work did not yet exist.[26]

The prologue does, however, lend some support to a missionary reading. Thomas insists that debate should occur on common ground with the interlocutors. When a believer engages someone who does not share the faith, it will often be helpful to resort to the common ground of what is accessible to reason. He writes, "since some, for instance, the Muslims and the pagans, do not agree with us on the authority of scripture, through which they might be convinced, . . . we must revert to natural reason, to which all must assent, although it is deficient in things divine" (I, 2).[27] Later in the prologue, Thomas argues that the Muslim religion could not be true because of Mohammad's false teachings concerning eternal life. Such passages provide the point of departure for a missionary reading. The difficulty is that these remarks do not inform the content or structure of the body of the book.

Insuperable problems beset any attempt to link the work to a missionary project.[28] I will list here only the most striking objections.[29] First, if the work had been written in response to Raymond's request, one would expect a letter of dedication to accompany it. Second, as Jordan and Gauthier note, the Dominican order stipulated that those involved with missionary work be conversant with the intellectual beliefs and cultural practices of those whom they sought to convert. Yet the *Summa Contra Gentiles* ignores completely the details of Muslim religion. Gauthier rightly observes that if Thomas had written a missionary manual devoid of concrete reference to "the real situation," "the error would have been gross."[30] Third, nearly all the missionary interpretations of the text find confirming evidence in the pervasiveness of the phrase "contra gentiles" in the manuscripts. Yet this in no way supports the desired conclusion.

As Jordan convincingly argues, the Greeks for Thomas are a "metonym" for all gentiles and the *gentiles* themselves represent "historically, pre- or extra–Christian man, and, metaphorically, the human mind under the tutelage of nature."[31] Jordan's reading finds partial support in the prologue itself, where Thomas discusses the difficulty of uncovering the meaning of the arguments of the *gentiles*: "In this way the ancient teachers were accustomed to destroy the errors of the *gentiles*, whose positions they could know because they themselves had been *gentiles* or lived among *gentiles* and were learned in their teachings" (I, 2).[32] In another section of the prologue, Thomas quotes the scriptural passage, "Now you do not walk as the gentiles do, in the emptiness of their sense, having their mind obscured in darkness" (Eph., 4:17).[33] Clearly, both passages link the *gentiles* or *gentes* to "pre- or extra-Christian man," especially to the ancients, not specifically to the Muslims. The first passage is noteworthy for another reason. In it, Thomas explicitly links the full appreciation of particular teachings to participation in a way of inquiry, even a way of life. Given the Thomistic and Dominican emphasis upon the need for detailed knowledge of those with whom one engages and Thomas's ignorance of Muslim culture, the work could not possibly be intended for missionary use. Indeed, the errors that Thomas labors to correct in the first three books are most often those of the early Greek natural philosophers and the Arabic interpreters of Aristotle.[34] The final book, which treats of properly revealed teachings, focuses on neither contemporary nor widespread heresies, but on those heresies opposed to the "most profound truths" of the Catholic faith. Gauthier concludes, "the catalogue of errors refuted by Saint Thomas . . . establishes definitively that the *Summa Contra Gentiles* is not a missionary work."[35]

If the motive is not missionary, what is it? In a review of some of the literature on the *Contra Gentiles*, Feret points out the "anachronism" of attempting to classify Thomas's project in terms of modern divisions of apologetics, philosophy, and theology.[36] The early debates over the *Contra Gentiles* focused on the issue of Thomas's fidelity to the division of the work according to the "twofold mode of truth." Questions persist concerning the inclusion in the first three books—the books that treat of what is accessible to reason—of such topics as creation in time (II, 31–39), the ultimate end (III, 48–63), the revealed law (III, 113–42), and divine grace (III, 143–63). All these topics seem to be inaccessible to reason. Most commentators have either accused Thomas of being unfaithful to the plan articulated in the prologue or they have attempted to excuse his occasional lapses.

M. Blanche and R. Mulard hold that the *Summa Contra Gentiles* is an apologetic work that nonetheless treats all matters under the formality of the revealed.[37] They suggest that the questionable topics included in the first three books should be seen as digressions. The writings of Blanche and Mulard are responses to the thesis of Guy de Broglie, who argues that the chapters in the third book on the ultimate end of human life demonstrate the natural desire for God. In his article, de Broglie argues that the segregation of the first three books from the fourth constitutes a formal distinction between philosophy and theology. He states that "the essential and central theses of the first three books" form "a Christian philosophy which has its own consistency."[38] The thesis is unfounded and beset with the difficulties that attend the very notion of a Christian philosophy. Nowhere does Thomas refer to the matter of the first three books as philosophical.[39] The thesis that the first three books constitute a Christian philosophy does have the advantage of indicating that reason is not operating autonomously and that faith is not being set aside. But is it adequate to their complex structure? As Corbin notes, de Broglie's argument, especially concerning the natural desire for God, "proceeds continually by an equivocal displacement."[40] Precisely such equivocations lead Gauthier to claim that there can be no philosophic demonstration of the desire for God. Gauthier thus thinks Thomas has been unfaithful to his original plan but that he corrected the error in the later *Summa*. Thomas sensed the danger involved in "seeming to make the beatific vision, the revealed law, and grace truths accessible to reason."[41]

Noting Thomas's regular practice of citing scripture in the first three books and his explicit adoption in the second book of a theological approach to the study of creatures, Maurice Bouyges argues that "the work is not a philosophic summa" but "a philosophical exposition of Catholic doctrine, deliberately submitted to the control . . . of revelation."[42] Bouyges sees the citation of scriptural texts in the so-called philosophical portion of the work as pointing out to non-Christians the compatibility of what they already hold with Christian revelation.[43] He goes on to suggest that the distinction between the first three books and the fourth is a rhetorical one, having to do with a segregation of matters "discussible and not discussible" before non-Christians.[44] Hence, Jews, Muslims, and Christians share the positions discussed in the first three books, while the fourth book addresses the properly Christian doctrines of the Trinity, the Incarnation, and resurrection of the body. The thesis is problematic. The Muslims, for example, share with Christians a belief in the resurrection of the body. In the first three books, moreover, Thomas does not refer to Jewish and Muslim religious texts in order to establish the common basis for discourse. When Thomas uses the first person plural, he speaks on behalf of Christians, not some larger amalgam.[45] Finally, the thesis makes little sense of the great preoccupation of the first three books: Aristotle and his interpreters.

The division does accommodate the Aristotelian corpus. As we have seen, Aristotelian themes, especially those concerning wisdom, permeate the prologue. As Gauthier has noted, nearly all the authorities who merit Thomas's dialectical attention are Aristotelian commentators: "Aristotle, again Aristotle, always Aristotle . . . the great principle of Thomist hermeneutics."[46] Might not the distinction be motivated by the desire to distinguish in order to unite (to use Maritain's phrase) the two traditions of wisdom: the Aristotelian and the Christian? The division of the work in accordance with the twofold mode of truth follows from the Aristotelian pedagogical principle that inquiry should proceed from "the more manifest to the less manifest." What natural reason can investigate is more manifest to us than revealed truths are. Even more important is the assertion that the distinction is internal to "what we confess" (*quid confitemur*) about divine things (I, 3). In the passage where Thomas posits reason as a common ground of debate, he speaks of the believer's "descent" to reason. Some have taken the reference to "descent" as a sign of the apologetic character of the work. Yet it need not be read in this way. Mark Jordan's suggestion that the *Contra Gentiles* be understood in terms of Thomas's struggle "to find a pedagogical form that would provide an organic unity to the teaching of Christian truth" is to the point.[47]

IV. THE UNITY OF WISDOM(S)

The unified presentation of the two traditions of wisdom is prominent in the introductory chapters of the prologue, chapters that immediately precede the discussion of the "twofold mode of truth." The first chapter of the *Summa Contra Gentiles* announces the theme of the work: wisdom. It describes the relationship between the pursuit of wisdom and other fields of human inquiry. Wisdom is a way of life enacted by those possessing the requisite virtues. While Thomas begins and ends the chapter with Proverbs 8:7, "My mouth shall meditate truth, and my lips shall detest impiety," the chapter has many citations of Aristotle. Thomas rehearses a number of Aristotelian claims: that the office of the wise man is "to order and to govern," that among related disciplines the art or science that guides the rest is called wisdom, and that wisdom without qualification belongs to the science that studies the end of the entire universe.

Thomas embraces the Aristotelian conception of wisdom, with its teleological account of human nature and human inquiry as culminating in a knowledge of the divine. Thomas does not adopt a defensive posture toward the life of reason. Indeed, in the next chapter the philosophic conception of wisdom blends almost imperceptibly with the theological tradition of wisdom. Yet the use of Aristotle is not as straightforward as it might at first appear. Thomas seems to have quietly and without argument settled certain problems in Aristotle's thought. There is a tension in Aristotle over whether the architectonic discipline is politics or metaphysics. In the opening of the *Ethics* (I, 1, 1094a27–b11), he argues on behalf of politics, since it determines and secures the end for the commonwealth and stipulates what is to be studied. Later in the same work, however, he asserts that it would be absurd for contemplative life to be subordinate to the practical life, since the former pursuit is intrinsically superior to the latter (VI, 13, 1145a6–12). Thomas unequivocally assigns the role to the teacher of theoretical wisdom. Thomas's understanding of the contemplative life in terms of the practice of intellectual virtue makes possible the analogy between practical and theoretical lives. Still, there appears to be no analogy between wisdom and crafts, since the latter are practical and have as their end the production of goods. How is contemplation capable of ordering practice as well as theory?[48] Thomas extends the political motif of governing and ordering beyond its Aristotelian scope of ordering the speculative *scientiae*. It now has under its purview the ordering of all things in light of the end of the universe. How does Thomas propose to overcome the tensions in Aristotle's thought between the contemplative and the practical lives, between philosophy and politics?

Thomas introduces additional elements that are at best implicit in Aristotle. He notes, for instance, that the end of the universe is also its origin, and that the ultimate end of the universe is "intended by its first author."[49] Thomas grounds the *telos* of the universe in the providential intelligence of its efficient cause; thus a doctrine of creation undergirds the claim that the theoretical study of the universe provides access to a practical, teleological apprehension of its governance. After asserting that the good of the universe is itself the good of the intellect, namely, truth, Thomas adds that divine Wisdom "assumed flesh and came into the world in order to manifest the truth."[50] What is the relationship between the philosophical pursuit of wisdom about the first principles of the universe and a particular, contingent event within the universe?

Does Thomas here intimate that concrete historical events have become central to the pursuit of the good life? An ascending motion toward the divine characterizes the narrative structure of the philosophical life; how does the descent of God alter that structure? Can the two be reconciled?

Thomas proceeds to praise the pursuit of wisdom as "more perfect, more noble, more useful, and more full of joy" than all other human pursuits (I, 2).[51] Through the pursuit of wisdom one "possesses a certain portion of true beatitude" and "reaches especially to divine likeness" (*ad divinam similitudinem praecipue accedit*). The life of wisdom has as its model the life of God. How is that assertion to be reconciled with Aristotle's repudiation of a related Platonic thesis in *Ethics*, I, 4?[52] Does the grounding of the human and natural in a divine model indicate at least on this issue the subordination of Aristotle to Plato? More important, what is the basis for Thomas's remarkably confident assessment of the efficacy of wisdom in attaining the highest good? The description of the life of wisdom as the intersection of the human and the divine is compatible with Aristotle's *Metaphysics*, I, 1. Yet Thomas's account is more optimistic: not only does wisdom establish friendship between God and us, but it also leads us to immortality (I, 2). Does the pursuit of wisdom unite philosophy and theology? What justifies the passage from one to the other? Clearly Thomas has in mind theological, not just philosophical wisdom. He speaks not of wisdoms but of wisdom. Although there may be many claimants to wisdom, and these may be related analogically, there can strictly speaking be only one wisdom. Wisdom secures knowledge of the highest causes, unifies all learning, and teaches authoritatively about the whole.

Often unnoticed in the discussions of the "twofold mode of truth" is the presupposition of a primordial unity of wisdom. Both natural and supernatural principles are "contained by the divine wisdom" (*haec ergo principia etiam divina sapientia continet*). Thomas writes,

> The knowledge of the teacher contains what is brought forth into the soul of the student by the teacher. . . . The cognition of principles naturally known is divinely given to us, since God himself is the author of our nature. (I, 7)[53]

The argument, which underscores the significance of his previous statement that God is both the end *and* the origin of the universe, envisions the twofold mode of truth as two ways in which God instructs. Philosophical wisdom is made possible by the first gift of God through creation. This teaching influences the very structure of the first three books. While they treat what is accessible to reason, their order of presentation reverses the philosophical order. Whereas Aristotle's corpus moves from natural philosophy through psychology to metaphysics, the *Contra Gentiles* starts with God in himself (*secundum seipsum*) and then addresses the coming forth of creatures from God (*de processu creaturarum ab ipso*) and finally their return to the first principle (*de ordine creaturarum in ipsum, sicut in finem*) (I, 9).

As Corbin has noted, the ordering of the first three books reflects an *exitus-reditus* structure. Corbin observes that most exegetes have focused upon "the horizontal division between reasons and similitudes," and have overlooked the "vertical division according to the moments of the *Exitus-Reditus*." The second division, which constitutes a "circular movement," opens up a larger perspective on the structure of the text.[54] Only in light of that movement can one see the unity of the distinction of modes of truth as secondary to a primordial unity. The distinction holds "not on the part of God, who is truth, unified and simple, but on the part of our knowledge" (I, 9).[55]

Still, the prologue emphasizes not so much the primordial unity as the incompleteness of the first mode. Following Aristotle, Thomas notes that our knowledge is tethered to its origin in sense. Thus, we can achieve but a partial knowledge of divine things. We can know that God is (*quia sit*) and other things following upon the existence of a first principle, but we cannot know God's essence (*quid sit*). A comprehensive knowledge of divine things exceeds the grasp of human wisdom. The desire, which culminates in metaphysics, to uncover and contemplate the highest causes remains incomplete. In the words of Maritain, Thomas insists that "for us the intellectual life concludes with an avowal of poverty."[56]

Thomas focuses on the famous aporia of *Ethics* X, 6–8, concerning the contemplative life. That life fulfills the definition of happiness more than the life of virtue does, but human nature is ill-suited to complete participation in the life of contemplation. What are the consequences of that aporia for our understanding of the twofold mode of truth? The first mode accentuates the incompleteness of philosophy, its internally acknowledged limitations. Aristotelian philosophy is not a closed, exhaustive, Hegelian system. As Josef Pieper puts it, for Thomas natural reason culminates in a *philosophia negativa*.[57] Theology can engage philosophy on two levels: dialectically, with respect to this or that issue, and hierarchically or teleologically, with respect to the end it seeks. The first mode, then, is not a comprehensive system; instead, it is characterized by the persistence of difficulties. The gap between *quia* and *quid* in our knowledge of God points to the limits of philosophy. Thomas will soon draw a moral lesson from this fact. In ascending to knowledge of God, the human intellect should not presume that what escapes its reach is unknowable. As John Sallis puts it, an "awareness of ignorance belongs essentially to human wisdom."[58]

Throughout the prologue, Thomas highlights these aporias. Were it not for revelation, the highest things would be known only by the few, after a great deal of time and effort, and even then with an admixture of error. Even for those who are able and willing to pursue wisdom, the philosophical life is one of great labor (*cum magno labore*), which can never achieve undiluted intelligibility. Thomas cites a host of impediments to the life of wisdom: the dominance of the passions in the vicious, intellectual debility, the necessities of bodily and social life. While it may partially enlighten the few, philosophy leaves "the human race in the blackest shadows of ignorance" (I, 4).[59] Does the dialectical understanding of the telos of philosophy help to establish the unity of the two modes? It certainly opens the way for interaction between the two modes, for the inclusion of one within the other. Accordingly, Thomas depicts revelation as answering philosophical questions. Only divine providence directs human beings "to a higher good than human fragility is able to experience in the present life."[60] Thomas underscores the way providence meets the fragile condition of human nature with respect to the highest things. Given the natural disproportion between the human mind and the divine nature, God's act of revelation (*revelare*) is an act of mercy (*clementia*, I, 4).[61] The teaching of faith is a first glimpse of, and an incentive to pursue, knowledge of God: "no one tends toward something with desire and eagerness, unless it is known to him."[62]

The hortatory rhetoric of the prologue calls to mind the ancient practice of protreptic. Yet the protreptic of the *Contra Gentiles* is in some ways distinctively Christian. Revelation offers not only information but also moral correction. It curbs presumption and despair. By revealing the secret wisdom of God, it gives hope and incites us to "tend with zeal" to the highest things. By revealing how greatly God exceeds our natural capacity, it serves as a "repression of presumption, which is the mother of error." As Thomas puts it, God is known truly "when we believe God to be beyond all that we are able to know about him" (I, 5).[63] The identification of presumption as the mother of error is

Augustinian. Thomas combats the proud skepticism that conflates the humanly knowable and the intelligible itself.[64]

The "gradation of intellects," both within the human species and among the hierarchy of intellectual beings, is instructive and humbling. If it is foolish for an idiot to deny what a philosopher grasps, then how much more foolish (*multo amplius nimiae stultitiae*) is it for human beings to reject what exceeds the capacity of their limited faculties? Thomas addresses not only the limits to our knowledge of higher things, but also the defects "we experience in coming to know things every day." The analogy between human and divine pedagogy is intended to counteract the immediate dismissal of transcendent truth as foolish and unworthy of consideration.

The distinctively Christian character of the protreptic is evident in Thomas's emphasis on the connection between wisdom and teaching. For Aristotle, the capacity to teach is a sign of wisdom; for Thomas, the wise not only can but must teach.[65] Thomas quotes Hilary: "I am aware that the chief duty of my life—what I owe to God—is that my every word and sense may speak of him."[66] The passage echoes the Dominican understanding of contemplation as overflowing into the active life of instructing others.[67] Thomas's emphasis on the link between moral and intellectual error calls to mind Augustine's conception of Christian doctrine as the healing of souls.[68] The Christian protreptic of the work is explicit in another quotation from Hilary:

> By believing these things, begin, press on, and persist. Even though I know that you will not reach an end, I will congratulate your progress. He who piously pursues the infinite, although he will not ever achieve it, will nonetheless make progress by proceeding. But do not intrude into that secret, and, presuming to comprehend the summit of understanding, plunge into the mystery of endless truth. Instead, understand that these matters are incomprehensible. (I, 8)[69]

The passage advocates a kind of learned ignorance with regard to divine things. The transition from philosophy to theology does not forestall wonder and foreclose inquiry. Theology's eclipse of philosophy does not deliver, or make present, the fount of being. Instead, it accentuates mystery and celebrates the interplay of presence and absence. One makes progress through a knowing that does not exhaust, an understanding that fails to comprehend.

Is the protreptic nature of the prologue a key to the intention of the text? Mark Jordan thinks so. He locates the work within the ancient genre of philosophical protreptic.[70] Jordan sees the text as an enactment of the life of wisdom celebrated in the prologue. The work is thus a school for the training in virtues necessary for, and in some measure constitutive of, beatitude. The *Contra Gentiles'* "principle of economy" follows upon the desired rhetorical end: "those topics are treated extensively and most technically which have a direct bearing on persuasion to the highest good."[71] The intended audience, according to Jordan, is Christian. Such a reader would find the truth of the Catholic faith confirmed in many ways and would also be given the wherewithal to instruct others. Thomas's regular practice of confirming with scriptural authority arguments established by reason indicates that "complete persuasion to wisdom is accomplished when the reader sees that the intelligibility of argument leads into the intelligibility of scripture."[72]

The aspiration, then, for contemplative happiness provides a point of departure for dialogue between reason and revelation. Corbin comments: "There exists a unifying structure and this structure is justly constituted by the discovery of the natural desire for God." Corbin calls this "the great novelty of the *Contra Gentiles*," to which the *Summa Theologiae* "will give its definitive figure." Does the location of the topic of the natural desire for God in the third book mean that reason determines the structure of the whole, that the content and shape of revelation gain their intelligibility from reason? Should the fourth book be conceived as an addendum to the first three, as necessary for, but not determinative of, the whole? Repeating Thomas's view that creation itself is a kind of circle, Guindon notes that the natural desire for God is what enables Thomas "to complete the circle."[73] Lafont concedes that the "consideration of wisdom allows the essentially Christian aspect of mystery to be respected."[74] But given the placement of the pivotal discussion in the first section of the book, Lafont queries: "is the wisdom of the *Contra Gentes* clearly theological?"[75]

The chapter from the prologue on the reasonableness of believing in revealed teachings seems to support the interpretation that reason is the key to the whole (I, 6). While Thomas explicitly denounces the project of demonstrating the truth of revelation, he does hold that divine revelation makes its presence known "by fitting arguments" (*convenientibus argumentis*). The enumeration of some of the convenient arguments is, however, unlikely to satisfy the immediate expectations of the philosopher. The

Christian religion has efficaciously persuaded both the simple and the wise "to believe things so lofty, to perform deeds so difficult, and to hope for things so elevated." It confirms transcendent truths through visible works, both in miracles and in the wise speeches and prudent actions of "idiots." Confirmation occurs not just by the raising of the material and the human to the spiritual and the divine but also by the manifestation of the higher in and through the lower. Once again, concrete historical events, utterly alien to Aristotle's metaphysics, play a crucial role. The model of divine pedagogy is the Incarnation, in which God takes on flesh in order to manifest the truth. Thus, if revelation in some sense continues and completes the philosophical aspiration, it does so in unexpected ways, through a reversal of the movement natural to philosophy.[76]

What is one to make of apparent differences between philosophy and theology, between their contents and methods? Does Thomas in any way prepare the reader for the reversals and transformations introduced by revelation? The most successful attempt to read the first three books in light of the fourth is that of Anton Pegis, who describes the way Thomas orders the first three books to the central Christian mystery, the Incarnation.[77] Hence, Pegis avoids engaging in what Corbin has identified as the interminable debate over whether Thomas is faithful to the schema he outlines in the third chapter. Indeed, Pegis offers something like a narrative account of the structure of the first three books in relationship to the fourth. He concurs with Gauthier on the prominence of Aristotle in the first three books, but he holds that Thomas transforms Aristotle's "systematic" conception of nature into a historical view of nature, which is a result of, and is always open to, divine initiative.

Thomas's reworking of Aristotle is evident in the difference between Aristotle's prime mover and Thomas's *ipsum esse subsistens*. Aristotle achieves the notion of God as prime mover, but his God is coextensive with matter, motion, and time. Pegis even goes so far as to speak of "Aristotelian materialism." As the prologue intimates, Thomas accommodates the Platonic notion of God as exemplary cause and model of the good life. But even the Platonic view of divinity falls short of the Thomistic position.[78] Thomas's notion of God, which does indeed begin from Aristotle's conception of the prime mover, sees God as an utterly transcendent being, source of all existence, including matter. Thomas's conception of divine transcendence and of the created dependence of all other things engenders a novel emphasis upon time and history; thus, Thomas transforms "the firm and rigid intellectualism of Aristotle in a historical and created system."[79] As Pegis notes, Thomas repeatedly underscores the way God is "present and active in history." Pegis concurs with many other commentators in seeing beatitude as the leitmotif of the philosophical portion of the *Contra Gentiles*. But Pegis detects a transformation of the Aristotelian question of beatitude in the *Summa Contra Gentiles*. Thomas's question is not simply what is the good, but what is the relationship "of the universe to God and of man to beatitude . . . in the world of divine initiative."[80]

Corbin adds illuminating details to the project begun by Pegis, namely, that of seeing how the first three parts are ordered to and completed by the final book. He notes, for instance, that the order of the fourth book parallels that of the first three books, which treat, respectively, God in himself (*l'unité de l'essence divine*), God as efficient cause (*la sortie des créatures*), and God as final cause (*l'ordination des créatures*).[81] The fourth book treats, first, the Trinity of divine persons; second, the Incarnation and sacraments; and, third, the resurrection of the body.[82] If the interpretations of Pegis and Corbin are accurate, then the fourth book is more integral to, and determinative of, the structure of the whole than many commentators have realized. The reading of the last book should, then, provoke a reconsideration and reestimation of the previous parts. Conversely, the first three books should display their own incompleteness apart from the fourth book and thus prepare the way for it.

What are the implications of the readings of Pegis and Corbin for our consideration of the method and structure of the *Contra Gentiles*?[83] Corbin's distinction between a horizontal and a vertical principle of order suggests two approaches to the text: dialectic and narrative. The vertical principle—linked to the "twofold mode of truth"—proceeds through reasons to similitudes in an effort to extend understanding of the teaching of the faith as far as possible; it takes its starting point from the received opinions of the Philosopher and his commentators. What is striking about the method of this segment of the text is how closely it adheres to Aristotle's conception of dialectical inquiry. This is crucial for a number of reasons. First, many misreadings of the first three books arise precisely from a failure to attend to the dialectical nature of the inquiry. Second, the prominence of dialectic in Aristotle's own texts makes it possible for Thomas to go beyond Aristotle without opening himself to the charge of infidelity. There is a middle ground between fundamentalist fidelity and what Pegis calls Thomas's "doctrinal mutation" of Aristotle.[84] Third, as the prologue intimates, the possibility of dialogue between revelation and reason is in part attributable to the dialectical or aporetic character of ancient philosophical discourse, especially discourse about the highest things.

V. DIALECTICAL INQUIRY

Two passages from the prologue indicate the importance of dialectical method in the *Contra Gentiles*. First, there is the statement in the opening chapter that the work will both teach the truth and combat errors. A second passage underscores the importance of the dialectical engagement of interlocutors. In the chapter describing the work's method of proceeding, Thomas five times uses a version of the phrase "to convince an adversary" (*adversarius convinci possit*, I, 9). Some have supposed that the emphasis on the correction of errors and the persuasion of adversaries buttresses the apologetic thesis.[85] In a careful study of the use of the term *convincere* and its cognates in Aquinas, Gauthier demonstrates that *convincere* is not part of an apologetic project of convincing unbelievers but is intrinsic to Thomas's depiction of the office of the wise. Gauthier writes,

> The necessity of the double office of the sage is thus founded not on the need to persuade an adversary, but on a requirement internal to the manifestation of truth itself: in order to be in the complete possession of truth, it does not suffice to have accomplished the first task of the sage; to express the truth, it is also necessary to be acquitted of the second task—to show the cause of the opposed error.[86]

Convincere means, "to overcome completely," "to refute," or "to prove incontestably." The goal is not to persuade adversaries who may be dead or who would be unlikely ever to read the *Contra Gentiles*, but to render particular arguments more persuasive to the reader, to inculcate intellectual virtue and uproot the sources of intellectual vice. The engagement of conflicting views and the refutation of adversaries are characteristics of dialectical inquiry. As Aristotle puts it in *Topics* I, 2, to raise searching difficulties on both sides assists in the detection of truth and falsity. In the Christian pedagogy of the *Contra Gentiles*, dialectic "will make the Christian confident of the intelligibility of his faith."[87]

Contemporary scholarship on Aristotle increasingly highlights the nonsystematic or aporetic character of his texts. As Aristotle puts it in the *Metaphysics*, it is not possible "to loosen a bond" of which one is ignorant (III, 1, 995a30). The loosening occurs through dialectic, which "is a process of criticism wherein lies the path to the principles of all inquiries."[88] Dialectic begins from *phainomena*, the received opinions (*endoxa*) of the wise or the many, and the data of sense experience. But what is the philosopher's task with regard to received opinions? Is it merely to align them and show their compatibility? Or is it to test and verify them? Some commentators have seen dialectic as harmonizing phenomena and unmasking attempts to escape from ordinary experience.[89] Others hold that *phainomena* are in need of certification, which occurs through critical examination. The latter reading conflicts with Aristotle's remarkable confidence in *phainomena*. It does not follow, however, that, as the first view would have it, the philosopher merely sorts out and unifies the phenomena. As Kurt Pritzl argues, Aristotle is committed only to the view that phenomena contain partial or obscure truth. Pritzl shows convincingly that phenomena stand as the first term in a *'oti-dioti* relationship, that is, they supply the facts of which the philosopher seeks an explanation.[90] Inquiry for Aristotle does not rest until one has an explanation.

In certain respects, philosophy finds itself inevitably opposed to ordinary language and experience, to the fragmentary character of pre-philosophical knowledge, and to the conceptual sedimentation of ordinary knowledge. Philosophical inquiry transforms the fractured and haphazardly related discourses characteristic of pre-philosophical life. The transition involves not only a conscious reappropriation of ordinary language but also the commencement of critical appropriation of the various traditions to which one is heir. Nonetheless, the communally accessible realm of speech and sense experience is the indispensable starting point for philosophy. To begin philosophy by denying its ground in pre-philosophical experience shows want of education (*apaideusia*).

Physics I provides a paradigm of constructive dialectical inquiry.[91] Aristotle begins by sorting the various received opinions (*endoxa*) concerning the principles of natural things. The opening discussion examines various kinds of "dialectical problems," which arise from conflicts of opinion between the wise and those of most people or between one wise person and another (*Topics* I, 11). The wise disagree over the number of the principles and what they are. Some views of the wise, for instance, the Eleatic view that all is one, conflict with obvious features of experience and hence with the opinions of the many. Aristotle criticizes positions, dismisses some, and affirms portions of others. He ends the initial discussion with the irenic observation that all agree that the principles must be contraries

(I, 5, 188a27–30). In his commentary on the opening chapters of *Physics* I, Thomas acknowledges the dialectical character of the investigation; he refers to Aristotle's procedure as one of disputation (*disputare*) and to the various opinions (*opiniones*) from which the inquiry begins.[92]

Aristotle does not rest in harmonious opinions. It is "necessary to examine how this can be reached on the basis of rational argument" (I, 5, 188a30–31). Thomas observes that Aristotle is moving from an examination of opinions to an investigation of the truth (liber I, lectio 10). The move suits Pritzl's description of dialectic as searching for the explanatory reasons of the received opinions or observations, the *dioti* of the *'oti*. In providing the reasoned account of the principles, Aristotle frequently recurs to knowledge implicit in our way of describing the world, to the ways "we" speak about changeable things. But he grounds the descriptive in the explanatory schema of substance and accident. Thomas holds that in this section of the first book, Aristotle determines the truth through induction, through an analysis of exemplary instances of change (liber I, lectio 12). In the final stage of the book, Aristotle shows how his own account resolves the original difficulties and where and why alternative views went wrong. A standard feature of Aristotelian dialectic involves the interpretation or reinterpretation of the views and questions put forward by his predecessors. He strives to show not only that his view is true, but also that it can salvage what is of value in the positions of his rivals. Thomas observes that, after determining the truth, Aristotle shows that his proof is the sole way (*solum ista via*) of resolving the difficulties of his predecessors (liber I, lectio 14). The ability to resolve doubts, Thomas adds, is a sign of the truth of one's position; so long as doubts persist, the proof remains uncertain. Thus, the convincing of opponents (*convincere*) is integral to philosophical inquiry.

Examples of Thomas's appreciation of the role of dialectic in Aristotle could be multiplied. Thomas also embraces allied features of Aristotle's method of inquiry. He is deeply opposed to linguistic univocity and homogeneity of method, which become the dominant features of late medieval and early modern conceptions of discourse.[93] Thomas inherits and amplifies Aristotle's conception of language as analogical; he also embraces the Aristotelian teaching on the need for a plurality of methods. In spite of these obvious points of dependence, commentators often trace the misguided view of Aristotle as a "systematic" thinker to Aquinas. This is of course an exact inversion of Pegis's thesis concerning the relationship between Aristotle and Thomas. Is there a noticeable difference in method between Aristotle and Aquinas? More pointedly, is Aquinas guilty of substituting pellucid demonstration for dialectical inquiry? To Chenu's assertion of the historically conditioned character of the *Contra Gentiles*, Gauthier opposes his thesis: "rarely has a work been less historical . . . , rarely has a work escaped so completely from history in order deliberately to situate itself on the atemporal plane"[94] Thomas's Aristotle has been "recreated to coincide with atemporal reason."

Josef Pieper, on the contrary, argues that the *quaestio disputata* stands in the literary tradition of the Platonic dialogue. Thomas's engagement of all pertinent authorities, of authorities from various traditions, is an exemplary instance of what Alasdair MacIntyre has called "tradition-constituted inquiry."[95] Jordan and Allard suggest that the *Summa Contra Gentiles* is noteworthy for its multiplication of arguments and its rich citation of varied authorities on behalf of single propositions. The lengthy dialectical segments of the work provide a field for the induction of principles, for their testing, refinement, and application.

The dialectical method of the *Contra Gentiles* is not a substitute for the demonstrative model of science articulated in Aristotle's *Posterior Analytics*. The *Contra Gentiles* contains many demonstrations, a number of which are crucial to its teaching. Nonetheless, the dialectical path to the principles of the science, not the demonstration of conclusions from principles, predominates in the second and third books. The question whether Thomas substitutes demonstration for dialectic is wrongly put, since it supposes some sort of divide between a tentative Aristotelian dialectic and a rigorous Thomistic science. As Thomas's comments on the method of *Physics* I indicate, dialectic leads into a determination of truth.[96] In its various forms, dialectic provides occasion for induction, for what Arthur Madigan calls "organizing insights."[97] Without such insights, demonstration could never begin. The operation of the intellect, moreover, even in its apprehension of first principles requires experience; dialectic's culling, sorting, and arranging of various phenomena facilitate the operation of the intellect.[98]

While subsequent chapters will address in detail the dialectical segments of the book, some indication of the fruitfulness of such an approach can be provided here. The dialectical structure is especially evident in the second and third books, which address puzzles concerning human nature and the human good. What drives the discussion is a series of encounters with inherited opinions. The consideration of human nature is puzzling in a number of ways. Thomas begins with a common treatment of the human soul and angels as members of the genus of intellectual substances and proves numerous attributes of these substances (II, 46–55). What he means by "genus of intellectual substances" is unclear. Are souls and angels equal participants in the genus? Thomas proves numerous attributes of intellectual substances. Some have taken the proofs, especially the one concerning incorruptibility, to apply fully to both souls and angels. But this fails to explain why Thomas, after having proved that all intellectual substances are incorruptible (II, 55), much later proves that the soul is incorruptible (II, 79). At this juncture, one is forced to reconsider the previous, common consideration of the soul and angels. Indeed, one is forced to read more carefully the intervening, dialectical segment of the argument.

In the intervening chapters (II, 56–78), which highlight the distinctive attributes of the human soul, Thomas engages not only the texts of Aristotle but also the opinions of Plato, Alexander, Galen, Avicenna, and Averroes. He begins with the opinion of Plato, whose goal was to "salvage the nature of man" (*natura hominis salvetur*). Although Thomas is opposed to Plato's position, he embraces his project; indeed, he proceeds to disagree with various theses by showing that they fail to explain the phenomena in question, that is, they fail to "save the nature of man." Debate often surrounds lingering aporias in Aristotle's own texts. Through dialectical engagement of Aristotle's commentators, Thomas brings forth, clarifies, and applies relevant principles.

The authority of Aristotle is also prominent in the most extended dialectical segment of the book, the one concerning the ultimate end of human life, which occupies nearly forty chapters (III, 25–63). Commentators have persistently overlooked the dialectical structure of the section. Much attention has been given to the prominence of Aristotle, yet rarely is it noted that Aristotle is cited on both sides of the issue, as providing grounds for both affirming and denying a transcendent ultimate end. The dominant mode of argument is, moreover, *via negativa*, and where it is positive, it is dialectical, aporetic. As in the previous discussion of human nature, here, too, the articulation, clarification, justification, and application of principles occurs through dialectical engagement with inherited opinions, namely, those of Alexander, Averroes, and Augustine.

A determination of what Thomas holds and how he argues to it is impossible apart from a careful consideration of the dialectical structure of the text, one that begins from initial aporias concerning the human good, engages various opinions, and proceeds to resolutions. What distinguishes the discussion of the natural end of human nature is the lack

of a peremptory answer. Aristotle's description of the contemplative and
active lives partially fulfills his own definition of happiness. Yet the gap
between aspiration and achievement remains. Like the question of the
eternity of the world, the question of complete happiness is a dialectical
problem (*Topics*, I, 11, 104b12–18). As Jan Aertsen has noted, there is a
"dialectic within the natural desire for God."[99]

The third book amplifies the prologue's intimation of the aporetic
character of philosophical discourse at its pinnacle. Attention to the
aporetic character of the discussion, not just in its method but also in
its conclusion, would have aided commentators interested in seeing how
Thomas can avoid either closing human nature upon itself by denying
the natural desire for God (Gauthier) or demonstrating the natural desire
which seems to undermine the gratuitous nature of the gift of supernatural elevation (de Broglie). The aporias, which indicate the limitations of
philosophy, provide an opening for a dialogue between revelation and
reason; because they are no more than aporias, they cannot provide
grounds for a philosophical anticipation of revelation.

The books treating of human nature and the human good are crucial
to the structure of the *Contra Gentiles*; the teaching of these books is likely
to be misconstrued if it is abstracted from its dialectical context. Dialectic
is not absent from the remaining books. It figures prominently in two
discussions from the first book, in the relationship between God and the
world and in the divine names.

Numerous teachings concerning the divine intellect bring Thomas
into apparent conflict with Aristotle and into explicit disagreement with
his commentators. God knows singulars, things that are not, future contingents, and the infinite, all of which Aristotle is purported to have
denied. Thomas responds to these challenges in a number of ways, by
arguing, for instance, that Aristotle has been misconstrued or that a
principle has been extended beyond its scope in Aristotle's texts. He
holds, accordingly, that composition and division are not essential to
truth (I, 58), that to know lowly things is ignoble only for imperfect
beings (I, 70), that the unknowability of the infinite applies only to finite
intellects (I, 69), and that future contingents are not actually future for
God (I, 67). In these discussions, Thomas analyzes the meaning, scope,
and equivocal uses of terms; he thus employs the standard dialectical tools
outlined by Aristotle in *Topics* I, 13–18. The most protracted and most
polemical section of the first book concerns God's knowledge of singulars
and lowly things.

Throughout these discussions, Thomas underscores the analogical character of human discourse about God and the way literal, univocal speech about God misleads. Indeed, Thomas devotes a large portion of the first book to the question of language about God (chapters 14 and 30 through 36). The resources of, and limits to, human speech about God evince the achievement and incompleteness of philosophy with respect to the highest things. The movement from affirmation through negation to affirmation by supereminence is dialectical; it involves an interplay of presence and absence. It also anticipates the more patently aporetic second and third books. In each case, dialectic exhibits the intermediate status of human nature with respect to the whole.

In the fourth book, which treats principally of the Trinity and Incarnation, one might expect Thomas to dispense with dialectic. After all, theology is the study of revealed doctrine. Nonetheless, apparent conflicts in the received data of revelation make dialectic unavoidable. Where dialectic is not prompted by apparent disagreements in accepted authorities, it is motivated by encounters with heretical positions, which, in spite of their unorthodoxy, enable Thomas to articulate, clarify, and develop principles. The adversarial setting, typical of dialectical reasoning, is prominent in the fourth book, as are the dialectical strategies of distinguishing various senses of words and the investigation of differences among things. The dialectical presentation of theological truth serves a rhetorical purpose. After refuting various heretical opinions on the Trinity, Thomas compares the opinions and shows precisely where they agree and disagree with authentic teaching. His concluding comment brings out the usefulness of dialectic in theology: "From this, too, a judgment of the Catholic truth can be had. For, as the Philosopher says, even false statements testify, since they stand apart not only from true statements but even from one another" (IV, 7).[100]

The theological structure and intent of the work further complicate the inquiry. As Thomas notes in the introduction to the second book, the theologian considers creatures as they relate to, and manifest, God, not as they are in themselves. The latter inquiry is the purview of the philosopher. By beginning from what is absolutely prior and proceeding to what is naturally posterior, the theological order reverses the natural order of pedagogy. It might seem that the theological ordering would constitute a sort of cosmic deduction, the consequence of which would be the virtual elimination of dialectic. The work begins from God and then traces the *exitus* or descent of things from God. Yet Thomas regularly reverts to the philosophical order of learning, especially in the second and third books, where the inquiry into human nature achieves clarity only by recourse to Aristotle's natural philosophy, which treats human beings as rational animals. One might be tempted to speak of a dialectical relationship between the theological and the philosophical modes of proceeding. We have already suggested that lingering problems in the philosophical discussion of the good provide an avenue for dialogue between philosophy and theology. Can we speak of the relationship in more adequate terms?

VI. NARRATIVE CONTINUITY

Theology's dialectical engagement of philosophy begins from the human and ascends through "reasons and similitudes" to the divine. Revelation makes the continuation of the ascent possible. As we have already noted, however, the continuation of the ascent occurs through a transformation of the philosophical approach and through a reversal of the philosopher's expectations. Theology subsumes the philosophical life within a more encompassing narrative conception of the life of wisdom. In order to see the value of this way of reading the *Contra Gentiles*, it will be helpful to begin with two of the most prominent motifs of the prologue: the life of wisdom and the nature of divine instruction.

The prologue exhorts its readers to appropriate the intellectual virtues. The depiction of the life of wisdom takes a Platonic turn, when Thomas notes that the model of the life of wisdom and of the good life for human beings is God.[101] The doctrine of God as pure *esse*, as comprehending all perfection in a transcendent unity and as absolute source of all things, pervades the first two books. The first book begins and ends with a discussion of the life of wisdom and blessedness, initially as it is sought by humans and finally as it is possessed by God. God is the transcendent paradigm of the Good: "The divine virtues are called the exemplars of ours; for the things contracted and particularized are the likenesses of absolute things" (I, 93).[102] In this passage, Thomas embraces a Platonic reversal in discourse about the Good, which begins from the natural and the human but then sees these as reflections of the divine.

The reversal is implicit in the prologue itself. After introducing the twofold mode of truth, Thomas stresses the fundamental compatibility of the two modes by adverting to the notion of God as a teacher, who contains in himself the truths of both modes (I, 7). A transcendental unity of truth precedes the distinction into natural and supernatural. This indicates something that Corbin thinks is characteristic of the later *Summa*, namely, the subordination of the human ascent to the divine descent. The ascent of reason through the "reasons and similitudes" is made possible by the first manifestation of God in creation. Instead of overstating the dominance of the *scission* of the twofold mode, Corbin would have done well to have followed through more completely on the claim that the *exitus-reditus* motif is a clue to an alternative way of reading the book.

Thomas continues the consideration of God as model and transcendent ground of wisdom and goodness in the second book's treatment of creation. He persistently refers to God as an artist and to creation as a manifestation of his wisdom, goodness, and beauty. In order to say anything about divine creation, Thomas must rework the language of physical production; he negates certain features of Aristotle's account of making or generating: preexisting matter, and the notion of generation as a movement from potency to act, a movement that involves succession and endures through time. Divine creation *ex nihilo* involves the sheer communication of being; it introduces a unilateral dependence of the created act of being upon its source (*ipsa dependentia esse creati ad principium* [II, 18]). The whole of the created order is radically contingent. As creator, God is the source and measure of all things, simultaneously artist and exemplar. Indeed, things are said to be true insofar as they conform to their notion in the divine essence. The discussion of creation continues the reversal of philosophical discourse begun in the first book.

The theological reversal of the philosophical order of the study of creatures brings narrative to the fore. Nature is now seen as a manifestation of the wisdom of the divine artist:

> All creatures are compared to God as artifacts to an artist. . . . Whence the whole of nature is like a certain artifact of the divine art. It is not, however, opposed to the nature of an artifact that the artist should work in a different way on his product even after he has given it its first form. Nor therefore is it against nature that God should work otherwise in natural things than as the customary course of nature operates. (III, 100)[103]

The first and last discussions of creation underscore its narrative structure. Thomas devotes the longest section of the initial treatment of creation to detailed analysis of the arguments for and against the eternity of the world. As is well known, Thomas holds that natural reason can do no better than to provide dialectical arguments on both sides; it cannot resolve the issue. For philosophy, it remains an aporia, a dialectical problem. The limitations to natural reason make room for the foundation of the Christian narrative, the teaching concerning the temporal beginning of the world. Creation has a narrative intelligibility, with a beginning, middle, and end. The final discussion of creation confirms the reading. Thomas argues against the creation of an infinity of souls on the ground that infinity is contrary to the very notion of an end (IV, 97).

The famous distinction between essence and existence is of course part of Thomas's teaching on creation; yet the emphasis in the second book is not upon that distinction but upon the order of created being (*esse ut ordo*). For, creation is a result of divine artistry and is a manifestation of divine wisdom. In his account of God's motive in creating, Thomas avoids the opposed errors of seeing creation as a result of necessity or of arbitrary will. Creation is rooted in the divine freedom and ordered to a good, namely, the communication of God's own goodness. The second book, moreover, often uses aesthetic terms, such as *conveniens, decenter, manifestatio*. The three famous Thomistic marks of the beautiful— *integritas, claritas*, and *proportio*— exercise a pervasive, if understated, influence on the book.

The manner of citing scriptural texts further supports the narrative reading. In the first three books, the largest number of citations by far are to the wisdom literature of the Old Testament, to the books of Job, Wisdom, Proverbs, Psalms, and Ecclesiastes. Still, there are instructive departures from the general pattern of citing the wisdom literature. In the discussion of creation in the second book, for example, the most frequently cited work is Genesis, while the Gospel of John is preeminent in the final book, at least until the end, when Revelation is cited. The practice of confirming philosophical arguments with scriptural texts allows the reader to pass, as Jordan puts it, from the intelligibility of reason to that of revelation. It also allows dialectic to pass into the narrative of scripture, into a story that encompasses the whole of time.

Does the neo-Platonic model of *exitus-reditus* capture these scriptural features of the narrative structure of the *Contra Gentiles*? As we shall see, the *exitus-reditus* reading is helpful only at a very general level. The neo-Platonic conception of emanation and return, which is often depicted as resulting from a necessary, organic process, downplays the constitutive elements of dramatic narrative, namely, freedom and contingency.[104] Pegis's accent upon Thomas's shift from an Aristotelian (or even Platonic) to a Christian understanding of the relationship of God to the world is helpful here. According to Pegis, created being is always open to divine initiative. As Thomas puts it, the artist is free to work on his product even "after he has given it its first form." The passage, taken from the discussion of providence in the third book, argues for the openness of creation from above. The preceding discussion in the third book on the ultimate end of human life shows that creation, at least that part of it which is rational, is open from below. The third book thus sets the stage for the dramatic interaction between creator and creature. The entire discussion of human destiny occurs in a book devoted to the topic of God's providential rule. God ordains all things to their final state by orchestrating temporal, historical events. Thus, the third book inscribes the dialectical investigation of human destiny within a narrative account of divine providence.

In his study of the *ordo* of *esse*, Thomas focuses primarily upon the human person and frequently deploys the neo-Platonic image of the human person as a "horizon and confine of the material and the spiritual" (*horizon et confinium corporeorum et incorporeorum*). Inhabiting a middle realm in creation, human beings are microcosms of the whole. Thomas ends the discussion of the unity of soul and body by stating: "In this way the marvelous connection of things is able to be considered" (II, 68).[105] That the narrative of the cosmos pivots upon human nature is also clear in the third book, where Thomas argues that the return of embodied intellectual creatures makes possible the *reditus* of all creatures to God. Thomas returns to this principle in arguments on behalf of the appropriateness of the Incarnation. He associates the fittingness of the Incarnation with the pivotal role of human persons in the perfection of the universe (IV, 55).

In these apparent concessions to the primacy of nature and rational argument, Lafont detects a structural subordination of theology to philosophy. Two comments are in order. First, Thomas's distinction between two modes of truth can be understood as distinguishing revelation from its pedagogical presuppositions. If we do not have some appreciation of the natural world, especially of human nature, how will the claims of revelation be intelligible to us? An understanding of what revelation teaches and of the significance of that teaching presupposes the truth of certain philosophical arguments. Conversely, a study of the achievements and limits of philosophy brings out what is distinctive in Christianity.

Second, Pegis's thesis concerning Thomas's ordering of the first three books to the mysteries of the fourth suggests an alternative reading. We have already noted the way dialectical argumentation concerning the eternity of the world paves the way for the Christian narrative of creation *ex nihilo*. A similar pattern surfaces in the discussion of the Incarnation, where Thomas first shows dialectically that the arguments against the possibility of the Incarnation are without merit and then adduces numerous arguments on behalf of the fittingness of the Incarnation. Hence, dialectic passes into a narrative that highlights the concrete, historical, and personal mode of divine pedagogy. Thomas depicts the Old Law in pedagogical terms, as engendering self-knowledge. God offers redemption only after man has been left alone so he might experience that he himself was not sufficient for salvation: "neither by means of natural knowledge, . . . nor by means of his own virtue" (IV, 55).[106] Thomas proceeds to locate human life within the three epochs: before the law, under the law, and under grace. The Christian understanding of human nature is rooted in historical events that were unknown to the philosophers.

As Pegis suggests, Thomas orders many of the dominant themes of the first three books to the mystery of the Incarnation. Consider the issues already mentioned as meriting sustained, dialectical consideration: God's knowledge of, and providence over, singulars and lowly things; his life as the paradigm of wisdom; the nature of the human person as a microcosm of the whole of creation, and as aspiring to a knowledge of God. All these prepare the ground for the central mystery of the fourth book: the Incarnation.

The fourth book inscribes the previous considerations within the drama of redemption. The Incarnation, the most admirable mystery, bridges the "immense distance of the natures" of God and man (IV, 54). The Incarnation introduces a dramatic reversal in the narrative of human history: it raises human beings beyond their merits or expectations and overcomes isolation through a transcendent communion. The reversal expresses the wisdom of God, which from the perspective of a more limited narrative can be understood only as "foolishness." In the Incarnation there is "such a profundity of wisdom that it exceeds all human understanding."[107] As the prologue to the *Contra Gentiles* hints, historical events, events that embrace and transform the condition of the whole of humanity, are central to the scriptural fulfillment of philosophy's dialectical quest for wisdom and happiness.

2

GOD: SUMMIT, SOURCE, AND EXEMPLAR OF THE LIFE OF WISDOM

I. INTRODUCTION

The prologue underscores both the accomplishments of, and the limitations to, speculative philosophy. Reason can reach conclusions about God; its inquiry remains incomplete. The method and structure of the first book reflect the thesis that human inquiry is located between presumption and despair. The discussion of whether God can be known by natural reason amplifies what the prologue had adumbrated: the philosophic life stands midway between the presumption of attaining and comprehending the highest good and the despair over its inaccessibility. Thomas combats equally the claims that God's existence is self-evident and that his existence is unknowable apart from faith. As Louis Mackey puts it, "The locus of the proof is situated between two negations. God is not self-evident—wholly and overwhelmingly present—nor indemonstrable—utterly gone and beyond recall. God is recoverable, and Thomas's proof is the recovery."[1]

That our notion of God fails to establish his existence does not show a defect in God but rather in "our intellect," which must reach God obliquely from effects (I, 10–11). The inverse relationship between the orders of being and knowing requires that philosophical inquiry be self-reflective. At every turn in the discussion of God, Thomas is preoccupied with the status of the language he is presently using to reach and describe God. In the divine names, the unlike likeness of our speech about God issues in an interplay of presence and absence. The recurring need to consider the sensible sources of our language renders inappropriate an abstractly deductive treatment of God's nature. Instead, the ascent to God is repeatedly interrupted by descent to what is first in our experience. The pattern enables Thomas to write not just about God, the goal of the pursuit of wisdom, but also about the distance that separates our discourse from its signified. The humble arts of grammar and logic are central to the first book. An analogically ordered multiplicity of names simultaneously informs us about God and avoids the error of conceptual idolatry.

The structure of the first book is dialectical, as it juxtaposes antipodal errors: the error of idolatry, of conflating the world and God, and the error of denying God's intimate causal contact with, and providence over, singulars and lowly things. In the first section, Thomas castigates views, proffered by some *gentiles*, that would circumscribe God by the limits of human imagination or conceptualization. In the midst of this discussion (I, 22), Thomas argues that God is subsistent being (*esse subsistens*). Both philosophy and scripture countenance this description of God; for, in conversation with Moses, God refers to himself as "I am who am." "This sublime truth" (*haec sublimis veritas*), as Thomas calls it, illustrates the convergence of reason and revelation. The combination of abstract (*esse*) and concrete (*subsistens*) modes of signifying indicates that God is neither an abstract concept nor one being among many. Having corrected tendencies toward idolatry, Thomas proceeds to consider the divine perfection. The most extended dialectical segment of the book is devoted to debates with Aristotle's commentators over God's relationship to the world. In an apparent paradox, Thomas uses God's absolute independence and self-sufficiency as the basis for refuting the view that God is aloof from the world. He accuses his opponents of having an imperfect understanding of perfection, that is, of projecting standards of human perfection onto God. The end of the book, on God as the subsistent exemplar of the life of wisdom, returns us to the dominant motif of the prologue. But it does so only after having introduced a reversal of perspective. God is no longer seen solely as an end to be attained, but also as the source and exemplar of the life of wisdom.

II. THIS SUBLIME TRUTH

The proofs for God's existence are borrowed from arguments given by philosophers and Catholic teachers (I, 13). The primary demonstration in the chapter on the existence of God is the Aristotelian one from motion.[2] The argument is an extended version of the terse and more famous first way of the *Summa Theologiae*. Even in the *Contra Gentiles* the proof is compressed; it summarizes in a few pages premises Aristotle develops through several books of the *Physics* and *Metaphysics*. The brevity of treatment reflects a reversal in structure and a transformation of intention. Since the *Contra Gentiles* considers philosophy under the light of revelation and reorders philosophical questions to serve theological ends, it reaches God not at the very end of its inquiry but at the outset. Brevity is significant for another reason. Thomas begins the chapter on the existence of God by noting that he is simply restating familiar arguments. The chapter is devoid of dialectical disputation. Only those issues most controverted among Aristotle's commentators and those touching directly upon misconceptions of the divine nature merit detailed dialectical attention. Thomas typically ends a dialectical discussion by mentioning proponents of the errors he has just refuted. No such list accompanies the arguments for the existence of God. In the traditions with which Thomas concerns himself in the book, there was no disagreement over the existence of God. The brevity of the argument and the absence of dialectic support the view that the *Contra Gentiles* is not an apologetic work designed for unbelievers.

The argument for God's existence moves from the phenomenon of motion in the sensible world to a transcendent, causal source of motion. Thomas focuses upon the two key premises of the argument: (a) everything that is in motion is moved by another, and (b) procession to infinity among movers and things moved is impossible. The clearest argument in support of the first premise begins from the definition of motion as an actualization of the potential as potential (*Physics*, III, 3, 201a10). Aristotle's definition captures the in-between status of motion, its ordered incompleteness. Motion is a process ordered to the actualization of a potency, to the acquisition of some thing, state, or capacity. Prior to motion, a substance is potentially receptive of a change; after motion, it has actually undergone the change. What is capable of change or able to move must be brought into act by something already in act, since the potential is never reduced to act except by that which is in act. If this were not so, a moving thing would have to be "at once in act and potency with respect to the same thing."

If there were an infinite regress of moved movers, motion could never have begun: "in an ordered series of movers and things moved," the removal of the first mover cancels the motion of all other members of the series. On the supposition of an infinite series of movers, there is no first mover; all are intermediate movers. The infinite series simply postpones an answer to the question concerning the cause of motion. Thomas also argues that an infinite series leads to something impossible, namely, that a body would traverse an infinite distance in a finite time. There are two stages to this argument. The first stage shows that whatever moves is divisible and is thus a body.[3] A thing in motion must be partly in that from which it is moving and partly in that to which it is moving. If it were completely in either, it would either not yet have begun to move or already have completed its motion. What is in motion is divisible; possessing parts, it has size and must be a body. The second stage argues that since "every body that moves some thing is itself moved while moving it," the entire infinite series must move simultaneously during the time that one member of the series is moved. But that one member, being finite, is moved in a finite time and thus the whole series is moved in a finite time.[4] Why is this problematic?

If the chain of bodies, which may for the sake of argument be considered one body, traverses an infinite distance D in a finite time T, then in a portion t of time T the same body at the same velocity will traverse some finite distance d. In double the time t, the body will cover twice the distance d. Both the time and the distance remain finite. If we continue to increase the time t, at some point t will equal the finite time T. As it does so, the distance d will go on increasing in proportion to the increase in time. No matter what the increase in distance may be, since the increase is proportional to finite increments of time, the distance remains finite. Thus, in the same time and at the same velocity, the body traverses both a finite and an infinite distance. An infinite series of moved movers is thus not possible.

Thus far Thomas has relied solely upon Aristotle's *Physics*; yet the proof in that text does not necessarily reach God. It may reach an absolutely unmoved mover or reach only some unmoved part of a self-moved mover.[5] The scope of the *Physics* is limited; it considers change only in substances composed of matter and form. Hence the reduction of potency to act is not absolute or coextensive with being. A self-moving being must have some cause of its motion; such a cause is an absolutely unmoved mover, which moves as an object of appetite. For the latter argument, Thomas turns to the *Metaphysics*, which reaches an "absolutely separate" being that moves other things as an object of desire.[6] Thomas adds proofs that reach God as first efficient cause, as supreme being, and as providential governor.

After having established the existence of God and prior to considering his nature, Thomas asserts that, "the way of remotion is especially to be used in the consideration of the divine substance, since by its immensity it exceeds every form that our intellect attains" (I, 14).[7] The ordinary manner of coming to know a substance is to locate it within a genus and then to discover the differences that demarcate it from other members of the genus. Such a procedure is not available in this case, since God transcends every genus. His transcendence allows only for an ever more refined knowledge of what he is not, a knowledge achieved by the multiplication of negative differences. The divine nature is thus contracted, but not in such a way that we can apprehend affirmatively what it is.

The way of remotion is founded on the proposition that God is "wholly unmoved" (*omnino immobilis*, I, 14). From the denial of motion and change in God, Thomas immediately infers a number of other negations: God is eternal, has no passive potency, and is neither material nor composite. Following Aristotle, Thomas holds that time is the number of motion; where there is no motion, there cannot be time. An unmoved being thus transcends time (I, 15). Only incomplete, imperfect beings move; for, they must lack what they move to attain and they must be actualized by something already in act. The supposition of divine mutability would render God dependent on a being prior in act (I, 16). But God is absolutely first. The doctrine of potency and act also underlies the repudiation of composition in God (I, 18). Whatever is composite is potentially dissoluble.

Thomas proceeds to argue that God is not a body (I, 20). The chapter is surprisingly long, given that matter and potency have already been denied of God. The argument unites the Aristotelian view that a body is a continuum, composed of parts, possessing quantity and thus potentially divisible, with the neo-Platonic view that what is most noble or most intelligible is not a body.[8] All who have erred on this question have been led astray by their imagination. Thomas concludes that, in considering incorporeal things, it is necessary to relinquish (*derelinquere*) the imagination. Since Thomas holds that the imagination is integral to human thought, his position might seem contradictory. But it is consonant with the view that we must use the way of remotion in knowing God.

The only way to stop following the imagination is to employ negations of the images we inevitably use in our thought and speech about God. There is no possibility of supplanting images with pristine concepts. The initial list of things denied of God is at least partly designed to counteract the tendency to limit God to the imaginable. This tendency, which lies at the root of idolatry, explains why the thesis that God is a body merits lengthy consideration. The thesis has misled many: the early natural philosophers who posited only material causes, the *gentiles* who supposed the elements to be gods, and the Manichees and certain Jews, who conceived of God in bodily terms.

Having corrected certain fundamental misconceptions about God, Thomas provides two apparently positive assertions: that God is his essence, quiddity, or nature, and that his being is his essence. Yet even these are formulated as negations of composition. Chief among the compositions to be denied is that of individual and essence. In every being that is not its essence, there is composition and the "essence is signified through the mode of a part, as humanity is in man" (I, 21).[9] Forms do not subsist. They need to be individuated through principles extrinsic to them. The divine essence, however, is not individuated by anything extrinsic, but is itself "singularly existent" (*per se singulariter existens et in seipsa individuata*). The statements "Socrates is humanity" and "Socrates is whiteness" violate the grammar of finite being. If Socrates were identical with humanity, no other human beings could exist. The mode of attribution appropriate to composite entities is that of an attribute inhering in a subject, as in the statement "Socrates is white." Since there is no composition in God, there is no distinction between essence and individual. This is not so much an affirmation, however, as it is a denial of the relevant composition. God's simpleness is not another attribute but more like what Burrell calls a "formal notion," which "defines the manner in which properties might be attributed to God."[10]

In finite beings, there is composition not only of individual and essence but also of essence and being. There is a difference between to be and to be this sort of thing. Since "being signifies an act," every nature that is distinct from its being is brought into being by something extrinsic to it. In that case, essence is to being as potency is to act. If God were composite in this way, his existence would be derivative, his essence would participate in being. But pure being participates in nothing. Thomas's use of authorities is instructive. He combines Aristotle's language of potency and act with the Platonic language of participation. Cornelio Fabro argues that Thomas subordinates predicamental (Aristotelian) causality to transcendental (Platonic) causality.[11] Yet, the Platonic account of divine causality that Thomas inherited had already been corrected to some extent by Augustine and Dionysius. Indeed, Dionysius' attention to the various ways in which our names signify, or fail to signify, the divine essence fits nicely with Aristotle's emphasis on modes of signifying. Both of these correct the Platonic tendency toward conceptual literalism. The chief authority for the notion of God as subsistent being is not, however, philosophical but scriptural:

> Moses was taught this sublime truth by God. When he sought the Lord saying, "If the sons of Israel should ask me, 'What is his name?' What shall I say to them?" The Lord responded, "I am who am. Speak thus to the sons of Israel: he who is sent me to you." Thus, the Lord showed his own proper name to be "He who is." For any name whatsoever is instituted to signify the nature or essence of some thing. (I, 22)[12]

The account of God as subsistent being brings together, even as it transcends, various discourses about God.[13] The propriety of the name "He who is" can be traced to numerous grounds: its consignification of the present tense implies God's timelessness; its failure to predicate any attribute of God befits the indeterminacy of the divine essence; its identification of God as none other than his being unites concrete actuality with an unparticipated source of being.[14] The convergence of the "sublime truth" taught to Moses with the conclusions of natural theology exhibits the overlap of faith and reason, of the God of scripture and the God of the philosophers. Although the connection was noted prior to Thomas, it finds its most adequate metaphysical underpinning in his description of God as subsistent being.[15]

The strategy of contracting the divine essence through a series of negations prompts Thomas to amplify his previous assertion that God is indefinable. Only what is in potency can be determined by the addition of substantial differences (I, 24). But God is pure act, not amenable to further determination or actualization. Neither is God in some genus (I, 25). The differences that contract a genus are outside the nature of the genus. But nothing is outside of being; thus, what is pure being cannot be a genus. Since God is indefinable, he is incapable of being demonstrated in a strict *propter quid* demonstration, the starting point of which is a proper definition. He can be demonstrated only from his effects (*quia*). These remarks underscore the way God escapes ordinary modes of discourse.

The notion that God is his very being, that he has no essence distinct from his being has confused some readers. In a recent book, Christopher Hughes argues that it is a necessarily false claim.[16] He holds that "nothing subsistent could be just existent: a merely existent substance is too thin to be possible."[17] In the case of God, however, Thomas does not have in mind the sort of simplicity that approaches nonbeing, say that of the elements. Rather, the divine simplicity indicates that God escapes and exceeds the limited perfections of being had by creatures. The notion of God as pure being is apt to mislead. Much of the first book is devoted to anticipating misconceptions. Lest we be confused about the way in which God as pure being escapes all particular genera, Thomas argues that God is not the being of all things. If God were the being of all things, then all would be "simply one" (I, 26).[18] There would be no generation or corruption, only alteration, and all things would "exist from eternity."

There are four origins of the view that God is the being of all things. First, there is the "perverse understanding" of authoritative texts, such as the one in which Dionysius writes, "The act of being of all things is the super-essential divinity."[19] But if this implied that God were the being of all things, then he would not be said to be "above all, but among all, indeed a part of all." Yet Dionysius explicitly affirms the utter transcendence of God. Thomas clearly wants to salvage the authority of Dionysius, but can he do so on the basis of Dionysius' own texts? If isolated from the whole, certain passages in Dionysius seem to support a kind of pantheism. Yet other passages contradict that teaching. The strategy is to acknowledge tensions or ambiguities in his texts, and then to show that certain unwelcome tendencies, tendencies that Dionysius himself rejects, can be counteracted by the doctrine of God as subsistent being. If Thomas goes beyond Dionysius and corrects him on certain issues, he does so in order to salvage the truth that Dionysius was himself attempting to express. Such is one pattern for the dialectical engagement of authorities.

Second, there is the confusion of reason. Since what is common is specified through addition and since God receives no addition, some suppose that God is not a proper being but the common being of all things. However, what is common to many is not separate from them except in reason. The common "can be thought but cannot be without addition." *Esse commune*, the being common to all creatures, does not subsist apart from concrete substances. Yet God is a concretely existing being, distinct from all others. God's pure being is not to be understood as the impoverished fact of existence, indifferently said of all existing things. Fran O'Rourke puts the contrast between *esse commune* and *esse subsistens* nicely: "The individuality of divine being derives from the all-inclusive fullness of its perfection, that of *esse commune* from its limited reception in finite beings."[20] Thomas concurs, when he describes divine being as

> without addition not only in thought but also in the nature of things; not only without addition, but even without any receptivity to addition. God is thus proper, not common, being; for his being is distinguished from all others in that nothing can be added to it. (I, 26)[21]

The passage makes clear that the understanding of divine simplicity as an impoverishment of being is itself impoverished.

The third error arises from the difficulty we have in understanding divine simplicity, since what is most simple for us is not a complete thing but a part.[22] Simplicity is predicated of God, however, as of a perfect, subsisting thing. The notion of subsistent perfection is conceptually jarring; it reveals how inadequate is the transference to God of our ordinary ways of speaking. Finally, error arises from misunderstanding the locution "God is in all things," which indicates presence not as part but as cause.

Thomas is acutely aware that the more abstract our notion of God, the more likely we are to fall into error. The temptation to abstraction arises naturally in the movement beyond the imagination, a movement necessary to overcome materialism. The abstract mode of signifying leads to the identification of God as the formal being of all things and thus once again to idolatry. In the subsequent chapter, God's absolute priority and utter simplicity underlie the argument that he cannot be the form of a body. Once again, Thomas associates the error with the idolatry of the *gentiles*, who posited the "whole world to be God, not by reason of the body, but by reason of the soul."[23] Thus, natural theology castigates misleading practices of divine worship (I, 27).

The initial treatment of the divine essence begins from straightforward errors, which arise from succumbing to the imagination, and moves on to more sophisticated, metaphysical misconstruals, which understand simplicity in an abstract and impoverished manner. The method of remotion corrects the tendency to conflate our ordinary ways of thinking and speaking with language about God.[24] In keeping with the office of the wise, who teach truth and refute error, Thomas consistently identifies the sources of fallacious arguments. His goal is to point out and eradicate the sources of error and so to correct the starting points of intellectual vice. Only after he has corrected these errors and manifested their sources in habitual ways of proceeding does he turn to a positive discussion of the divine perfection. The chief conclusions of the way of remotion point the way toward a positive notion of God as absolute, subsistent perfection.

III. PERFECTION AND THE DIALECTIC OF DIVINE NAMES

Underlying the negations of any composition in God is the affirmation of the existence of a transcendent first cause. The combination of affirmation and negation provides the basis for an account of God as subsistent perfection. The highest member of any genus is the measure of the perfections of the individuals in that genus. But God, transcending every genus, is the measure of all being and is thus universally and absolutely perfect. The mode of excellence, moreover, is proportionate to the mode of being; as pure act, God lacks no perfection. Thomas adduces authoritative texts from Exodus and Dionysius which identify God as the "fullness of goodness." He grounds his account of the divine perfection not only in what he has previously established concerning the primacy and simplicity of God, but also by anticipation of what he will show in the second book concerning God as creator: "In the genus of efficient cause, there is reduction to one cause, . . . from which are all things" (I, 28).[25] Just as there is no a priori, immediate access to God's existence, so too the discussion of God's perfection cannot proceed wholly deductively but must advert to the origin of our knowledge in sensible things. The theological order of proceeding, which moves from God to things, from the absolutely prior to the posterior, reverses the order of natural reason. The reversal presupposes and can never fully eclipse the natural order.

The account of the divine perfection does not violate the original injunction concerning the use of remotion in discussion of God. The very term "perfection" is said of God only by extension from its original mode of signifying. The etymology of *perfectum* signifies something thoroughly made (*per factum*). Hence its original meaning applies only to that which "by becoming reaches a complete act." It can be extended, however, to apply to what "is completely actual without any making" (I, 28).[26] The applicability of the name "perfection" to God is not as straightforward as one might assume. There is a complex relationship between the order of being and the order of names. Creatures are both like and unlike God. He combines the causal principle that every agent produces its like with Dionysius' notion that creatures have a diminished participation in, and dimly reflect, God.[27] The likeness of creatures to God enables us to speak about him; their unlikeness underscores the inadequacy of our discourse. Scripture itself alternates between affirming and denying likeness. Quoting Dionysius, Thomas comments:

> The same things are similar and dissimilar to God. They are similar insofar as they imitate as much as they can him who is not perfectly imitable . . . ; they are dissimilar as things caused fall short of their causes. (I, 29)[28]

The Dionysian language of teleological imitation is an important component of Thomas's account of the divine names. Given the unilateral dependency of creatures on God, it is more appropriate to state that creatures are like God than that God is like creatures. The former way of speaking emphasizes dependence, receptivity, and motion toward a model or source. That all human speech about God consists of unlike likenesses explains why Thomas expends more effort correcting sophisticated errors about God and why a detailed treatment of the resources and limits of human discourse precedes the discussion of divine perfection.

In his preferred description of God as *ipsum esse subsistens,* Thomas introduces us to the grammatical violence involved in our attempt to speak about God.[29] In that description, we simultaneously deploy concrete (*subsistens*) and abstract (*esse*) modes of signifying. In our experience, existing things are concrete, while simple things are abstract. The perfections that we discover in creatures in divided and particular ways are present in God simply, indistinguishably, and concretely. While we can know that this is so, we cannot directly or simply conceptualize what we know. We must use both concrete and abstract modes of signifying in our language about God.

The detailed treatment of naming focuses upon the difference between the *res significata* and the *modus significandi* of names (I, 30). Two words may share the same *res significata* but have different *modi significandi.* For example, "to run" (*currere*) and "running" (*currens*) signify the same thing but do so in different modes. The infinitive signifies abstractly, whereas the participle signifies concretely. Since all our knowledge originates in sense, our mode of signifying is tied to the sensible world of composite entities. Yet the perfection signified (*res significata*) in a name such as "good" may apply to beings that transcend the realm of composite creatures. In speaking of God, we must simultaneously affirm the *res significata* and deny the *modus significandi* of the name. We may then proceed to apply the *res significata* to God in a more eminent way. There is an order of affirmation, remotion or negation, and affirmation by supereminence. Thomas articulates the basis for the way beyond mere remotion thus:

> Since it is possible to find in God every perfection of creatures, but through a more eminent mode, whatever names designate a perfection absolutely and without defect are predicated of God and of other things, such as, goodness, wisdom, being, and others of this sort. . . . Names that express perfections in the mode of supereminence . . . are said of God alone: such as the highest good, the first being, and the like. (I, 30)[30]

Since we have access to God as cause and exemplar only through his effects and images, even the way of supereminence fails to grasp God. The causal primacy of God in relation to creatures makes possible an intentional ordering of names to that which escapes human comprehension.

Although univocal naming of God is impossible, the causal dependence of creatures upon God, whose perfections they dimly reflect, salvages our names from mere equivocity.[31] Our names of God are analogical.[32] It is legitimate to speak of analogy when there is an order of the names either to some other thing, as "health" is predicated of many things, or to some one of the names, as "being" is said principally of substance and secondarily of accident. Since there is nothing independent of God and creatures to whom the names might refer, the former is not viable. The causal dependence of creatures upon God makes the latter possible. Causal likeness, then, is the foundation for the analogy of names. The order of naming is the reverse of the order of reality. Names originally imposed to refer to creatures apply to God secondarily; yet, since God is the source of all perfection, the perfection signified by the name is realized more fully in God than in creatures (I, 34).

The divergence of the mode of naming from that of being gives rise not only to the complex process of affirmation, negation, and affirmation by supereminence, but also to a multiplicity of names. We must reach and speak about the simplicity and pure actuality of God from his manifold and diverse effects. To assume that a multiplicity of nonsynonymous names contradicts the divine simplicity is to confuse the orders of naming and being. We can make informative propositions about God because we do not attribute the intellect's mode of signifying to the thing signified (I, 36).

While the intellect can distinguish between *res* and *modus*, affirming the former and denying the latter, the intellect cannot overcome its natural mode of signifying. It is not possible to strip away the reference to creatures, for this would merely eviscerate the import of the name. The arguments establishing a transcendent ground of the being and perfections of creatures give order, focus, and intelligibility to the pointing. Yet *in via* the pointing can never become a grasping. Natural theology culminates, or fails to culminate, in an interplay of presence and absence, an interplay that accentuates mystery and precludes finality. The names, as Mark Jordan argues, are used "under erasure." But this does not mean that they simply negate themselves or deny their own meaning in playful non-sense. Their self-silencing is, as Jordan writes, "the fulfillment of the possibility of the sign." He amplifies, "The more intelligible the signified, the more inadequate the mode of signification. . . . The opposition persists only because the image is tied to the original. There would be no hierarchy if there were not both likeness and unlikeness."[33]

The process of extending to God a name originally imposed with respect to creatures presupposes, and must never abandon, the moment of remotion or negation, even if the extension issues in an affirmation. René Roques' observations about Dionysius apply to Aquinas as well,

> It is necessary that negation penetrate to the heart itself of affirmation in order that affirmation might succeed. In this transcendent and purified affirmation, negation itself is justified. By this means, negative theology presents itself as a theology of eminence . . . , as the true theology of Transcendence.[34]

The interplay of negation and affirmation, absence and presence, can be more than arbitrary play only if affirmation grounds negation and there is an intelligible order among the names. Nonetheless, as Roques urges, affirmation would not succeed without negation having penetrated to its heart. It can succeed only by failing to make present the signified; for human discourse cannot deliver the actual presence of the transcendental signified. It can deliver only an idol.[35]

As Marion and Jordan both note, the divine names serve an important pedagogical function in theology. They inflame rather than satiate desire. Enacting the project described in the prologue, the names curb the proud assimilation of God to the human intellect and foster instead a spirit of reverent worship. The humble art of grammar reveals the limits of human knowledge; philosophy cannot transcend the complexity and plurality of names. The culmination of philosophical discourse is no stasis, but repining restlessness. Yet Thomas notes that the overcoming of the plurality of names is "promised" in scripture: "On that day there will be one Lord, and his name will be one" (Zach. 14:9) (I, 31).[36] Thus, the teleology of ancient philosophy, the partially frustrated yearning of created nature, passes quietly into the revelation and promise of scripture.

What is striking in the initial treatment of divine perfection is the primacy of goodness. The notion of perfection, which has principally to do with completeness in actuality, is intrinsic to the notion of the good. That God is good is evident from his nature as unmoved mover, which moves as an end or desired good. The communication, moreover, of both goodness and being arises from goodness. The dual motion of creatures from and to God grounds the assertion of God's goodness. Thomas here deploys the neo-Platonic principle that the good is diffusive of itself, but he recasts it as a principle, not of efficient causality, but of final causality.[37] He is thus able to unite it with Aristotle's conception of goodness as actuality. Thomas even finds an Aristotelian confirmation of the revamped neo-Platonic principle, for Aristotle states that "a sign of the perfection of something is that 'it can produce its like' " (I, 37).[38] As O'Rourke notes, Thomas brings together claims that remain disparate, if not opposed, in Aristotle: "it belongs to act to fulfill itself by actualizing others, and the good is what all things desire; act as expansive or communicative and act as desirable are identical in the act of existing."[39]

Not only is God good; he is goodness itself, the good of every good, and the highest good. These predications move from the concrete to the abstract and back to the concrete mode of signifying. Thus, Thomas moves from what can be said of God and creatures, "good" (I, 37), to what can be said only of God, "goodness itself" (I, 38). Then he turns to God as the ontological ground, "good of every good," and transcendent exemplar, "highest good," of all that is good (I, 40–41). Thomas thus deploys Aristotelian means to an end embraced explicitly only in the Platonic tradition. Aristotle does indeed refer to the life of God as most fully actual and most pleasant. Yet, in spite of his definition of the good as that which all desire and his assertion that all desire to know, he never identifies God as exemplar of the good life.[40] For Thomas, the speculative pursuit of first causes is identical to the practical pursuit of the good.

Thomas then argues that God is one (I, 42). He argues (a) that there cannot be two highest goods, (b) that two perfect beings would be indistinguishable, and (c) that there cannot be many first movers. The logic of necessary being requires singularity: "nothing belonging to this designated thing insofar as it is this thing belongs to another."[41] But God is *per se* a necessary being.[42] As is customary, Thomas ends the chapter with authoritative texts from scripture and with a citation of the errors which oppose the truth. He states that while the *gentiles* posited a multitude of gods, many of them also affirmed a hierarchy among the gods with a highest god at the summit. Thomas irenically observes that even scripture calls lesser beings—angels, for instance—gods. Only the Manicheans propose two first principles, neither of which is subordinate to the other.

Subsequent to the consideration of God's goodness and unity is that of his infinity. Since God is neither material nor potential, the infinity of a multitude or of a continuous quantity is excluded. There remains the infinity of "spiritual magnitude," according to which, as Augustine states, "it is the same to be greater as to be better." The infinity of "power and goodness or completeness of one's nature" is not understood as a privation, but as a negation. The negative argument on behalf of God's infinity begins from the principle that "every act inhering in another receives its termination from that in which it is."[43] If the accident "whiteness" were self-existent, it would be infinite. But only God is self-existent, that is, only God is in nothing and is determined by nothing. His perfection has no term. In the following passage, Thomas speaks in more positive and in more Platonic terms about the perfection of God,

> Everything possessing a certain perfection is more perfect to the extent that it participates in that perfection more fully. But that mode is not possible, nor is it even able to be thought, by which a certain perfection is possessed more fully than it is possessed by that which is perfect through its essence and whose act of being is its goodness. (I, 43)[44]

According to Thomas, the thesis that the world is eternal confirms the view that God's power is infinite, since the eternity of motion requires that God move during an infinite time. The contrary thesis, that the world has a beginning in time, suggests another defense of God's infinite power. The more powerful something is, the more it is able to reduce potency to act. But "what is utterly nonexistent is infinitely distant from act."[45] He who brings things into being from no preexistent matter is infinitely powerful. Thomas concludes by noting that the "ancient philosophers attest to this truth," for "all posited an infinite first principle of things."[46] The first philosophers, however, fallaciously supposed the first principle to be a discrete or continuous quantity; in so doing, "they did not recognize their own voice" (*propriam enim vocem ignorabant*). Later philosophers eschewed the notion of an infinite body.

While one of Thomas's goals in the *Summa Contra Gentiles* is to correct the errors of the *gentiles* or the philosophers, he is eager to grant credit where due and to highlight the dialectical progress of philosophy. The statement that the early philosophers did not "acknowledge their own voice" applies Aristotle's conciliatory assertion that truth is like the proverbial door that no one can fail entirely to hit. The eagerness to credit opponents with having apprehended part of the truth is more than the application of the rule of charity; it is not to be confused with some grand scholastic synthesis or an uncritical amalgamation of opinions. Instead, Thomas's own view, which emerges from the dialectic, demonstrates its superiority to extant positions by providing an account of where and why rival positions go astray. Thomas also strives to show that what is true in rival positions finds surer foundations in his own account. The strategy mirrors the dialectical structure of *Physics* I.

Thomas turns next to a discussion of the divine understanding (I, 44). The principal argument for ascribing understanding to God runs thus: "Every mover moves through a certain form which it intends in moving." God is the unmoved mover of the entire universe. But the universal form requisite for moving the whole of creation can exist only in an intellect.[47] Hence the first mover must be intelligent. Since understanding is an immanent act, and since in God operation is indistinguishable from essence, God's understanding is identical with his essence. Whatever inhibits perfect understanding—imperfect conformity of intelligible species to object, incomplete union of species with intellect, embeddedness of the object in matter—is utterly foreign to God. In God, there is an unmediated unity of the most perfect operation with the most intelligible operation (I, 45).

Since God wants nothing for his completion and since movement from himself to other objects of knowledge would entail change and presuppose imperfection, God primarily and essentially knows only himself. The divine essence is the proper, immediate object of God's understanding; hence, God knows all things through one, simple, timeless act of understanding. A number of difficulties attend the simultaneous affirmation of the simplicity of divine knowledge and of God's comprehensive understanding of a multitude of objects. Thomas denies that the multitude can have distinct being or be independent forms or exist primarily in a separate intellect (I, 51). A fruitful starting point can be found by adverting to the nature of human understanding: "By understanding, the intellect forms in itself a certain intention or notion of the thing understood, which the definition signifies." (I, 53)[48] The divine essence is the intelligible likeness of all things; through knowing it, God knows all existing things.[49]

Thomas continues the analogy to human understanding in a subsequent chapter where he argues that God knows all things together. Even the human intellect can understand many things through one species. In the act of knowing, the human mind provides a suggestion of the timeless unity of divine knowing. As Dionysius writes, "Knowing itself, the divine wisdom knows all things, material things immaterially, divisible things indivisibly, and many unitedly." (I, 58)[50]

The analogy from human understanding is a necessary but imperfect starting point for an account of the divine intellect; the method of remotion is prevalent again. God's knowledge is not habitual (I, 56), or discursive (I, 57), and he does not understand by composing and dividing (I, 58). Thomas underscores the unlike likeness of human and divine when he writes that discursive reasoning, which is characteristic of rational animals, results from the imperfection of the intellectual power in us (I, 57). Nonetheless, the link provides the indispensable point of departure for an ascent to the divine intellect.

IV. GOD AND THE WORLD

Having moved from the world to God, Thomas reverses direction and considers God's relationship to the world.[51] The complex relationship between affirmation and negation is operative in Thomas's sustained dialectical defense of the position that the transcendent simplicity of the divine understanding need not preclude a proper knowledge of all created things, even the lowliest. As David Burrell has shown, Thomas counters the Arabic and Jewish understanding of God's relationship to the world by substituting a model of practical reasoning for that of speculative reasoning.[52] The shift is allied to Thomas's repudiation of emanationist metaphysics, which mitigates the role of divine will in creating. Thomas repeatedly speaks of God's knowing by causing.

Since an effect is known when its cause is known, God knows all things as cause of them. God causes all things either immediately or mediately, but he also knows from the inside whatever is caused immediately by intermediate causes. As Thomas puts it,

> Since he knows himself, God knows what is from him immediately. When this is known, again God knows what proceeds from it immediately; and

thus concerning all mediate causes to the last effect. Therefore, God knows whatever is found in reality. (I, 50)[53]

If God were to have only a common knowledge of things, his knowledge would be imperfect and potential. To know the reality of something is to know its "ultimate perfections, by which its proper being is completed" (I, 50).[54] The distinction of things, moreover, is not from chance, but from a knowing cause. Denying the neo–Platonic postulate of intermediate creators, Thomas asserts that a secondary cause could not be the source of the distinction of things because it already exists "in a world of distinct effects." Its position in relation to other things is determined prior to its existence. The distinction and order of the whole, which pertains to the proper as well as the common being of things, is attributable to the cause of the whole. God must then have a proper knowledge of things. As Thomas puts it,

> The divine intellect of God is able to comprehend in his essence what is proper to each thing by understanding that in which each thing imitates his essence and that in which it falls short of his perfection. (I, 54)[55]

The divine essence, then, is the proper likeness or exemplar of all things, even of singulars. The account of exemplary causality, Thomas notes, salvages to some extent the Platonic doctrine of ideas.[56]

The longest and most polemical sections of the first book concern God's proper knowledge of singulars.[57] As we have already seen, Thomas attempts to reconcile the immediacy, simplicity, and primacy of God's self-knowledge with his proper knowledge of a plurality of existing creatures. In a subsequent discussion, he responds to opinions denying God's knowledge of singulars. He reiterates and amplifies many of the arguments posited on behalf of God's proper knowledge of things. From the fact that God knows as cause, it follows that God knows singulars, since "universals have being only in singulars."[58] The apparent dignity of human knowing, which consists in abstracting universals from singulars, is actually a consequence of the poverty of the human intellect, which must gather knowledge from things. God's knowledge, on the contrary, is prior to and a cause of things (I, 65). The denial of God's knowledge of singulars results from the failure to make sufficient use of the method of remotion; the failure is rooted in an anthropomorphic conception of divinity. God's perfection requires a fundamental reversal in our conception of the mode of knowing.

In arguing that God knows things that are not, Thomas continues to deploy the principle that God's knowledge is productive. As an artist knows unfashioned things, so God knows uncreated things.[59] In knowing himself, God knows all the ways in which he might be imitated. He also knows things that have yet to come into being. Thus, God knows things that do not yet exist and things that will never exist. Thomas contrasts the "ever-abiding simultaneous whole" (*totum simul semper manens*) of eternity with the "duration of time," which is "stretched out in the succession of before and after."[60] The now of eternity is proportioned to time as the indivisible to a continuum (I, 66).

Recourse to God's productive or practical knowledge of things aids Thomas in numerous discussions, yet it seems to create insuperable difficulties for God's knowledge of future contingent singulars. Would not God's productive knowledge render all events necessary? Anticipating the difficulty, Thomas notes that the contingent lacks all necessity only in the future; when a contingent event is present, it cannot not-be. Lest one misunderstand the sort of necessity operative here, Thomas distinguishes between absolute necessity or necessity of the consequent, and conditional necessity or necessity of the consequence. The former would eliminate contingency altogether, while the latter insists only that, if Socrates is sitting, then he is necessarily sitting, not that he is compelled to do so. Since God is immediately and timelessly present to the whole of time, God knows future contingents as present contingents. Thus, his knowledge does not destroy contingency.

But what is Thomas's response to the apparent contradiction involved in holding that God produces all events, yet some events are contingent? The problem is especially acute with respect to the free choices of rational beings. Thomas does not avoid the issue. God's knowledge extends even to the motions of the will precisely because his causality extends to these. He writes,

> Since each thing operates through its form, from which is the act of being of the thing, it follows that the fount and source of the whole of being, from which is also every form, must be the principle of all operation; for the effects of secondary causes are reduced more principally into first causes. (I, 68)[61]

Thomas does not presently expatiate on how God can be the cause of operation without determining the action. That will come in later books. Here he makes only the initial, negative assertion that the "dominion that the will has over its acts . . . excludes" only "the determination of the power to one thing and the violence of an exterior agent."[62] It does not exclude "the influence of a higher cause from which is its being and operation" (*influentiam superioris causae, a qua est ei esse et operari*). His positive thesis is this. All being is from God; if operations are to be actual, they must participate in the source of all being. God's causal activity is immediately operative wherever there is being in act.[63]

Thomas turns next to God's knowledge of the infinite (I, 69). Once again, he seems to be at odds with Aristotle, who argues that the infinite as infinite is unknowable. Thomas concedes that the infinite is indeed unknowable according to the mode in which Aristotle described its knowability, namely, in terms of the "measurements of its parts." But God does not know in this way. He knows all things by knowing himself as pure, infinite actuality. Since God knows the unlimited variety of ways in which creation might imitate him, his knowledge extends beyond what is actual to what is potential. The method of remotion, which is necessary for the analogical application of terms to God, enables Thomas to avoid direct contravention of Aristotle.

A number of teachings concerning the divine intellect bring Thomas into apparent conflict with Aristotle and into explicit disagreement with his commentators. God knows singulars, things that are not, future contingents, and the infinite, all of which Aristotle considered unknowable. Thomas does not directly rebut Aristotle's position; rather, he strives to circumscribe the scope of the principle, or to argue that it is not relevant to the divine mode of knowing, or to interpret Aristotle as providing only a partial response to a question. He argues that composition and division are not essential to truth, that to know lowly things is ignoble only for imperfect beings, that the unknowability of the infinite is applicable just to finite intellects, and that future contingents are not actually future for God. The dialectical strategies employed here follow the suggestions of *Topics* I, 13–18 concerning the analysis of the meaning, scope, and equivocal uses of terms.

At the end of the discussion of God's knowledge of the infinite, Thomas lists four ways in which human knowledge falls short of the divine: (a) our intellect is absolutely finite, (b) it knows through diverse species, (c) it cannot know many species simultaneously, and (d) it is limited to the knowledge of what is. Thomas never asserts that Aristotle is guilty of conflating human and divine modes of being or ways of knowing. Instead, he insists that transformation is necessary in the movement from the former to the latter. The strategy is compatible with the teaching of the analogy of names, wherein remotion and negation are necessary in the application to God of names crafted from the natural world and for human purposes.

In this context, Thomas argues that God knows lowly things (I, 70). What grounds the view of God's intimate causal presence to the world is the previous account of God's utter independence and transcendent perfection. In response to the suggestion that such knowledge would be ignoble, Thomas notes that the stronger a power is, the more it extends to remote effects. His principal argument is grounded in the radical contingency and inferiority of the entire created order. The most noble things in the universe are more distant from God than the lowest creatures are from the highest. If lowliness were an impediment or inappropriate to divine knowledge, God would not know anything other than himself. Were God to know only the more noble creatures, he would be deprived of an even more noble knowledge, that of the order of the whole, which cannot be without lower creatures. Once again the criterion deployed by those who would circumscribe God's knowledge is more appropriate to the imperfect order of human knowing, wherein the concentration on lowly things is a result of the incapacity of the knower. But God knows both low and high alike, effortlessly and in the same way. Continuing his attempt to show that there is no contradiction between his own teaching and that of Aristotle, Thomas addresses Aristotle's statement that "vile things are better ignored than known" (*vilia melius ignorantur quam cognoscuntur*). Thomas argues that the passage applies solely to cases where vile things are impediments to knowing noble things.

Between the two discussions of God's knowledge of created beings stands a consideration of God as truth, which is introduced by an aporia: the Philosopher holds that truth resides in the operation of the intellect composing and dividing, yet Thomas has already denied composition and division in God. The operation of composition and division is essential to our mode of knowing; what is essential to the notion of truth itself is that the "thing be as the intellect says it to be."[64] The definition of the true as the "adequation of the intellect and thing" (*adaequatio intellectus et rei*) may be said of God, even if the adequation is not achieved through the operation appropriate to human reasoning. God has unitedly, immediately, and perfectly what our intellect possesses discursively, mediately, and imperfectly (I, 59).

The reversal of the analogy between human and divine understanding continues in the discussion of God as truth. The perfection of the work of the intellect is called truth; something is called true when it "follows properly the act of its own nature." In both ways, God deserves the name truth. A created thing is called true insofar as it can give a "true account" (*veram aestimationem*) of itself; it does so, by imitating "its model" in the divine mind.[65] That which is the model for all others is called true not by reference to some higher, preexisting model, but according to itself. Hence God is not just true but the truth. That God is both a subsistent being and the transcendent model of all perfections requires once again the simultaneous use of concrete and abstract modes of signifying.

The divine truth is pure, admitting no error or deception (I, 61). The strongest reason for supposing the divine intellect to be inerrant relies, not upon an analogy to human understanding, but upon an exact reversal of it. In the determination of truth, things are measures of the human intellect. Adequation requires a unity of knower and known, a unity that is absolute in God. The application of adequation to God, however, reverses the causal relationship between the mind and things. Thomas writes,

> Through its knowledge, the divine intellect is the cause of things. Its knowl-
> edge is the measure of things, as art is the measure of artifacts, each one of
> which is perfect insofar as it is consonant with art. The comparison of the
> divine intellect to things parallels that of things to the human intellect. (I, 61)[66]

The principle that things have the same disposition in truth as in being entails that God is the highest and first truth. Thomas adds that the measure of a genus has most perfectly whatever is possessed by the members of the genus: God's truth measures all truth.

Thomas's discussion of the divine truth recalls the prologue, wherein contemplation of truth is said to be the end of the universe. Truth is absolutely one in God, whose truth is the ground, measure, and end of all truth. No human science can claim to study truth as one, although the goal of all human science is that truth through which and according to which all other truths are true. The Aristotelian themes of the prologue have been transposed to a neo-Platonic context, in which God is the efficient cause, the exemplary cause, and the measure of all things. The ascent to the highest good requires a doubling back, a recognition that the ascent presupposes a descent; the summit of the philosophical ascent is also its base.

Having discussed God's understanding and truth, Thomas turns to God's will (I, 72). Whatever is capable of grasping the good by under-standing has will. Without will, God could not be said to direct things to an end. Thomas thus deploys an Aristotelian principle on behalf of a conclusion never stated by Aristotle. To deny God's capacity to will is to disparage the divine perfection: only volitional beings can be said to enjoy their own perfection, that is, to rest in goods appropriate to their being. In the *Metaphysics* XII, 7, Aristotle's depiction of the life of contemplation as the "most pleasant" comes close to this position without ever stating that God has will.[67]

Thomas argues that the divine will is God's essence (I, 73), that the principal object of the will is the divine essence (I, 74), and that, in willing himself, God wills other things (I, 75). Whenever someone loves something for its own sake, he desires that it "become better and be multiplied." Although the divine essence cannot be increased or multiplied in itself, it can be multiplied according to likeness. God wills the good of the whole universe. But the order of the universe consists in the order among singulars. The Book of Genesis confirms that God takes pleasure in, and cares for, each single work (*vidit Deus lucem quod esset bona*) and all his works together (*vidit Deus cuncta quae fecerat, et erant valde bona*). The quotation from Genesis indicates what is at stake in the debate with Aristotle's commentators: the understanding of God's creative and providential relationship to the world (I, 78).

Crucial to the critique of emanationist accounts of God's relationship to the world is the question of the modality of God's will. According to Aquinas, God wills his being and goodness by an absolute necessity, while he wills other things by a necessity of supposition. Since God wills other things for the sake of his goodness and wills the latter with an absolute necessity, must he not will the former with an absolute necessity? The suggestion has often been eagerly embraced in the neo-Platonic tradition. Thomas holds, however, that God's goodness is complete without them. The only thing necessarily willed is that whose nonexistence eliminates the good. But there is no such good other than God. Thomas's transposition of the neo-Platonic doctrine of the diffusiveness of the good from efficient to final causality is operative here. The good does not flow of necessity from God as light from the sun; instead, the good results from the intention of a rational being. The created order, moreover, falls far short of the divine perfection; there is an infinity of other ways in which creation might imitate God. No thing or order of things imposes necessity upon the divine will (I, 80–81).

God wills things distinct from himself by suppositional, not absolute, necessity. If God wills the existence of the universe, a universe to which the divine goodness has no necessary order, then he necessarily wills its existence. From God's willing the existence of a particular universe it follows that he wills whatever is necessary for its completion. The last principle provides the basis for Thomas's argument that God's will does not eliminate contingency from things. God wills whatever is needed for the completeness of the universe; but completeness requires a plurality and hierarchy of creatures, some of which operate contingently. The logic of suppositional necessity salvages contingency and freedom.

Concerning the divine will, Thomas writes,

> Thus can we proceed in assigning the reason of the divine will. God wills man to have reason that man might exist; he wills man's existence for the completion of the universe; he wills the good of the universe to be because it is consonant with his goodness. (I, 86)[68]

The first two reasons come from the role of suppositional necessity in creation, while the third reason—the reason for creation itself—is ascribed to the fitting or becoming. From an analysis of what is appropriate to particular creatures and to the relationship of creatures to another and to the whole, we can surmise certain probable reasons why God made what he did. But we can give no account other than the divine goodness in response to the questions of why this universe rather than another and why a creation at all. The rationale of the divine goodness ultimately escapes the human intellect. Indeed, our access to God's will and goodness is through its manifestation in the order in which we presently find ourselves.[69] We know enough to construct probable arguments and to negate the reduction of things to the twin extremes of absolute necessity and mere whim. The account of God's willing of other things stands between an emanationist account and one that highlights the sovereign, arbitrary will of God.

Given the limitations to human knowledge, how can we know enough to place limits upon God's will? Thomas argues that God cannot will what is "repugnant to the nature of being" (*aliquid repugnat rationi entis*), for example, that affirmation and negation be true simultaneously and in the same respect. The coextension of goodness and being implies that God cannot will what cannot be good, only what is or can be good. Divine goodness underlies the suppositional necessity that God wills whatever is required for the completion of something. Thus, per se contradictions, for instance, "man is an ass," are impossible. God's inability to will what is per se impossible is not, then, a limitation in the pejorative sense.[70]

In contrast to the consideration of the divine intellect, which culminated in a discussion of God as truth, the divine goodness does not follow the divine will. God's goodness has of course already been treated; indeed, it was the first name attributed to God, the name said to be synonymous with perfection. What is the reason for the disparity in the two orders? As the teaching of the divine names reveals, our knowledge of the divine perfection arises from our knowledge of the world. We know that God is perfect because we know that he is good. God is known to be good as goal and source, as a desired end and as communicator of goodness. The first book thus provides an ample, metaphysical account of the claim made in the prologue that God is both final and first cause of the universe. It also points toward a unification of the theoretical and the practical lives, of the account of the human good in Aristotle's *Ethics* and that of the divine life in the *Metaphysics*.

The resolution of unsettled questions among the philosophers provides a vantage point from which one can reconsider the notion of nobility, perfection, and excellence. For the ancients, the contemplative ascent to the Good or the first cause is the most noble way of life. The completion of the ascent renders one indifferent or averse to a return to lower things. Thomas agrees that the ultimate end of the entire universe is to ascend to that from which it came forth. This is the perfection of finite creatures, to whom the etymology of "perfection"—"thoroughly made"—literally applies. God's sheer actuality and unadulterated nobility require no such indigent process. His superabundant perfection is evident in his overflowing to create and conserve lowly creatures. The descent to lowly or vile creatures is no longer esteemed a burden to be forced upon unwilling philosophers (Plato) or an unbecoming object of divine knowledge and concern (Aristotle).

V. GOD AS SUBSISTENT EXEMPLAR OF THE LIFE OF WISDOM

In the context of his discussion of the divine will, Thomas takes up the question of whether God possesses any passions or virtues. According to their genus, passions imply the change of the sensitive appetite and cannot be said of God. Many passions are also alien to God because of their species, for example, sorrow, which is caused by the presence of evil, or hope, which presupposes the absence of a desired good. The passions of delight, joy, and love can be said of God, once the elements peculiar to passion have been negated. Delight and joy result from a "good . . .

possessed in act" and consist in a "certain resting of the will in something willed."[71] Containing all goodness in himself and resting in himself, God has both delight and joy (I, 90). Love, as Dionysius states, is a "unitive power" (*unitiva virtus*). Thomas writes,

> The more intimate to the one loving is that from which union is, so much more firm is the love. . . . That by which all things are joined to God, namely, his goodness, . . . is what is supreme and most intimate to God, for he himself is his goodness. (I, 91)[72]

Thomas subordinates efficient to final causality and understands the latter as arising from God's abundant love. In fact, the *exitus-reditus* structure of creation is rooted in the metaphysical account of God as love. The communication of love is the motive for creating, for giving being to other things; having created, divine love draws all things to itself.

Just as certain passions are analogically applicable to God, so too some virtues apply: Giving each thing its due, God is just; containing the model of things made, God has art; bestowing goodness on things, God possesses liberality; and showing himself as he is in deeds and words, God is true. At this juncture, Thomas returns to the status of the divine names (I, 93). Insofar as the passions or virtues are "contracted to human things," (*ad res humanas contrahantur*) they do not apply to God. When generalized, some do apply. In speaking of the divine virtues, Thomas adopts Platonic language: "The divine virtues are called exemplars of ours; for the things contracted and particularized are the likenesses of certain absolute things."[73] The ensuing discussion, which shows that God is a subsisting, living being, indicates that the abstract mode of signifying is insufficient and, when used exclusively, misleading.

Thomas next considers God's possession of contemplative virtues, especially wisdom. As in the prologue, so too here he combines scriptural and Aristotelian arguments concerning wisdom and God's possession of it. Wisdom is knowledge of the highest causes; since God knows himself perfectly, wisdom is especially attributed to him. Scripture states that wisdom is a gift of God, while Aristotle says that it is a divine, not a human, possession. Thomas ends the discussion of passion and virtue by arguing that, just as God cannot will what is incompatible with his being or goodness, so he cannot will evil and he hates nothing. If he were to do either, he would contradict his own will, which is to communicate the likeness of his goodness to creatures (I, 96).

The treatment of the divine life comes next and is the penultimate topic of the first book (I, 97). The oddity of its location is clear from Thomas's initial justification of God's having life, namely, that the acts of understanding and willing presuppose life. If the order of presentation were deductive, the discussion of God's life would seem more appropriately to have followed the discussion of his being, and to have preceded that of his intellect and will. There are at least three reasons why the divine life is treated where it is. First, our access to God begins from what is most evident to us, not from what is prior in being. We know that God lives because we know that he understands and wills. Second, the divine life comes at the end of a litany of perfections, which are habitually signified by us in abstract terms. Immediately prior to the discussion of God's perfection is the section on the divine names, which argued that, in speaking of God, we must employ both abstract and concrete modes of signifying. By emphasizing that God is a concretely living being, the section on the divine life provides a dialectical corrective to the entire section on the divine perfection. Third, the discussion of God's life prepares the way for a consideration of the kind of life enjoyed by God, a life of supreme blessedness, comprehending and excelling all other modes of felicity. The blessedness of God's life of wisdom marks the culmination of the first book, as the praise of the human pursuit of wisdom had introduced it.

In every respect, God's life, the life of wisdom, is most blessed (I, 100). Blessedness follows upon the perfection of operation, for which there are four criteria. First, it must "maintain itself in its operation," that is, nothing must take place in the cause but the operation itself. This is true only of contemplative operations. Second, the principle of the operation must be that of the highest power. Third, the object of operation must be the "highest intelligible" (*felicitas est in intelligendo altissimum intelligibile*). Finally, the form of the operation must be such that the operation is performed "perfectly, easily, firmly, and delightfully." God's life fulfills the Aristotelian and the Boethian definitions of blessedness: "a state perfected by the congregation of all goods."[74] Yet God's life excels all limited participations in blessedness, indeed every conceivable blessedness; for he possesses perfections not through achievement or accumulation but eternally, immediately, and simply. Since blessedness arises from intellectual nature and only God is a subsistent intellect, God's blessedness is supreme, unmitigated, indistinguishable from his very being.

The culmination of the first book—with its references to wisdom and the life of blessedness and with its commingling of pagan and Christian sources—recalls the teaching and repeats the rhetoric of the prologue. Wisdom is a way of life, replete with joy, that satisfies all human longing, unites man to God in friendship, and warrants the name of blessed. The first book is itself an enactment of that life of wisdom, an enactment that culminates in a recognition of the pursuit of wisdom as a participation in the exemplary cause of the whole, a sharing in the life of that first and highest cause whose contemplation is the goal of philosophy. The previous arguments on behalf of God's desire to communicate his goodness to creatures provide grounds for an unexplained and audacious assertion of the prologue: the life of wisdom establishes friendship between us and God. Still, the dominant mode of discourse in the first book is *via negativa*, a mode that accentuates the gap between the human pursuit of wisdom and the divine possession of it (I, 102). As Thomas puts it, "false and earthly felicity" is nothing but a "certain shadow" (*quandam umbram*) of divine blessedness. The philosophical pursuit of the highest good is, as Josef Pieper argues, ultimately a *philosophia negativa*. The mode of supereminence, however, points beyond the limits of our language to the sheer actuality and utter bliss of the divine life, a life of which we can experience only intimations and which we can possess only in hope.

VI. NARRATIVE FOUNDATIONS IN THE FIRST BOOK

The importance of dialectic is evident in the very structure of the first book, which combats antithetical errors: the idolatrous reduction of God to what is imaginable, and the anthropomorphic assumption that divine perfection entails the distance of God from the world. References to the *gentiles* figure prominently in the first section of the book, where Thomas castigates their view that God is a body or the soul of the world. The persistent danger here is that of idolatry, of conflating our ways of knowing with the divine essence. The opening section thus introduces what becomes a pervasive feature of the first book: the concern over the resources of, and limitations to, human speech about God. Precisely that issue is operative in the most dialectical section of the book, which treats of God's relationship to the world. Thomas argues that those who distance God from the world assume too great a likeness between human and divine perfection. Focusing upon Aristotle and his commentators, Thomas deploys various dialectical strategies from the *Topics* to show that there need be no conflict between the view that he and the Christian tradition espouse and the texts of Aristotle.

The convergence of philosophical argument and theological authority is a paramount concern of the first three books. In the first book, the two most conspicuous instances of convergence have to do with God as subsistent being and as the exemplar of the life of wisdom. The convergence is also evident in the pervasive references to the Old Testament wisdom literature, especially to the books of Job, Proverbs, Psalms, and Wisdom. In this life, neither philosophical nor theological discourse can overcome the plurality of names, the multiplication of concepts, inherent in human speech about God. Scripture, which informs us that a day will come when God's name shall be one, promises a transcendence of the limitations to human discourse.

The prominence of scriptural passages in crucial segments of the first book invites the following questions. Does scripture merely confirm conclusions reached by an autonomous philosophy? Or is scriptural teaching the impetus for the search for rational explanation? The latter thesis underlies Gilson's view of Christian philosophy, the Thomistic version of faith seeking understanding (*fides quaerens intellectum*). Thomas's thorough reworking of the philosophical order of questions—his ample consideration of issues treated laconically by Aristotle—undermines the view that the first three books constitute an autonomous philosophy. This does not mean of course that one can detect theological premises in the arguments of the first book. Thomas wants to show that philosophical argument partially confirms, and in no way conflicts with, the Christian conception of God and his relation to the universe. To do so, he must avoid employing theological data as premises. Yet the order of questions is theological, not philosophical; the emphasis is upon those issues that bear directly upon the Christian conception of divinity.

The passage of dialectical inquiry into the narrative of scripture helps us to discern the dominant principle of inclusion of topics in the first book. Thomas is most concerned with those teachings about God that touch implicitly on the narrative shape of revealed truth. The two stages of the first book establish: (a) God's utter transcendence of, and freedom from, all things and (b) his detailed knowledge of, and providential care for, created beings, even the most lowly. The first stage secures the foundations of a narrative that begins and ends beyond time and is written by the omnipotent architect of the whole. The second stage counteracts a deistic misconstrual of God's relationship to the world, a misconception that undermines the very possibility of viewing creation in narrative terms. If God were distant from the world, indifferent to its parts, then particular, contingent events would have no cosmic significance.

The chapter on the compatibility of divine causality with contingency and human freedom, while merely a prelude to an ampler consideration in the third book, is crucial to the structure of the *Contra Gentiles*. Divine and human freedom is integral to its narrative; without freedom, there could be no dramatic interaction between us and God. Similarly, Thomas refuses to reduce God's reason for creating either to necessity or to arbitrary will. In so doing, he suggests an alternative model of God as artist; the reason for creation is to be discerned through detailed investigation of God's artifacts. Finally, the chapters on divine love and wisdom eliminate one of the chief sources of a tragic view of the human condition: the jealousy and animosity of God. Instead, God is the superabundant source of all goodness, freely bestowing gifts upon creatures.

Beyond these particular themes, the first book provides numerous clues as to how we ought to read the whole. Thomas deploys a plethora of dialectical strategies; he also combines Aristotle's view of the disparity between the orders of knowing and being with the Platonic language of exemplar and image. The successive moments of negation and supereminence in the divine names engender a reversal of discourse, which results in the realization that God is the superabundant source of the very starting points of our inquiry. Not only must we double back to secure the sensible foundations of our discourse about God, but we are also invited to reconsider things as effects of divine wisdom and goodness. The very foundation of our ability to name God is the limited likeness of creatures to God (I, 29). The language of exemplar and image, model and copy becomes increasingly prominent in the second section of the first book: in the discussion of God as preexisting source of all perfection, as supreme truth measuring the truth of all created things, and as subsistent exemplar of the life of wisdom.

If the text takes its point of departure from an understanding of wisdom as knowledge of the highest causes, it concludes by pointing out that the pursuit of wisdom is a participation in, and reflection of, the divine life. The text urges a reappropriation of image in light of exemplar. The pattern of alternating ascent and descent has important ramifications. The pattern is of course suitable to embodied rationality; it is a reminder that the body is a constituting condition of our search for wisdom. The pattern is also pertinent to our understanding of divine and human perfection. At the center of Thomas's linguistic corrective of philosophical miscontruals of the divine stands his positive alliance of the good as perfective with the good as communicative. Freed of anthropomorphic suppositions, descent need no longer be seen as opprobrious. Might the prominence of the twin motions of ascent and descent not also foreshadow the central Christian mystery in which the way up is the way down?

3

DIVINE ARTISTRY: THE METAPHYSICS AND AESTHETICS OF CREATION

I. INTRODUCTION

The first book culminates with God as the subsistent exemplar of the life of wisdom, a life that we cannot attain fully by our own power. How then are we to gain access to it? The way that is commensurate to our natural capacity is through a detailed study of God's effects, which is the subject of the second book of the *Summa Contra Gentiles* (II, 1). While the first book considered God's immanent operations, the second treats of his transitive operations, which are evident in creation. These themes are somewhat familiar from the prologue to the first book, with its commingling of philosophic and theological conceptions of wisdom. Here, however, participation in divine wisdom is said to result from a mode of consideration markedly different from that of the philosopher:

> Since the Christian faith teaches man principally about God, and makes him know creatures by the light of divine revelation, there arises in him a certain likeness of God's wisdom. Thus it is said: "Beholding the glory of the Lord with open face, we are transformed into that same image," II Cor. 3:18. (II, 2)[1]

While the philosopher considers creatures as they are in their own nature, the theologian investigates them by the light of revelation and is interested in them insofar as they come from, and are related to, God.

What impact does the theological approach have on the structure and teaching of the second book? The alteration of the philosophical approach to human nature can be seen in two ways. First, there is a reordering of the structure of inquiry, which is motivated and shaped by the concern to develop a distinctively theological pedagogy. Book two moves from God to creation, to the nature of intellectual substances, to the embodiment of the human soul, and finally to the activities and operations of the embodied intellect. In the discussion of human nature, Thomas is preoccupied with the metaphysical principles of the human person. Indeed, the first two books of the *Contra Gentiles* constitute a theocentric treatise in metaphysics.[2] Yet, the theological approach to creatures never exhibits a hasty or adventitious referral of things to God; there is no direct or simple access to the divine. Second, Thomas relates human nature to God by revealing the harmony, integrity, and brilliance of the created order. The beauty of created things, especially as manifested in the human person, leads believers to marvel at and revere the author of creation. The theological study of creatures destroys errors about the nature of God, fosters an appreciation of God's wisdom and power, and incites souls to a love of divine goodness. Although properly theological doctrines are relegated to the fourth book, the descent of theology to reason in the first three books has as its end the reordering of philosophy to theology. As the prologue intimated, the office of the wise no longer falls to the first philosopher, but to the theologian. Indeed, Thomas radically subordinates mere "human philosophy" (*humana philosophia*) to the "highest wisdom" (*maxima sapientia*), which the former "serves."

The subordination of "human philosophy" to the "highest wisdom" alters the order and mode of consideration of creatures. As is clear from the prologue, there are similarities between theology and metaphysics. Thomas's theocentric metaphysics can be understood as perfecting the science of metaphysics. The *gentiles*, including Plato and Aristotle, never complete the return from the first principle to dependent beings. By contrast, Thomas articulates a detailed metaphysics of created being. The consequences are telling. As Josef Pieper suggests, creation "determines and characterizes the interior structure of nearly all the basic concepts in St. Thomas's philosophy of being."[3] In the second book of the *Contra Gentiles*, Thomas envisions creation as a manifestation of the wisdom and beauty of divine artistry. Yet he also underscores the difference between a philosophical and a theological approach to creatures when he states the latter is "more akin to God's knowledge" (II, 4).[4] The second book ends appropriately by ascending once again to God, the transcendent exemplar of the whole of creation.

II. THE DIALECTIC AND NARRATIVE OF CREATION

Following the treatment of the existence and nature of God in the first book, the second book begins by considering those attributes that pertain to God as creator. Thomas argues that there is active potency in God and that his power is not distinct from his substance or his action (II, 7–9). These follow immediately from the simplicity of God. Echoing the previous discussion of the divine names (I, 30–36), Thomas argues that power is attributed to God according to the "diverse conceptions of our intellect" and that the relations that we predicate of God do not really exist in him (II, 10 and 12).

Were God really related to creatures, change and multiplicity would be introduced into the divine nature. Thomas avails himself of Aristotle's teaching in the *Categories* where he states that, strictly speaking, "relatives in their very being refer to something else."[5] While most relations are bilateral, some are unilateral. The knowable, for instance, is called relative "not because it is related to something but because something else is related to it" (II, 12).[6] Similarly, creation consists in an unilateral dependence of the creature upon God (*ipsa dependentia esse creati ad principium*, II, 18). The radical dependence of created beings upon their transcendent principle insures that the pedagogical reversal from what is prior to us to what is prior according to nature reflects the actual order of reality.

Given the limits of human discourse, however, the reflection is not pellucid. In order to speak about creation *ex nihilo*, Thomas must rework the language of physical production, which by moving and operating induces a change of form in preexisting matter. The way of remotion (*via negativa*), articulated in the discussion of the divine names, is equally operative in the passages on creation. Physical production applies to agents that bring forth determinate species in preexisting matter. God (*ipsum esse*) is the universal cause of being, in contrast to whom every creature is merely "being through participation" (*ens per participationem*). All finite agents operate through powers inherent in them; God, on the contrary, acts through his whole substance. In God, there is no movement from potency to act, nor is there anything existing outside of him upon which he might act. It follows that in the act of creation there is neither motion nor change, indeed there is no succession whatsoever (II, 15–19).

The theme of the limits to philosophical discourse resurfaces in the dialectical consideration of the eternity of the world, where Thomas argues that philosophy cannot settle the question. As Aristotle remarks in *Topics*, I, 11, the question of the eternity of the world is a "dialectical problem." Thomas considers three sorts of arguments for the eternity of the world: from the perspective of God and creatures, and from making itself. The first argument runs thus (II, 32): God acts eternally and immutably; therefore, his effects must always exist. Moreover, God is a sufficient cause of creatures, a cause whose power cannot be impeded. There is no apparent reason for God to delay, and in eternity there is no differentiation of moments to determine why things should be made at one time rather than another. Necessity, furthermore, arises from the end, which in creation is the communication of God's goodness. The more "enduring" is the participation of the creature in that goodness, the more the communication of goodness approximates the divine infinity.

Thomas's responses to the first set of arguments are as follows (II, 35). The assertion that the novelty of an effect entails change in God rests on a misconception of divine action. Divine activity is distinctive. Between God's will and its effect, there is no intermediate, motive power, as there is in us. God's acts of understanding, willing, and making are indistinguishable. It might seem to follow that whatever God wills is automatically brought into being. But this is to construe the will in mechanistic terms. Effects come forth from God in accordance with the determination of his intellect and the ordaining of his will. As art "determines all conditions," including the time of the making of the artifact, so too does the divine intention. The same response turns back the arguments that an effect follows immediately upon the activation of a sufficient cause and that the temporal beginning of the world could result only from divine delay. The next position holds that the absence of moments of time removes the possibility of a reason for creating at one time rather than another. Thomas concedes the point, but he denies that it eliminates a reason for not producing things eternally. Such a reason can be had from the end intended in creating, which is the communication of divine goodness. The subsequent objection supposes that the representation of goodness is in terms of equality. On the contrary, the representation suits the manifestation of the transcendent in what is transcended. The temporal beginning of the world fittingly manifests God's transcendence of creatures. He explains:

> The preeminence of divine goodness over creatures is most fully expressed in creatures' not having always existed. From this it is patent that all things other than God have him as the author of their act of being [*esse*]; that his power is

not bound to the production of certain effects, as nature is to natural effects; and, consequently, that he is a voluntary and intelligent agent. (II, 35)[7]

From the standpoint of creatures, the following arguments can be adduced (II, 33). Certain creatures, namely, separate substances, have of their nature "no potency to nonbeing," and hence they must exist always. The coming into being of anything requires change and a preexisting subject in which the change can occur. So, some receptive being must always have existed. If time is eternal, so is motion. But the "now" of time is always both an end of past time and a beginning of future time. Time and motion, then, must be eternal. The very argument against the eternity of the world implicitly supposes the eternity of time, since in order for the world to begin there must have been a time before it was.

In response to these arguments, Thomas holds that the necessary nature of certain creatures is not absolute but suppositional, consequent upon their actual existence (II, 36). The doctrine of the absolute dependence of all created being (esse) foils an argument for the eternity of the world. Each instant of time is a beginning and an end only if every assignable point in time has this character. But the assumption begs the question. Is it not possible for a point of time to be a beginning of future time and no "terminus of past time"? The necessity of the before that precedes time is real only in our imagination, which similarly must imagine space above the heavens.

Finally, from the perspective of making, the eternity of matter seems to be a necessary consequence of the principle that "nothing arises from what is not." All making presupposes a preexisting subject, which is called prime matter (II, 33). Thomas takes the arguments from the nature of making as a point of departure for discussing the slow, dialectical progress of philosophy toward a metaphysical notion of making (II, 37). The first philosophers considered making in an extrinsic fashion, as the alteration of accidental dispositions. Later, they came to understand making more intrinsically as the production of individual substances from preexisting potency. Finally, philosophers achieved the notion of one first cause, which produces universally from no preexisting things. The last understanding of making is proper not to natural philosophy but to metaphysics, which studies "common being and things separate from motion."[8] In metaphysics, the term "making" is transferred from its original imposition in natural philosophy to cover any production of a nature.[9]

Having undermined the philosophical attempts to prove the eternity of the world, Thomas briefly rehearses and rebuts attempts to prove that the world is not eternal (II, 38). Most of the arguments focus upon the impossibility of an actually existing infinite, which appears to be implicit in the assertion of the eternity of the world. Thomas counters that the objection applies to the actual and simultaneous existence of the infinite, but not to the successive existence of the infinite. Taken in this way, any infinite is finite. Having deflated the philosophical pretensions to resolve conclusively the question of the eternity of the world, Thomas states that the best probable argument against the eternity of the world is taken from the end of the divine will, which is to "manifest" (*manifestare*) his goodness and power (II, 38). The transcendence of the divine goodness over creatures is most evident from the temporal beginning of the world (II, 35). He adds:

> We are able to avoid the assorted errors of the gentile philosophers, some of whom posited an eternal world; some, an eternal matter of the world, from which at some time the world began to come forth, either by chance, or by some intellect, or even by love or strife. (II, 38)[10]

The opening words of *Genesis*, "In the beginning God created heaven and earth," provide scriptural confirmation for God's absolute priority in creating. The citation of scripture at the end of the dialectical discussion of creation opens philosophy to the narrative of scripture. In that narrative, the nothingness from which creatures come is an "infinite privation of being."[11] So crucial is the proper understanding of nothingness that Fabro writes: "The tension between Being and nothingness within the finite existent provides the authentic standpoint of theoretical thought. According to the various ways in which they interpret this tension the various fundamental philosophies differ among themselves."[12] Thomas mentions only the ancient natural philosophers as opponents of the doctrine of creation *ex nihilo*, yet their teaching concerning the eternity of matter is characteristic of the dominant pagan narratives of the origin of things. In them, creation is typically conceived as the introduction of order and intelligibility into a preexisting state of chaos and confusion. Even though more philosophical models, for example, Plato's *Timaeus*, assert the primacy in dignity and nature of the world of ideal forms, the notion persists that disorder is temporally coextensive with, and initially resistant to, a higher order. Only the Christian narrative, as John Milbank argues, unequivocally eclipses the notion that "ontological violence"—a conflict or battle between order and disorder, intelligibility and unintelligibility—lies at the origin of things.[13]

The distinction between being and essence in all created things underscores their radical contingency. Thomas couples the distinction of *esse* and *essentia* with an emphasis upon *esse ut ordo*. The notion of created being as an *ordo* enables Thomas to combat two equally noxious understandings of the motive for creation: that God creates by natural necessity and that he creates by chance. Creation is the result of divine freedom, yet freedom does not imply arbitrariness. There are, admittedly, no external rules to which the divine artistry must conform in creating the universe; since creation involves the bringing into existence of the entirety of the cosmos, God is indebted to no creature. There is then no absolute necessity in the fact or the manner of creation. Still, the cosmos is ordered to a good; in creating, God acts according to his wisdom. The wisdom and goodness of the divine artistry is exhibited principally in the order of the parts of the cosmos to one another (*in ordine partium ad advicem*, II, 24). There is a conditional necessity in the way the parts complement one another and subserve the beauty and order of the whole; each creature is conditionally due "parts, properties, and accidents," which it needs to be what it is (II, 29). Conditional necessity arises from the "naturally prior in relation to the naturally posterior" (II, 28–29).

Thomas does not engage in "possible-worlds" speculation about the motives and possibilities open and appropriate to God. He would find dubious the project of setting criteria for a best possible world. Our access to such information depends upon, and is constrained by, the nature of the one and only universe in which we actually live. In criticizing the "optimic possible world" account of the motive of creation, Laura Garcia writes,

> The hesitation to affirm that there is such a [best possible] world is in part due to the fact that we have so little to go on in determining what God's purposes are. Further, on Aquinas' picture of things, God's purposes cannot constrain him to create anything at all, much less to create any particular universe, since the only purposes he has necessarily are already fulfilled by his own existing.[14]

In discussing divine activity, Thomas opts for the metaphor of the artist and the language of the fitting and comely. For instance, in a chapter on the true first cause of the distinction of things, Thomas argues for the "fittingness" of God's having created a diverse and hierarchically arranged *ordo* of beings. Since God's perfection exceeds that of any and all created beings, multiplicity and variety more fully imitate the divine goodness.

The discussion of the integrity of particular creatures and the harmony and splendor of the whole underscores the goodness and beauty of creation. As the prominence of terms such as *conveniens, decenter,* and *manifestatio* indicates, aesthetic language permeates the description of the motive for, and the result of, creation.[15] Creation is not only a *manifestatio* or *communicatio* of the divine goodness and wisdom, but also an *explicatio* of the perfections of an absolutely simple being. Some Heideggerian critics have argued that the movement from Greek to Christian thought involves a shift from revelatory or aesthetic discourse to a discourse of causal production. The assumed opposition between the two ways of thinking, however, is itself a modern invention, which reached fruition in the divide between scientific and Romantic thought in the nineteenth century. The shift in method, to which the second book of the *Contra Gentiles* bears witness, from the study of nature to that of creatures accentuates the motifs of splendor and manifestation. As we have already noted, the Christian doctrine of creation is at variance with the account of productive generation in Aristotle's *Physics*. The language of production is inadequate to the notion of creation as a bestowal of *esse*, which is not an extrinsic, efficient cause, or merely a result of the union of matter and form.[16] Rather, *esse* is what is most intimately and most fully actual in creatures. Creation involves "transcendental appearing."[17] The entire motive of creation is the *communicatio* of goodness and the *manifestatio* of wisdom and beauty.

The aesthetic language also marks a transition from dialectic to narrative. The emphasis upon circularity in book two prepares the ground for just such a narrative. Jan Aertsen has emphasized the importance of "circularity" and "circulation" in Aquinas's metaphysics. Human beings perform the pivotal function in the circular path of creatures from and to their transcendent source. Aertsen does not, however, draw out the consequences of circularity for the Christian narrative. Thomas seems to view the pagan conception of time, implicit in the affirmation of the eternity of the world, not as circular, but as linear and indefinite. Even where it is cyclical, it is not circular in the sense of completion or perfection. As Thomas sees it, proponents of the eternity of the world have adopted certain awkward theories such as the "circular movement of souls" with the same souls returning to different bodies (II, 38). Temporal infinity is contrary to the very notion of an end; it precludes the possibility of seeing creation as a narrative whole, with beginning, middle, and end.

III. THE METAPHYSICS OF CREATED BEING

The initial consideration of creatures focuses on the being, nature, and properties of intellectual substances. Somewhat misleadingly, Thomas treats intellectual substances generally, without distinguishing between human souls and angels. He argues that the intellectual substance is not a body (49), is immaterial (50), is a subsistent form (51), and is incorruptible (55). Through an extended chain of arguments, Thomas shows that some intellectual substances, namely, human souls, are naturally the substantial forms of bodies. The soul thus differs significantly from the separate substance. If Thomas locates the soul in the hierarchy of intellectual substances, he also emphasizes its weakness and poverty. In order to exercise its proper activity of understanding, the soul needs powers that operate through bodily organs. The union of soul and body, then, is not accidental or violent. Lest we think of the union as a divine afterthought or a human lapse, Thomas brings to bear his metaphysics of actuality, which emphasizes the concrete integrity of composite, created substances. In the case of the human being, the "composite and the form subsist in the same act of being" (II, 68).[18] By this line of reasoning, Thomas hopes to align the theological understanding of human person as an embodied, spiritual substance with Aristotle's consideration of the human species as a member of the genus of animals. The latter consideration is part of natural philosophy, not metaphysics.

Tensions remain, however. Not until the end of the discussion of human nature, after he has already begun to treat specifically of separate substances, does Thomas show that the separate substances and the soul are not of the same species (II, 94). Among the arguments are the following. First, the being of the angelic intellect, in which the body is incapable of communicating, is not the same as the being of the soul, which is by nature the form of the body. Second, each angel is a species unto itself, while each human soul is but a part of the human species.[19] Third, proper operations reveal the species, but the mode of understanding from phantasms, proper to human intelligence, differs from that of the angelic intellect. What are we to make of the previous common consideration of souls and angels? Having reached this juncture in the discussion of intellectual substances, one is forced to reconsider the general indistinct discussion of the soul and the separate substance. That discussion, it turns out, prescinded from crucial differences between the two species of intellectual substances. It treated of human nature exclusively in relation to its intellectual part. An investigation into the nature of that intellect reveals it to be a part that is imperfect because it is separate from its whole.

From such an investigation, Thomas concludes that embodiment is natural to, and perfective of, the soul. The conclusion renders problematic the previous assertions concerning the immateriality, subsistence, and incorruptibility of the soul. Two passages from the latter part of the second book show Thomas's awareness of the difficulty. Having finished the argument on behalf of the unity of soul and body (56–78), he devotes three chapters to the incorruptibility of the human soul (79–81). Given the previous proofs for the incorruptibility of all intellectual substances, a second set of arguments seems redundant. Is Thomas's return to the question of the incorruptibility of the soul a concession to the gulf that separates souls from angels, a gulf that the intervening chapters has made untraversable? A second passage supports this line of interpretation. In the course of arguing for the existence of separate, intellectual substances, Thomas writes,

> It befits an intellectual substance according to its genus that it subsist through itself, since it has an operation proper to itself. . . . It is, moreover, of the essence of a thing subsisting through itself that it not be united to another. Therefore it is not of the essence of an intellectual substance according to its genus that it be united to a body, even if it is of the essence of that intellectual substance which is the soul. (II, 91)[20]

In spite of Thomas's persistence in speaking of the soul as an intellectual substance, these two passages severely qualify the initial inclusion of human souls in the genus of intellectual substances. Indeed, souls are not properly speaking subsistent; their incorruptibility is in need of additional arguments, different in kind from the sort of arguments posited for angels. Even the immateriality of souls cannot be inferred immediately from the nature of human persons of which souls are but parts. Although nowhere in the *Summa Contra Gentiles* does Thomas clarify his use of the phrase "genus of intellectual substances," elsewhere he makes a helpful distinction between natural and logical genus.[21] The former divides things as they are in being, while the latter allows for a unified consideration that prescinds from all that differentiates two things and focuses solely on whatever they share.[22]

The distinction between logical and natural genus exonerates Thomas of the charge of linguistic inconsistency. It does not, however, provide a rationale for the order and content of the second book. In order to uncover the rationale, a careful examination of the rhetorical structure and aporetic method of the book is necessary. The analysis will shed light on the theological strategy behind, and the philosophical basis for, the transition from the common consideration of intellectual substances to the treatment of the soul as substantial form of the body.

As we have already noted, the structure of book two is theological or metaphysical. Accordingly, an examination of the particular powers and operations of intellectual substances is subsequent to a consideration of them as created, derivative beings, whose natures are distinct from their being. The metaphysical analysis, which occurs in chapters 49–55, of the being and nature of intellectual substances precedes the division into separate and embodied. Thomas first argues for the immateriality and subsistence of intellectual substances. Then, lest we confuse them with God, he argues that intellectual substances are not pure act. Instead, they are composed of being and essence, act and potency. In material substances, there is a twofold composition: that of form and matter and that "of the substance thus composed and the act of being" (*ex ipsa substantia iam composita et esse*). A corollary of this claim is that the composition of being and substance, act and potency, is more universal than that of form and matter. As Thomas puts it, "matter and form divide natural substance," while potency and act divide "common be-ing." Having distinguished intellectual substances both from composite, physical substances and from God, Thomas concludes by arguing for their incorruptibility (II, 54).

In arguing for the immateriality of intellectual substances, Thomas repeatedly adverts to the difference between the kinds of receptivity proper to intellectual and material substances (II, 49–51). Were the in-tellect material, it would receive forms materially through "quantita-tive commensuration." The reception of one contrary would involve the physical displacement or destruction of another (II, 49). Yet the intellect receives forms universally and immaterially without quantitative commensuration. In the intellect, contraries are not opposed but are understood through one another. Unlike matter or sense, the intellect is self-reflexive; in knowing itself, the intellect is not related to itself as part to part, the way bodies influence themselves, but as whole to whole. Finally, the intellect is not moved or destroyed in its reception of forms but is "perfected and at rest" (II, 51).

It follows from these premises that the intellect has an operation in which the body does not communicate, that is, it operates through itself (*per se*). If it were dependent upon matter, it would have a material mode of being, which would in turn require that it receive forms according to a material mode. The proper operation of the intellect does not mean that the intellect can know without the body.[23] Deborah Modrak makes a helpful "distinction between a cognitive activity and the enabling condition required for that activity." The soul's *per se* operation does, however, entail its *per se* existence, that is, its subsistence (II, 51). The latter conclusion follows from the Aristotelian principle that whatever has a passion or operation proper to itself subsists. Accidents and principles of composites, for example, do not operate or suffer in virtue of themselves but only in virtue of the substances in which they inhere or of which they are parts. The conclusion that the soul is simultaneously subsistent and a part of human nature makes the soul a conspicuous exception to the natural order of composite entities. The philosophical burden of the second book is to make sense of the peculiar status of human nature.

The arguments for the immateriality and subsistence of intellectual substances move from assertions about the mode of receptivity appropriate to the operation of the intellect to conclusions about its nature and being. They have as their point of departure a contrast between material and intellectual modes of reception. The order observes the natural sequence of human learning, which moves from the sensible to the immaterial. Thomas reverts to the natural order in various segments of the second book. Although the general order of presentation moves from what is prior by nature, there are frequent concessions to, and reminders of, the natural order of human pedagogy.

If chapters 49 through 51 differentiate intellectual substances from below, the next three chapters distinguish them from above. Chapter 52, for instance, proposes that in created intellectual substances *esse* and *quod est* differ. Thomas reiterates the teaching about God from book one, namely, that God is *ipsum esse subsistens*, pure, infinite actuality, comprising every perfection. In God there is no potency, no composition, no distinction between *esse* and *quod est*. Transcending every genus, being is not diversified by specific differences as genera are, but rather insofar as it is "the being of this or that" (II, 52). No limited, caused substance is identical with its own being. Creatures participate in being.

Being is the complement of substance; creatures are in act through having being. As receptive of the act of being, substance is related to *esse* as potency to act. The distinction between the two sorts of composition can be seen in both intellectual and composite substances. Being is not the act of matter; it is the concrete actualization of the whole substance. Neither matter nor form nor being itself is that which is; rather, *quod est* is the whole substance (II, 54).[24] Being is the proper act of the whole substance. In composite substances, then, there are two compositions: first, of matter and form, and, second, of the substance thus composed and *esse*. In the twofold composition, form has a certain primacy. Thomas calls it the principle of being (*principium essendi*) of the composite, that by which (*quo est*) the composite exists. The metaphysical primacy of form is but the correlate of Aristotle's thesis in natural philosophy that form is more substance than matter, that form is to matter as act to potency. In immaterial, intellectual substances, there is no composition of matter and form. Still, they are dependent creatures, whose being is not identical with their substance. In them, form itself is the *quod est*, while being is *quo est* and *actus* of the substance.

Esse is not merely the fact of existence (*existentia*); nor is it simply a consequence of the composition of matter and form. Instead, *esse* has an absolute priority in the order of actuality. Just as in the metaphysics of creation *ex nihilo* Thomas corrects the language of physical production, so too he broadens the scope of "potency" and "act" and introduces principles more fundamental than those noticed in Aristotle's *Metaphysics*. Yet it is not as if, in addition to form and matter, we can experience some third thing called "being"; from sense experience, we can distinguish between what something is and that it is. But this reaches only the fact of existence. The absolute priority of *esse* is not an immediate datum of our experience of things. As Fabro convincingly argues, the proper context for the distinction between *esse* and *quod est* is not epistemological.[25] In establishing the distinction in the second book of the *Summa Contra Gentiles*, Thomas nowhere adverts to acts of cognition. Instead, the teaching is best understood as part of the Christian metaphysics of created being. The full import of the distinction comes to the fore only after the metaphysical or theological reversal of discourse has taken place.

IV. PROBLEMS CONCERNING HUMAN NATURE

The priority of *esse* is a crucial doctrine in Aquinas's metaphysics of created being. Some have made too much of the role of *esse*, however. Fabro and Gilson, for example, argue that the doctrine of participated being enables Thomas to secure the incorruptibility of the soul on properly metaphysical grounds.[26] Gilson writes, "the immortality of the human soul is an immediate evidence. It stands in no need of being proven. . . . Inasmuch as it is pure form, the human soul *is* in its own right. It is as any subsisting form is, since, in order to cease being, it would have to cease being a form."[27] The proofs for the incorruptibility of intellectual substances do indeed follow from the distinction between *esse* and *quod est*. The most prominent of the metaphysical arguments hinges upon the premise that form is the principle of being (*principium essendi*), the proper recipient of the act of being (II, 55). Corruption occurs only where there is separation of form and matter. Whatever is in something *per se* belongs to it "of necessity, always, and inseparably," as roundness is *per se* in a circle.[28] Since form is the proper recipient of being, substances which are nothing but forms cannot be deprived of being. A pure form such as the intellectual substance is the direct and immediate recipient of the act of being. Hence it is incorruptible. The claim of Fabro and Gilson seems incontrovertible. It fails, however, to account for Thomas's own dissatisfaction with this manner of proving the incorruptibility of the soul. The metaphysical arguments apply to the genus of intellectual substances. But the applicability of the metaphysical proofs to the soul is questionable; the soul can be said to be a member of that genus in only a loose sense. Another approach is needed to secure the incorruptibility of the soul. Thus, Thomas provides two sets of arguments for incorruptibility, one of which applies to the genus of intellectual substances (II, 55), the other to human souls (II, 79).

The circuitous route to the proof of the soul's incorruptibility involves a descent from the metaphysics of created *esse* to the psychology of Aristotle's *De Anima*, which is part of natural philosophy. Pegis is right to argue that "Aristotle never asks the question" whether a spiritual substance can be the form of the body and that Thomas's teaching on the "unity of the human person" involves transcending the framework of Aristotle's psychology.[29] Nonetheless, the argument of Aristotle's *De Anima* is the indispensable starting point for claiming that the intellect is immaterial and the human soul is subsistent. The turn to Aristotle has properly theological motives.[30] As Josef Pieper puts it, "Aristotle is for Thomas (in the measure in which he follows him) nothing more nor less than a clear mirror of the natural reality of creation."[31] In creation, God manifests his wisdom and goodness through sensible effects. In making creatures with determinate natures, God provides them with appropriate powers so that they might operate in accordance with their natures. The integrity of created natures, their ability to manifest their powers through bodily operations, follows from the suppositional necessity inherent in God's act of creating. The utility of Aristotle's inquiry into soul, which investigates natural substances from their activities and operations, is obvious. Taking seriously the Aristotelian point of departure of Thomas's psychology may well lead one to rethink the arguments for incorruptibility.[32]

The circuitous route to the separability of the intellect is a matter of rigorous dialectical inquiry. The bulk of the second book is devoted to what some have considered polemical attacks on the Arabic understanding of human nature. On the crucial issues pertaining to the unity of soul and body, Thomas is indeed preoccupied with the Arabic reading of Aristotle. But it is not as if Thomas systematically works out his position independently of his opponents and then refutes them. As we have intimated, the inquiry concerning the nature of the soul achieves clarity only at the end of the second book. Thomas refines and develops his position in and through dialectical encounters with the received opinions of Plato, Averroës, Origen, Aristotle, and others. The text is not fruitfully read as a systematic or demonstrative treatise, but rather as a dialectical inquiry, which is driven by the attempt to come to terms with a set of difficulties.

The discussion of whether the soul is the substantial form of the body amply attests to the aporetic character of the work. In an introductory chapter, Thomas considers various explanations of the unity of soul and body and ends by raising numerous difficulties for the thesis that the soul is a substantial form (II, 56). Twelve chapters later, he responds to the question and then, in consecutive chapters, resolves objections and argues that his conclusion is congruent with the words of Aristotle (II, 68–70). In between, he engages the views of Plato, Averroës, and Alexander of Aphrodisias.

In his attempt to understand how the soul as form can be united to the body, Thomas takes up and rejects three means by which union might be effected. First, he precludes union by mixture, which alters the things being mixed. The intellect would no longer be itself but would become bodily. Second, he excludes union by contact properly. Since things that are one by contact meet only at their extremities, soul and body cannot thus be united. Third, Thomas considers union of power, which arises from the relation of activity and passivity. Unity by power is an improvement over previous suggestions. It allows the indivisible to touch the visible and admits penetration, not just contact at the extremities. The sort of unity that arises through power is that of the unified actuality of things acting and being acted upon (II, 56). But it is not unqualified unity.

The remaining possibility is that the soul and body are one *in ratione*, that is, the soul is the substantial form of the body. This view, however, is beset with numerous difficulties. Thomas lists the following: (a) one thing cannot come from two actually existing substances, yet an intellectual substance and a body are actually existing substances; (b) form and matter belong to the same genus, but the soul and the body are in different genera; (c) everything whose being is in matter must be material, for the form's act of being is not outside the matter, but the intellect is immaterial; (d) what has its being in a body cannot exist separately, yet philosophers have proved that the intellect is separate; and (e) if the intellect were the form of the body, its operation and power would be in a body, but this is contrary to what has already been shown concerning the intellectual substance.

Difficulties such as these led Plato to eschew the notion of soul as form (II, 57). Yet Plato had trouble accounting for certain unmistakable facts about the apparently composite nature of human beings. Consequently, he had to "devise certain solutions, through which he might save the nature of man" (*natura hominis salvetur*). In spite of the apparently pejorative assessment of Plato's solutions, Thomas himself embraces the project of saving the nature of man. The second book enacts a dialectical project of saving the phenomena. The relevant phenomena include the evidence of sense experience, the testimony of the many as reflected in language and customs, and the various conflicting arguments of the philosophers. The method involves a large measure of sorting out and reconciling of phenomena, but its goal is to give an account of phenomena in the light of causes, to ground the descriptive in the explanatory. Thomas's account, then, is vindicated insofar as it makes better sense of the phenomena than do rival accounts.

This is not to say that demonstrative science is no longer an ideal; a perfected science of human nature would indeed be demonstrative. It is to say that the dialectical path to the principles, not the demonstrative route from principles to conclusions, is preeminent in the second book of the *Contra Gentiles*. Thomas's engagement of all pertinent authorities, of authorities from various traditions, is an exemplary instance of what Alasdair MacIntyre calls tradition-constituted inquiry.[33] The conception of inquiry to which tradition-constituted inquiry is most antithetical is, of course, that of Descartes, who sought to stand outside of all traditions, indeed outside of human language, to achieve clear and distinct ideas.[34] As is clear from recent interpretations of Aristotle, the Cartesian heritage remains an obstacle to the reception of the Aristotelian alternative.[35] The disparate conceptions of inquiry reflect different positions on the relationship between soul and body. As Nussbaum and Putnam put it, for Aristotle there is no mind-body problem:

> The mind-body problem . . . starts from a focus on the special nature of mental activity—therefore from just one part of the activity of some among the living beings. . . . Aristotelian hylomorphism, by contrast, starts from a general interest in characterizing the relationship, in things of many kinds, between their organization or structure and their material composition. It deals with the beings and doings of all substances. . . . It asks two questions in particular. . . . How do and should we explain or describe the changes we see taking place in the world? . . . What is it about individuals that makes them the very things that they are?[36]

One might admit that the description captures Aristotle but wonder about its applicability to Aquinas. Indeed, Thomas seems to begin with Descartes—soul as intellectual substance—and move toward Aristotle—soul as form of body. The prospects for the success of such a project would be at best unlikely. Once again, attention to the structure and method of the text mitigates difficulties. The theological order proceeds from what is prior by nature, not from what is better known to us. Concerning the inclusion of souls in the genus of intellectual substances, one might reasonably ask, how do we know that human intellects belong there? Thomas would suggest that we begin, not with metaphysics or unmediated introspection, but with the account of soul in the *De Anima*. Indeed, the study of separate substances and God presupposes knowledge of soul.[37] While Aristotelian themes are not prominent in the opening discussion of the genus of intellectual substances, they come to the fore in the subsequent extended dialectical inquiry into the nature of the soul.

For Thomas, the tradition of speaking about human nature begins with the Platonic view of the union of soul and body. Plato's position is a variation on the thesis that soul and body are united through contact of power. Soul is to body as mover to moved. Thomas counters that, if soul were to body as mover to moved, then soul and body would not be one in being. Things diverse in being cannot share an operation; soul and body do, however, share the operations of sensing and imagining. Thomas's criticisms are in accord with Aristotle's view that the operations of the soul have necessary material conditions. On Plato's view, moreover, the body is not part of the definition of man; instead, man is a soul using a body. Since the mover is not dependent upon the moved for its being, death would not involve the corruption of the human being.

Thomas also recurs to the Aristotelian observation that to sense or to know is to be passive. The experience of coming to know casts doubt on Plato's thesis that the soul is always an agent with respect to the body. Accordingly, Thomas suggests substituting the Aristotelian couplet of act and potency for the Platonic language of mover and moved. The unity resulting from the relationship between an act and that of which it is the act renders the very question of unity superfluous. As he puts it, that by which something is reduced from potency to act is "its form and act" (*est forma et actus ipsius*). The "body becomes a being in act through the soul" (*corpus autem per animam fit actu ens de potentia existente*). The Aristotelian view is not susceptible to the criticisms leveled against the Platonic thesis.

Thomas proceeds to repudiate the Platonic division of human nature into a multiplicity of souls (II, 58). He argues that the predication "man is an animal" is a *per se* predication. Yet, according to Plato, it would be accidental. Plato might respond that the various souls have a "unity of order." Even so, they remain distinct souls. The first soul to inform a body would render it a "being in act and a particular thing" (*ens actu et hoc aliquid*). The first soul, then, would render the body a complete substance and subsequent souls could accrue to it only accidentally.

Having considered the Platonic position, Thomas turns to another reason for denying that the intellectual soul is the substantial form of the body: Averroës' thesis that we know by turning to, and coming into contact with, a separate possible intellect (II, 59). The separability, immateriality, and native infinity of the intellect—all of which Thomas has strenuously defended in the opening discussion of the being and nature of intellectual substances—leads Averroës to posit its separate existence.

Thomas objects that, unless the intellect were in some way united to us, we would not understand it nor would it belong to us. Averroës anticipates the objection and offers an account of the union of the separate possible intellect with us. Since the species is the form of the possible intellect, there arises a union of the possible intellect and the "form understood in act." Whatever is united to the form is thereby united to the possible intellect. We are united to the possible intellect by the mediation of the phantasm, which is a "kind of subject of the understood form."[38] Hence the possible intellect is in contact with us through the mediation of the phantasm. Thomas concedes that the position provides some link between the possible intellect and us, since the possible intellect is in touch with the phantasm present in us. It does not follow, however, that it is we who understand, but rather that we are understood, or at least that the phantasm residing in us is understood. Averroës' thesis destroys entirely the integrity and unity of human nature, for a substance acts by means of its form. As Thomas puts it, "the one understanding is the one possessing intellect."[39] On this view, not a human being but a higher substance possesses intellect.

Thomas amplifies the *quia* argument, which moves from second to first act, by considering whether our specific nature is derived from the passive or the possible intellect. Averroës attempts to circumvent the previous problems by positing the passive intellect as the source of the specific nature and as the power through whose exercise we "acquire the habit of knowing" (*habitus scientiae*). The passive intellect, however, is a power in a bodily organ. Such a power does not suffice to distinguish us from beasts; nor, since the apprehension of bodily powers is relegated to the realm of individuals, can the habit of knowing, which is of universals, be in the passive intellect. But the crucial argument for Thomas is the one that argues from the operation of understanding to the necessary presence of a power in the soul. The supposition of the argument is that public sensible operations manifest the natures of substances. Following Aristotle, Thomas states that

> Operations of life are compared to the soul as second acts to first act. . . . In whatever thing, therefore, there is found some operation of life, it is necessary to posit in it a certain part of the soul which is compared to that operation as first to second act. But man has an operation beyond all other animals: to understand and to reason. . . . Thus it is necessary to attribute to man a principle that properly gives him what is specific to him. . . . This principle

cannot be the passive intellect, because the principle of man's proper operation must be impassable and not mixed with the body, as Aristotle proves. (II, 60)[40]

Proper operations (second acts) flow from the nature or form (first act) of a substance. Conversely, proper operations evince the nature of the substance. In order to account for the experience of understanding, one must posit the existence of a power formally inherent in the soul by which we understand. Lonergan rightly calls this the "peremptory argument" against Averroism. Its basis is the simple premise "this man understands" (*hic homo intelligit*).[41]

Thomas underscores the human intellect's reliance upon sense (II, 61). He emphasizes the poverty of the possible intellect, which does not know intelligible species directly but must abstract them from phantasms. Thomas takes seriously Aristotle's claim that human understanding cannot take place without a phantasm. Since the operation of understanding requires the presence of sensible phantasms, the possible intellect cannot be "altogether separate." Aristotle's comparison of intellect to intelligible things as "the eye of the owl to the sun" captures nicely the weakness of the human intellect.

The dialectical encounter with Platonic and Arabic views of soul and body enables Thomas to introduce and refine a number of principles: the relationship between first and second act, substantial form as principle of being and unity, the potential nature of the soul, and the dependence of the intellect upon sense experience.

Having brought forth these principles, Thomas attempts to resolve the question how the soul can be the form of the body (II, 68). In order for something to be the substantial form of something else, the form must be substantially the principle of being of the other and form and matter must be joined in one act of being. Thomas argues that the form communicates being to the matter. To the objection that soul and body cannot share one act of being because diverse genera have different modes of being, Thomas retorts that *esse* belongs to each in different ways: "to matter as recipient and subject raised to a higher state and to the intellectual substance as principle and as consonant with its proper nature."[42]

The argument that an intellectual substance may be the form of the body completes the descent from the generic consideration of intellectual substances to the proper treatment of embodied intellects. Thomas pairs the descent with an ascent. Midway through the chapter he descends to the lowest composite substances and ascends upward through them to human nature. He locates human beings within the whole of nature and shows inductively that, as a proper operation exceeds matter, so too does the being of the substance. Reaching human nature, we discover a form like the "higher substances," one which is not wholly encompassed by matter but which, in order to exercise its proper operation, needs powers that operate through bodily organs.

Thomas is now prepared to respond to the previously mentioned objections to the soul's being the substantial form of the body (II, 69). He denies the premises of the first two objections, which assert that soul and body exist independently and are in different genera. He holds that soul and body do not exist independently; rather, the intellectual soul is the actualizing form of the body. Intellect and body, moreover, are not species in different genera but the principles of a particular species. Both objections confuse the logical with the real order. The next set of objections focuses upon the apparent incompatibility between the immateriality of the intellect and the soul's actualization of a body: Either the intellectual substance is a form and thus material or it is immaterial and thus not a form. Thomas responds that, unlike other forms, the intellect is not wholly embedded in matter. The response supposes a distinction, which Thomas subsequently invokes, between the essence (*essentia*), which gives being to the body, and the intellectual power (*potentia*), which in its operation exceeds the body.

Commentators have raised questions about Thomas's account, about its internal coherence and about its fidelity to Aristotle. Recent scholarship on Aristotle has tended to deemphasize the importance of questions of the immateriality and immortality of the soul, in order to balance a disproportionate attention to these issues in the neo-Platonic and Christian reception of Aristotle's *De Anima*. In his reading of the *De Anima*, Thomas at least does not devote inordinate space to these questions.[43] In the *Summa Contra Gentiles*, the theological approach to human nature makes sustained attention to these issues unavoidable. But does the theological handling of these issues by Thomas undercut his claim of fidelity to Aristotle? First, what should be clear from the text is that Thomas strives to locate these issues within the larger context of Aristotle's thought. His typical initial response to alternative readings of Aristotle is to point to their exaggerated accentuation of certain features of Aristotle's thought at the expense of others. Second, one might wonder whether the contemporary aversion to certain parts of Aristotle's texts does not constitute an imbalance of a different sort. Thomas is primarily concerned to address an aporia that puzzled Aristotle more than it has most of his recent commentators. At least one contemporary Aristotelian notes the problem. Deborah Modrak writes,

> Aristotle seems to be fully cognizant of the tensions between the two tendencies in his theorizing about the human soul—(a) the desire to give a unified treatment of all the faculties of soul such that the internal unity of the soul and the unity of the living being who is ensouled is assured and (b) the desire to give an account of the intellect that captures its uniqueness and divinity. The first desire issues in the attempt to encapsulate the core concept of soul in the general definition and the second in the attribution of separability to active nous in 3.5.[44]

The tensions Modrak sees Aristotle addressing in the *De Anima* are precisely the foci of the second book of the *Contra Gentiles*. If Thomas goes beyond the *littera* of Aristotle's text, he does so by responding to difficulties which are unresolved in Aristotle's texts and by applying or circumscribing principles that Aristotle himself articulates.

But is Thomas's account coherent? Anthony Kenny and Gregory Coulter resurrect an old objection to the account.[45] They hold that Thomas is forced to make contradictory assertions about the soul: that it is both complete and incomplete (Coulter), or that it is concrete and abstract (Kenny).[46] Coulter notes that Thomas distinguishes between the soul's completeness in being and its incompleteness in nature, but counters that the distinction is inadequate, since it violates the principle that "as a thing operates, so it exists." Coulter wants to force Thomas into one of two mutually exclusive positions: either the operation requires the body and hence its existence must be dependent on the body, or it does not require the body and hence is independent in both being and nature. But Thomas refuses to make the human person an angel or a subrational animal. Coulter ignores altogether the dialectical character of Thomas's attempt to come to terms with the apparently incompatible features of the human person, features that Modrak argues Aristotle himself was at pains to explain. Nussbaum and Putnam put it thus, "Aquinas has correctly understood Aristotle's distinction between 'shared' functions (cf. 'the operation of the compound') and non-shared functions that none the less have material necessary conditions."[47] In fact, the intellectual operation reveals the ambiguous character of the nature and being of the human person. Hence Coulter's conclusion—that "the entire epistemological grounding for analyzing the nature of thing through a study of its acts is undercut"—does not follow.[48]

Kenny and Coulter are not sufficiently attentive to the way in which the language of composite substances must be reworked in the case of the human person. Coulter assumes that, simply because in all other instances of composite substances form is "incomplete with respect to existence as well as nature," this must be true of the human soul. Kenny puts his objection in terms of Thomas's apparently contradictory reference to the soul as both concrete and abstract. To say that the soul is subsistent is to speak of it concretely, while to refer to it as a part of the composite is to speak abstractly. The problem is deeper than grammatical confusion. He concludes, "the impossibility of a form without matter is a logical impossibility, not a matter of physics."[49] While Thomas speaks of the soul as having *esse per se*, he also states that it does not naturally exist by itself. Hence the use of *esse subsistens* must not be univocal. The passage in which Thomas states what is proper to an intellectual substance bears repeating:

> It befits an intellectual substance according to its genus that it subsist through itself, since it has an operation proper to itself. . . . It is, moreover, of the essence of a thing subsisting through itself that it not be united to another. Therefore it is not of the essence of an intellectual substance according to its genus that it be united to a body, even if it is of the essence of that intellectual substance which is the soul. (II, 91)

Clearly the notions of intellectual substance, of *per se* subsistence, even of *per se* operation, do not apply univocally to souls and angels. Indeed, Thomas's statement of what is essential (*de ratione*) to an intellectual substance indicates that the soul is not properly a member of that genus. Thomas does hold that the intellect's operation is separate in its exercise if not in its enabling condition. Its operation is sufficiently separate to posit its incorruptibility, but not separate enough to call its independent state natural or perfective.

While Coulter notes places where Thomas argues that the soul is not a *hoc aliquid* in the strict sense, he fails to follow through on the analogical usage of terms. He cites a passage from the *De Ente et Essentia*, where Thomas states that "substantial form does not have existence of itself" (*non habet per se absolutum*). Two responses to the passage suggest themselves. First, Thomas does not qualify the *per se* existence of the soul with the word *absolutum*. Second, Thomas may say things that are generally true of composites but that would have to be qualified in the case of the human person, just as the language of natural philosophy must be reworked in its application to higher sciences.

If pressed further on the issue, Thomas might well say that with respect to composites other than man, incompleteness in nature is sufficient to insure that the parts not exist independently. Indeed, Coulter's reading of composite substances so emphasizes the equality of the two principles with respect to being that it leaves little room for the primacy of form as the proximate principle of the existence of the composite. He twice refers to Thomas's "conceding that the human form is the only instance of this type of form within the entire order of the universe," as if it were problematic. It is indeed, but the problem is not a consequence of Thomas's theory; rather, it is integral to the phenomena of human nature. An attempt to save the problematic phenomena is precisely what leads Thomas to assert different things about the human composite than he does about composites generally.

V. COMPETING IMAGES, RIVAL PRINCIPLES

In the second book, Thomas frequently cites the neo-Platonic motif of the human being as the horizon of the corporeal and the incorporeal. Yet Thomas reworks the motif and its attendant metaphysics in light of Aristotle's view of soul and body. Indeed, the neo-Platonic metaphor might be said to be in competition with an Aristotelian simile in which the relationship of the intellect to the intelligible is said to be like that of the eye of an owl to light. The conflict is most evident in the dispute over the status of the agent intellect.

The dispute hinges upon Aristotle's De Anima III.5. For the Arabic tradition, the image of the horizon gives metaphorical expression to an ontological and epistemological fact. According to Averroës and Avicenna, human beings understand by participating in, or coming under the influence of, a separate and transcendent agent intellect, which is the same agent for all. It follows that numerous individuals will share in a numerically identical act of understanding (II, 73). Since the power of knowing is common, they will be different animals but not different human beings. Thomas supposes, on the other hand, that the "nature of man is one" and that the principle whereby something acts is a principle of being and of multiplicity or unity. If one of the goals of psychology, moreover, is to explain how we come to know, then the Arabic view has the unwelcome consequence of negating the very operation it seeks to explain. On the Arabic view, one can never say, "this man understands." But this is what all wish to elucidate.

Even if one were to posit a plurality of separate agent intellects so that each individual would participate in a distinct intellect, human nature would remain fractured. Only a proximate cause in each individual can account for acts of knowing (II, 76). The Arabic view runs afoul of the experience of knowing. As Thomas observes, the "effect, which is to abstract universal forms from phantasms, is in our intention."[50] The passage is somewhat misleading. At what level or in what sense abstraction is actually part of our intention is unclear. It is difficult to see how "to abstract" could be the explicit, conscious goal of acts of knowing. Indeed, Thomas describes abstraction as considering something apart from something else, as an intellectual holding in abeyance of accidental features of a substance in order to consider what is essential. What is consciously intended is the knowledge of the natures of sensible particulars.

According to Thomas, the Arabic position deflects human nature from its proper operation, which is to know sensible things. Avicenna, for instance, holds that "to learn is nothing other than to acquire a perfect aptitude for uniting oneself to the agent intellect."[51] Thomas notes that the position differs little from that of Plato, who denies the causal role of sense in knowledge (II, 74). But the dependence of intellect upon sense is precisely the sort with which we are most familiar. As Aristotle argues in *De Anima* III.7, phantasms are necessary for all understanding. Phantasms have a dual role: prior to knowledge, the possible intellect needs a phantasm from which it receives the intelligible species; once it possesses the species, the phantasm is necessary as an instrument or foundation of the species. Thomas agrees that the "intellect understands immaterial things" but adds that it "sees them in something material." The universal is beheld (*inspiciatur*) in the particular (II, 73).

Thomas traces deficiencies in the Arabic reading of Aristotle to tendencies endemic to Platonism. According to Aquinas, the fundamental flaw in Plato's view of human cognition is a confusion of the order of knowing with that of being. Since knowledge is of universals and sensible things are particular, Plato posits subsisting universals as objects of knowledge. Thomas endorses Aristotle's critique of Platonic ideas and substitutes an alternative understanding of the intellectual process as the "abstraction" of intelligible species from particulars. Recently, however, the application of the term "abstraction" to Aristotle's account of knowledge has been subject to scrutiny. Is the view of understanding in terms of abstraction faithful to Aristotle? Or does it, as John Cleary has argued, distort Aristotle's account in the direction of modern epistemological justifications of knowledge? Cleary's thesis is an important test for our previous argument that Aristotle's influence is dominant in Thomas's psychology. In a careful study of the use of the Greek term *aphairesis*, Cleary argues that its "core meaning . . . is derived from a logical technique of 'subtraction' whose purpose is to identify the primary and proper subject of any particular attribute."[52] What would Thomas say about this reading?

Cleary argues that abstraction does not imply the existence of abstract objects. Similarly, Thomas criticizes the Platonic assumption that the identity of knower and known requires that they must have the "same mode of being." Things united in reality can be understood apart from one another. Thomas goes on, "Although the nature of a genus and a species never exists except in individuals, nonetheless the intellect understands the nature of genus and species without understanding the individuating principles, and this is to understand universals" (II, 75).[53] Thomas does not refer to some mysterious psychological process. Instead, he focuses on the intellect's ability to isolate certain features of an object from others.

Given the apparent compatibility between Cleary and Aquinas, one is forced to ask why Aquinas introduces the terminology of abstraction at all. One passage at least seems to confirm Cleary's reading of Aquinas's misreading. In it, Thomas states that "materiality is repugnant to intelligibility" (II, 75).[54] In order to be made intelligible, forms of material things must be abstracted from matter. The passage raises the question: what does Thomas mean by abstraction from matter? Thomas speaks regularly of the specific matter, or signate matter, or the individualizing matter that is accidental to the nature of a substance and does not enter into the definition of the species. The activity of the agent intellect is responsible for sorting out essential from accidental features of objects and for moving beyond the sensible particular to an apprehension of the universal. Thus, the question "why abstraction?" is intimately connected with the question "why agent intellect?" The response runs thus. The capacity to understand natures apart from individuating conditions exceeds mere passivity to phantasms; it presupposes an active power in us. Aristotle posits the agent intellect, which renders "intelligibles proportionate to us" (*intelligibilia nobis proportionata*, II, 77). Without abstraction, knowledge would remain potential and never become actual. The phantasm is only potentially intelligible; it is, moreover, particular. But actual knowledge occurs only when the intellect in act is one with the object in act; understanding is contrasted with sensing as universal to particular. Knowledge requires, then, that the form be received in the intellect, that the potential be made actual, the particular made universal. As the passage indicates, Thomas equates abstracting with universalizing or immaterializing the species potentially present in the phantasm.[55]

At one point, Cleary notes that Aristotle admits only two ways of knowing: induction and demonstration. There is no place for abstraction as a third way of knowing. Thomas would concur but add that abstraction is simply a way of describing how it is that induction issues in universals. In fact, Thomas takes the pertinent Aristotelian passage as authoritative in his account of human knowledge: "from sense comes memory; from many memories, one experience; from many experiences comes the reception of the universal which is the principle of science and art" (II, 76).[56]

The aporetic inquiry into the nature and operation of the soul saves the appearances of the variegated phenomena constitutive of human self-experience. Thomas embraces Plato's project and shows Aristotle to be a better Platonist than Plato. The Aristotelian-Thomistic view nicely balances activity and passivity in human knowing. It does not begin from private subjectivity and then seek to establish the objectivity of knowledge. As Cleary rightly insists, Aristotle's conception of knowledge is object-oriented. The link between particular and universal, phantasm and intelligible species is never lost. In contrast to the neo-Platonic assertion of a direct connection between the human soul and the intelligible order, Thomas highlights the oblique route of the soul both to itself and to separate substances. In place of the conceptual realism of Plato, he posits a dialectical realism, which moves from what is first in our experience to what is first in itself. Thomas accepts the ontological characterization of human nature as a microcosm, existing on the horizon of two worlds; yet, when he turns to the order of human knowing, he prefers Aristotle's image of the owl's eye in the light of day. Despite the palpable difference between the human person and brute animals, Thomas locates the former within the genus animal. What distinguishes humans from other animals is not the soul's isolation from matter but its greater openness to the sensible world.

Thomas does not naively endorse the neo-Platonic language of man as horizon. He embraces the principle that a hierarchy of creatures best reflects the infinite perfection of the creator. He quotes Dionysius favorably: "divine wisdom links the ends of higher creatures with beginnings of lower creatures" (II, 68).[57] Yet the neo-Platonic penchant for blurring distinctions between levels of the hierarchy diminishes the intelligible splendor of the cosmos. As Umberto Eco puts it, "In a Dionysian universe, coruscating with beauty, mankind risked losing its place, of being blinded and then annulled."[58] Thomas insists upon greater metaphysical discretion. He accepts Aristotle's teaching on the concrete actuality and unity of composite substances and couples it with a metaphysics of actuality, unity, and perfection.

Thomas's dispute with the Arabic position on the unity of the agent intellect highlights the *integritas* of human nature. But the integrity of the human person renders onerous the attempt to establish the incorruptibility of the soul (III, 79–81). The first argument on behalf of the indestructibility of the soul merely reiterates the previous assertion that the soul is a member of the genus of intellectual substances. But Thomas adds to this single *propter quid* argument, a plethora of *quia* arguments, all of which begin from the operations of the human intellect. The dialectical inquiry into the nature of the human soul is a sign of the distance separating it from properly intellectual substances.

Certain objections to the immortality of individual souls raise questions about the relationship between soul and body and about the individuation of the soul by means of the body. Three are pertinent. The first objection argues that, since souls are multiplied in accordance with matter, their multiplicity will not remain once they are separated from the cause of that multiplicity, namely, the body. The response is that only when one thing derives its being from another does its unity or multiplicity depend on that other. If, as is the case with most composite entities, the being of the form depends on that of the matter, then the matter is the sufficient cause of the multiplication of the form. Although the human soul needs the body to perform operations and is united to it in one act of being, its very being does not depend on matter. Hence, it will be multiplied with the "multiplication of matter," that is, "at the same time as the matter and in proportion to it." Yet matter will not be the cause of its individuation (II, 81).[59]

The second objection supposes that, once the form is separate from the body, the only possible diversity must be of a formal character. But then, we would be specifically diverse, which is an awkward consequence. The rejoinder is that not every diversity of form entails a diversity in species.

The individuation of human forms does not create a "diversity in essential principles." Rather, the diversity occurs in the "commensuration of souls to bodies," in the adaptation of this soul to this body.

Thomas does not hold that there is individuation of the soul prior to or independent from the body; he does, nonetheless, hold that individuation is not fully explicable in terms of the body. While the induction of other natural forms is part of the process of generation, God infuses the human soul into the human body at an appropriate point in the development of the fetus (II, 87). This is yet another indication of how peculiar is the composition of human nature, of the creature that exists on the horizon of the material and the spiritual.

The image of horizon figures prominently in the response to the third objection, which is based upon the role of the phantasm in human knowing. Once separate, the soul will not have access to phantasms; it will thus be inoperative and incapable of existing. Thomas's response is that the separated soul will understand "in a different way," in the manner appropriate to separate substances: "in its mode of understanding, it will be completely assimilated to the separate substances" (*perfecte assimilibatur substantiis separatis quantum ad modum intelligendi, et abunde influentiam earum recipiet*). He adds, "Since the human soul . . . exists on the boundary of corporeal and incorporeal substances, on the horizon of eternity and time, it approaches the highest by withdrawing from the lowest" (II, 81).[60] The application of the image of horizon in its pristine Platonic sense runs counter to the previous assertion that the soul is naturally the form of the body. Thomas seems here to forget the pertinent Aristotelian comparison of the intellect to the owl in the light of day. As Anton Pegis observes, Thomas creates "a new difficulty in the process of answering an old one."[61]

The conflation of soul and separate substance returns us to the ambiguity of the opening of the second book. The final chapters of the book do serve to correct the misleading association of souls and separate substances. Not only does Thomas show that they are not in the same species (II, 94), but he also argues that the separate substances do not receive knowledge from sensible things (II, 96), are always in the act of understanding (II, 97), and are cognizant of singulars (II, 100). He ends by contrasting the knowledge of the angels with that of God. The ascending movement of the final chapters illustrates the inferior location of human nature in the hierarchy of intelligences. The conclusion of the book is the structural inverse of its beginning and serves to remind the reader that the descent to creatures is ordered to an ascent to the Good.

VI. THE BEAUTY OF CREATION AND CHRISTIAN EROS

Most of the interlocutors with whom Thomas engages in book two are philosophers. Origen is a conspicuous representative of the theological tradition. His position is that souls existed naturally and temporally prior to bodies and that their subsequent union is a consequence of, and punishment for, sin. Thomas agrees that sin has had adverse effects upon the human condition. He does not, however, concur that very being of the human composite is not a "natural good" (II, 83). In keeping with the integrity and fittingness of the created order, "God established each thing in a mode consonant with its nature."[62] Once again, Thomas adduces the passage from the creation narrative in Genesis: "God saw that it was good."

The prominence of the language of convenience and goodness in the study of creatures underscores the role of the beautiful in divine pedagogy. The very term *conveniens*, which pervades the discussion of creation, means a "coming together," a "convergence." The term and its cognates take on the meanings of "agreement," "harmony," and "suitability." These terms are of course at the heart of Thomas's understanding of beauty.[63] Creation manifests the truth, goodness, and beauty of the divine artisan. Thomas speaks, accordingly, of the created order as the "highest beauty." The notion of beauty is allied to that of the good. They are the "same in subject, since clarity and consonance are contained under the meaning of the good."[64]

The three Thomistic marks of the beautiful—proportion, integrity, and clarity—are operative here. Proportion has to do with the order of parts to one another and to the whole and with the coming together of things for an end. The multiplicity and the hierarchical arrangement of created being underscore the proportion of creation. Existing on the horizon of the material and the spiritual, human nature inhabits a middle realm. The fittingness of parts to one another and to the whole is palpable in the depiction of the soul as needing the sensitive powers and of the human body as possessing a dignity befitting the intellectual soul. The integrity or wholeness of human nature can be seen in the unification of soul and body in one act of being and in the adaptation of this body to this soul. Thomas associates clarity with splendor, manifestation, and illumination. Since greater unity is present wherever there is more complete dominance of form over matter, human nature exhibits the greatest unity in the physical cosmos. The embodied operations of the intellectual substance manifest the splendor of intelligence in the physical order. In arguing that the only body to which intellectual substances are united is the human body, Thomas appeals to the principle that the "nobler form belongs to the nobler body."

Performing the office of the wise, Thomas imitates the divine artistry of creation and begins from what is absolutely prior in being. Yet, the intricate structure of the second book amply attests to the impossibility of adhering strictly to this order. The twin motions of descending and ascending are wonderfully intertwined in the crucial chapter arguing for the unity of the intellectual soul with the body. The argument descends from a consideration of souls as intellectual substances to the possibility of their being forms of bodies and then ascends from the lowest of material forms upward to human nature. The pedagogical concessions to the natural, human order of learning remind us of our embodied nature and of our proper, pivotal place in the cosmos. The reciprocal motions of descent and ascent meet in human nature. Since soul and body are united in the very same act of being, the spiritual and material spheres of the cosmos are most fully united in us. The congruence of the order of creatures with the human capacity to wonder and know is especially evident in the discussion of the unity of soul and body. Thomas comments, "thus we are able to contemplate the marvelous connection of things" (*hoc autem modo mirabilis rerum connexio considerari potest*, II, 68).[65]

The prominence of the language of beauty befits the theological intent of the study of creatures, which is to foster awe, reverence, and wonder at the source of such a beautiful artifact. Beauty pertains more directly to perception than does the good; "the beautiful adds to the good an ordering to the cognitive power."[66] Yet beauty also inspires delight; it is that which, "when seen, pleases." In the contemplation of the beautiful, then, there is an integration of the true and the good, of intellect and will or passion. The effect of delight or pleasure is dilation or expansion of the soul and thirst or desire.[67] The encounter with beautiful things renders the soul increasingly receptive to, and inflames its desire for loving union with, the source of all beauty and goodness. John Sallis's remark about the pedagogical point of images in Plato is to the point: The "seeing of an image always involves a tension, an instability," which drives "us beyond the image to the original."[68] Is this not precisely the goal of the theological study of creatures?[69] The words from the opening of *Contra Gentiles*, II, are apt:

> If the goodness, beauty, and allurement of creatures thus entices human souls, then the divine fount of goodness, compared to the small streams of goodness

discovered in particular creatures, will draw totally to himself the aroused souls of men. Whence it is said in the Psalms: They will become intoxicated from the abundance of your dwelling . . . and you will give them to drink from the torrent of your delight because with you is the source of life. (II, 2)[70]

4

THE DIALECTIC OF HUMAN
INQUIRY AND THE NARRATIVE
OF DIVINE PROVIDENCE

I. INTRODUCTION

Thomas devotes the third book to a theme that received only indirect attention in the previous book: how the contemplation of creation inspires longing in rational creatures to behold the source of creation. The book amplifies the prologue's statement of the human aspiration for contemplative happiness and addresses the grand debate of ancient philosophy, the debate over the ultimate end of human life. Thomas recasts the debate as a subtopic within a theological inquiry into providence. The introduction to the third book summarizes key theological teachings. Creating from nothing, God is the "principle of the being of all things." The communication of himself to creatures is most evident in the rational creature, who is not simply ruled but has dominion over his own acts. He is thus a "similitude and image" of the divine, the creature upon whom the narrative of creation pivots, the focal point of divine governance.

The question of <u>the destiny of human beings</u> gives rise to the most extended dialectical inquiry in the entire work. Thomas attempts to untie the difficulties surrounding the destiny of an embodied rational creature, the only animal with access to the order of spirit. While Thomas shows that no finite good or set of goods satisfies the desire for happiness, he emphatically denies that a transcendent vision of God is naturally available or proper to human beings. Once again, the received opinions of Aristotle's commentators give rise to the dialectic. Most of the commentators have an unwarranted optimism concerning the ultimate end of human life. They devise various means of bridging the gap between the notion of perfect happiness and the natural capacities of human beings to achieve happiness. Through the deployment of various dialectical strategies, Thomas shows that all these means conflict with Aristotle's text and with reasoned argument. The gap cannot be bridged by any natural capacity. This does not mean that human nature is somehow unintelligible; for, human beings can articulate and live in accordance with ways of life that approximate perfect happiness.

Most of the attempts to bridge the gap between perfect happiness and human capacity resort to some sort of neo-Platonic description of how human souls can transcend their own order of being and participate directly in higher orders of being, especially the order of the separate substances. These descriptions of the *reditus* of human souls are correlative to their depiction of the *exitus* as a natural process of emanation. Such views are antithetical to numerous conclusions reached in previous books of the *Contra Gentiles*, especially the one from the second book on the soul as form of the body. Thomas counters the optimistic, neo-Platonic image of man as horizon of the worlds of matter and spirit with Aristotle's sobering comparison of the intellect to the sight of an owl in daylight.

Yet in the third book Thomas does more than salvage and amplify Aristotle's position. What allows him to go beyond Aristotle's view is the vantage point from which he considers the question of the ultimate end, that of divine providence. After establishing the negative conclusion that no philosophical argument can show the impossibility of God's raising human beings to a direct vision of the divine essence, Thomas turns to an explicit consideration of providence. The natural order of creation is not the final word on divine providence, since creation does not preclude God's supernatural intervention. Thomas argues that it is fitting for God to intervene in order to instruct human beings. The structure of the third book confirms Pegis's understanding of the way Thomas has recast Aristotle's question of the ultimate end of human life. In a world open to divine initiative, human destiny is inseparable from divine providence. The unity of divine providence encompasses the two modes of truth, the natural and supernatural modes of divine communication. The consideration of providence is essential not only to the structural unity of the work but also as a prelude to the drama of redemption in the fourth book. Since nature is open both from below and from above, there is no impediment to the Christian narrative, a narrative that raises human persons to a direct participation in the life of God.

II. THE UNIVERSAL CITY

Thomas locates the question of human destiny within a general discussion of teleology, of the way natural substances act for ends congruent to their natures. Although final causality is more evident in human making and acting than it is in nature, the claim that natural things act for an end does not presuppose conscious intention in them. Instead, the evidence for natural finality is garnered from the development, operations, and organization of natural species. The statement that subrational creatures are ruled by another refers to the ultimate, not the proximate, principles of their motion. Agents incline to something definite, determined by the active powers peculiar to their nature. Growth itself tends to something specific; it is not haphazard or endless; and it occurs in a determinate order. The intermediate stages between the first and the ultimate cause are themselves ends in relation to prior stages of development. Reference to material and efficient causes alone is insufficient to explain why organisms develop in a certain order.[1]

Similarly, the intelligibility of the parts of organisms is teleological. Healthy, mature organisms develop in such a way that their parts serve the good and well-being of the whole. Thomas refers to the leaves of plants which protect fruit and to bodily organs which protect animals. As it serves the survival and flourishing of the organism, the adaptation of organs is an example of final causality. Thus far in the discussion Thomas has merely summarized the teachings of the opening books of Aristotle's *Physics*. The treatment of final causality in nature is devoid of dialectic, as it was the occasion for little controversy among Aristotle's commentators.

After a brief statement concerning final causality in nature (III, 2–3), there is an abrupt transition to an extended discussion of the origin and nature of evil (III, 4–15). What explains the prominence given to the topic of evil? Its prominence signals a transposition of the order of questions in Aristotle's *Physics*, where the latter takes up, not evil, but chance and luck as "posterior to nature and intelligence." Chance is allied to natural evil, but Aristotle does not treat it under that category. Thomas's subordination of evil to good parallels Aristotle's subordination of chance and luck to nature and intelligence. His silence about evil in the previous treatment of the metaphysics of creation reinforces the notion that evil is not integral to the foundation of being, that it is accidental to, and parasitic upon, the natural orientation of all things to the good. Thomas defends the veracity of the passage from Genesis where God calls creation good and rebuts the Manichean heresy, which posits evil as an actually existing force, independent of and coextensive with the good (III, 7 and 15). Thomas's intention is, in the words of Ricoeur, "to set up a radical origin of evil distinct from the more primordial origin of the goodness of things."[2]

The transposition can be traced to two features of the *Contra Gentiles* III that distinguish it from Aristotle's treatises. First, the third book juxtaposes the topics of natural teleology and human happiness, while these are somewhat distant in Aristotle's corpus. Thomas inscribes the question of the ontology and source of evil within the question of the teleology of human life. Second, the third book considers all of these topics under the purview of divine providence. The discussion of evil in the opening of the third book not only refutes the view that evil is an independent force, opposing the good, but it also raises the question of what role evil plays in God's providential design, in the divine narrative of creation. About that question, subsequent parts of the *Contra Gentiles* will have much to say.

Throughout the discussion of the subordinate status and accidental origin of evil, Thomas describes evil as a privation, as a concomitant result of what nature and reason primarily intend. Natural evil results from matter's resistance to being assimilated to form or from the necessary, though only indirectly intended, corruption of one form in the generation of another. Evil is a "privation of order or due harmony." This is true of moral evil as well. Rational creatures can choose only under the formality of the good; whatever they choose is good in some respect. What is chosen, then, is simultaneously a positive, desirable good and a privation with respect to the order of reason. Thomas speaks of the privation being "attached to" the good.[3]

In defending the assertion that good is the cause of evil, Thomas provides both a metaphysical and a psychological account of moral evil. Since evil is a privation of something which a subject ought to have, its existence presupposes the operation of some power. But operative power has being and, to that extent, is good. The accidental origin of evil is traced to a defect in the power of an agent. Following Augustine, Thomas holds that there is "no efficient, only a deficient, cause" of evil.[4] The Augustinian position provides not so much an "explanation" of the source of evil as a confession of its inexplicability. Lonergan comments, "We can know sin as a fact; we cannot place it in intelligible correlation with other things except *per accidens*."[5] The resistance of evil to rational investigation is perhaps one reason for the schematic treatment of the question of its origin. To say more would be to risk implicit denial of the thesis that evil is nonbeing. The various attempts to do something with the nothingness of evil force a lapse into a tacit dualistic metaphysics. The strategies for addressing the nothingness of evil are allied to the metaphysics of creation. Thomas's metaphysics radically subordinates all created things to the divine goodness and depicts creation as a manifestation of the splendor and goodness of the creator. Evil is not.

As if to illustrate the subordination of evil to good, Thomas quickly returns to the examination of the pursuit of the good in nature (III, 16) and then to God as end of the universe (III, 17–24). The most famous argument from the third book, that human beings have a natural desire for God, is but part of an argument that all creatures seek and imitate God. The natural appetites of sentient beings are intrinsically oriented to the good. Each creature imitates and participates in the divine goodness by acting in accordance with its natural operations. There is, consequently, "no difference between saying" that every creature seeks its own perfection and that it desires to imitate God (III, 24).

The language of imitation marks a shift from Aristotelian to Platonic categories. Following Aristotle, Thomas begins the discussion of final causality in nature with examples from human art and action. The order follows that of Aristotle's *Physics*, which moves from what is prior in our experience to what is prior according to nature. In the discussion of final causality, Aristotle moves from examples in human action and art, to instances in nature, and finally to God as final cause of the whole of nature.[6] Even if there is ground for ascribing efficient causality to Aristotle's God, the language of divine artistry is absent. Thomas, on the contrary, both begins and ends with the language of artist and artifact. The action of all creatures is subordinate to the efficient, exemplary, and final cause of the whole (III, 2).

The Platonic notion of exemplary causality is operative in the account of cosmic teleology. Thomas cites Boethius's statement that "forms in matter come from forms which are apart from matter" and affirms Plato's thesis that separate forms are principles of material forms (III, 24).[7] Thomas is quick to add that these forms exist in an intellect and not independently, as Plato holds. The divine artistry is the ultimate reason why natural operations proceed in an orderly and directed manner, as do the "actions of the wise." From the primacy of God in the orders of exemplary, efficient, and final causality, it follows that God is the paradigm and exemplar of all actions, an end imitated and sought in every action of every creature. God is the end of all things, not as a conceived ideal or as something to be produced, but as "something preexisting to be attained" (III, 18).[8]

Thomas anchors the account of how things tend to become like God in the metaphysics of participated being. Yet Thomas repudiates the neo-Platonic view of creation as a fracturing of sheer actuality and utter simplicity.[9] Properly and positively, creation involves the concrete delimitation, actualization, and manifestation of being (*esse*). As participants in being, all things possess goodness of being. Since all creatures are composite, their act of existence is not to be equated with their goodness. The inclination to actualize proper capacities accompanies the natural desire to be. Each creature imitates God according to its measure, and becomes like the first goodness through its proper activities. The original and ordinary meaning of the term "perfection" applies to that process whereby finite, temporal creatures achieve goods which they initially lack.

In describing the various measures according to which creatures imitate God, Thomas descends from God, through intermediate beings, to those composite creatures least resistant to corruption. A creature's capacity for perfection is directly proportionate to the degree to which its first actuality participates in being itself (*ipsum esse*, III, 20). Creatures most nearly approach simplicity at either end of the hierarchy; while the simplicity at one end approximates the perfection of God, at the other it reflects a paucity of being. The diminished perfections of higher beings and the exalted virtues of lower creatures coincide in the human person, the most complex of creatures. The entire order of generation is ordered to the human soul, "to which matter tends as to an ultimate form."[10] To the order of generation corresponds an order of preservation and perfection (III, 22). Material things are present for man's use and for the perfection of his knowledge.

The natural powers of creatures enable them not only to actualize their immanent teleology but also to bring about certain effects. Thus they imitate the divine causality and are, in the words of Dionysius, made coworkers with God.[11] God's motive in creating is the wish to communicate goodness (III, 21).[12] The imitation of divine productivity is a sign of great perfection.[13] The fruition and superabundance of goodness in creatures results in the causal communication of that goodness to other and lower creatures. The metaphysics of participated being has moral and political ramifications: To be a creature, conditioned by finitude, is to be receptive and cooperative.

The rearrangement of Aristotelian topics and the subordination of natural teleology to divine governance befit the theological approach to creatures described in the opening of the second book. The perspective from which teleology is considered in the third book is not that of the natural philosopher but that of the theologian, who seeks a knowledge of things that is "more like God's knowledge." The examination of natural teleology from the vantage point of the exemplary causality of God provokes a reconsideration of the order of creation. Nature is a universal city in which the benevolent and wise rule of God is made manifest. The theme of manifestation can be seen in the preponderance of references to divine artistry. Once again, Thomas underscores the remarkable manifestation of divine wisdom in human nature. The section amplifies the teaching of the previous book on the human person as a horizon of the worlds of matter and spirit and draws out the crucial role of human persons in the universal city of creation.

III. THE FRAGILITY OF HUMAN HAPPINESS AND THE DIALECTIC OF HUMAN DESTINY

The initial unproblematic discussion of the pivotal role of human beings in the order of creation becomes enormously complex in the ensuing consideration of the end of human life. The longest section of the third book is a dialectical investigation of the ultimate end of human life, which Thomas identifies with the knowledge of God. But precisely how are we to understand this conclusion? Is it the result of a philosophical demonstration? Or has Thomas surreptitiously introduced theological premises into a segment of the book purportedly devoted to rational investigation? The questions raised in the opening chapter concerning the twofold mode of truth and the intention of the work converge in this segment of the text. Perhaps more than any other issue, the teaching on the ultimate end has exercised the polemical passions of commentators. In the literature on the *Contra Gentiles*, the teaching on the ultimate end is commonly seen as pivotal. It figures prominently in debates over Thomas's fidelity to the division of the work in accordance with the twofold mode of truth.[14]

In the initial argument for contemplation of God as the end of human life, the only authority Thomas cites is Aristotle and he cites him six times (III, 25). The argument explicates the Aristotelian observation that all human beings naturally desire to know. Thomas posits an array of

Aristotelian arguments: that the end consists in the coincidence of the proper operation with its most intelligible object, that the speculative sciences are lovable in themselves, that first philosophy is ordered to knowledge of God, and that the human intellect apprehends universal being and naturally desires to know its cause. The origin of speculative philosophy is the human proclivity to wonder about hidden causes.

The Aristotelian principle that nature does nothing in vain issues in an argument for contemplation of God as the end of human life. Contemplation of God fulfills the definition of the end given in the *Ethics*, I, 7. The end is desired for its own sake; it is the last thing sought in the chain of means–to–ends relations; and it is self-sufficient and lacking in nothing. It satisfies every appetite. No finite good or conglomeration of goods meets these criteria. It seems then that there is a natural desire, known to the *gentiles*, for an end that transcends what is given in nature.

If this were an adequate reading, one would expect Aquinas to be satisfied with such affirmations. However, the dominant mode of argument on behalf of a transcendent ultimate end is *via negativa*. Where the line of argument is positive, it is dialectical. The eleven chapters subsequent to the affirmation of contemplation as the end constitute a sustained argument by exclusion (26–36). Thomas considers an array of candidates, from goods of the body to the goods of prudence and art. All fail. Thomas concludes, "it remains that the final happiness of man consists in contemplation of truth" (III, 37).[15] Thus far the argument has not transcended the position of *Ethics*, X, 6–8. Thomas has yet to specify the kind of knowledge involved in the contemplation of God.

Thomas goes on to deny that felicity consists in the various kinds of knowledge of God available in this life (38–40). Ordinary knowledge of God arises naturally from reflection on the order in nature, an order that presupposes some orderer. This knowledge reaches only a vague apprehension of the existence of a first cause and admits many errors. Demonstrations are more reliable, although they tell us more about what God is not than about what he is. The few who grasp them remain in potency to further knowledge of the divine essence; demonstrations may even contain an admixture of error. Thomas adds, "if there are some who have found the truth of divine things by the way of demonstration, to which there has been no falsity adjoined, it is obvious that there have been very few."[16] Even the mode of cognition of faith is "more like hearing than vision."

Thus far the argument has proceeded by elimination. The only remaining qualified candidate for achieving happiness is contemplation of the highest truth. What follows is a debate over the precise character of the contemplative end and its attainability. There is no reconsideration of the other components of the good life, at least not until the consideration of the means to the ultimate end. Many have objected to this apparent reduction of happiness to the intellect. Some, like John Finnis, see the hierarchical conception of the goods constitutive of happiness as eviscerating lower goods, rendering them merely means to narrowly conceived intellectual pursuits.[17] Others, such as Martha Nussbaum and Hannah Arendt, see the aspiration for contemplative transcendence as an "escape" from the "frailty of human affairs."[18] A complete response to these objections must await further explication of Thomas's position on the good life. Still, an initial response can be supplied at this point. Following the ancients, Thomas underscores the erotic foundation of the life of wisdom. The end is an object of affection and longing. The desire to know is more consuming than any other desire; the more one knows, the more one desires to grasp the ultimate causes. As Josef Pieper puts it, "Only the presence of what is loved makes us happy, and that presence is actualized by the power of cognition."[19] The life of contemplation is rooted in a desire for union with the beloved; it involves submission to the beautiful. Thomas's view of contemplation as fostering reverence for the source of beauty and order accords well with Pieper's position.

The alignment of contemplation with a desire for control and power is utterly alien to the ancients. Such a reading unjustifiably imports into ancient texts a modern conception of knowing as tied to making.[20] The worry, then, is that productive, theoretical power will overshadow the contingency, particularity, and fragility of the life of action. Yet Aristotle speaks of contemplation as useless. Against those who would neglect contemplation because its results are so feeble and so paltry, Aristotle argues that, however small and tenuous our knowledge of the divine may be, it remains more desirable than the sure and comprehensive knowledge of lower things.[21] Where, then, is the basis in Aristotle's texts for aligning contemplation with power and control?[22]

Thomas's argument brings to the fore the dialectical character of Aristotle's inquiry into the ultimate end. In fact, Thomas's criticisms of the Arabic commentators on Aristotle resembles Nussbaum's critique of a "species-independent criterion" of the good. She speaks of an "aspiration to leave behind altogether the constituting conditions of our humanity, and to seek for a life that is really the life of another sort of being—as if it were a higher and better life for us."[23] In chapters forty-one through forty-five, Thomas engages the optimistic Arabic assessment of the human ability to know the separate substances, and, through them, to know God: "By seeing the separate substances, one will participate in the mode of knowing by which the separate substance, through understanding itself, understands God."[24] The knowledge of separate substances would provide an alternative way of knowing God, achievable in this life, by the exercise of natural powers. By resolving, or abstracting from, our notion of sensible substance, we can attain the quiddity of separate substances. Just as we abstract the quiddity of sensible things from sensible particulars, so too we can abstract from the quiddity of sensible things to reach the notion of quiddity simply. We would thus reach a "quiddity that has no other quiddity," which is the quiddity proper to a separate substance (III, 41).[25]

According to Averroës, the mind, by unraveling phantasms, can strip away sensible accretions from the core and disclose a concept identical to that of a separate substance. The process of resolution, however, produces not a purified, positive concept, but a diminished, negative one. The importance of the account of abstraction in the previous book is clear. The proper and proportionate object of human knowledge is always the essence of sensible substances. The phantasms, from which we know the natures of sensible things, include matter and form. Sensible and separate substances share only the rational character of quiddity as quiddity. Yet the abstraction that makes the consideration of quiddity as quiddity possible reaches only the remote genus of separate substances.

Each of the speculative sciences has a mode of consideration proper to it, and the differences in their modes of defining are differences in kind, not merely in degree. Thomas thus defends Aristotle's view that the sciences are irreducibly plural and that discourse is analogical. A conceptual literalism is at the root of Averroës' view that the ascent through the sciences brings the mind into direct contact with increasingly higher orders of reality. Thomas counters this sort of realism with what Fabro calls "dialectical realism."[26] The orders of being and knowing are opposed to one another. As Aristotle's characterization of mathematics as an abstraction indicates, the more abstract our mode of knowing, the more removed the mind is from the real.[27] Thomas does not ground metaphysics in an act of abstraction but in a negative judgment. The concrete yet common investigation of being, evident in the very grammar of the phrase *ens inquantum ens*, does not bring the mind into direct confrontation with reality. Magnitudes and separate substances, for example, would have the same rational character only if the former existed separately, between forms and sensible things, as some Platonists hold (III, 41). But this is manifestly contrary to Aristotle's texts. Invoking the Aristotelian principle that all knowledge arises from sense, Thomas argues that the indirect route to separate substances through effects establishes only their existence, not their nature. Their quiddities "exceed all sensible effects."

Thomas proceeds to consider Alexander's view that, as we come to know all intelligible species, we are united to the agent intellect (III, 42). At the end of the process the agent intellect becomes the form of the habitual understanding. Through union with the agent intellect, we are able to know whatever it knows, including separate substances. The "peak perfection," which results from a "natural process of generation," enables us to understand the separate substances "like some sort of God."

Even if such a process were descriptive of human knowing, it would not achieve the desired union. Since we cannot attain knowledge of all objects from the senses, the process would be interminable. Is it not more reasonable to suppose that the ultimate felicity attainable in this life is that acquired through the speculative sciences and not by a natural process of generation? The very notion of perfection as a process of generation is of course a piece of emanationist metaphysics, something that Thomas has already discredited. A process of generation perfects a substance according to its own genus, not a higher one.

Thomas is aware, then, of the danger Nussbaum associates with the "aspiration to leave behind altogether the constituting conditions of our humanity." Thomas's partial affirmation of Nussbaum's thesis can be seen in his dispute with Averroës over how to interpret Aristotle's comparison of the intellect to an owl in the light of day. Whereas Averroës argues that the comparison indicates only the difficulty of knowing the most intelligible things, Thomas holds that it extends to the impossibility of our knowing them by our own power (III, 45). Aristotle's emphasis on the ineliminable role of the phantasm in human knowing and on the naturalness of embodiment for the human intellect guides Thomas's explication.

Thomas's sympathy with those who resist the evisceration of the constituting conditions of humanity can be seen in another way. The conflict with Aristotle's commentators over the achievability of the human end through a natural process has ramifications for the narrative of the good life. Some have suggested that the neo-Platonic narrative of *exitus-reditus* applies to the structure of the *Contra Gentiles*. Yet, the neo-Platonic schema is too closely allied to emanationist metaphysics to provide a fitting vehicle for the Christian narrative. Just as Thomas takes issue with pagan accounts of the necessity of creation and the eternal existence of matter, so too he resists the position that the return of creatures to their source results from principles inherent in nature. Such a process can perhaps be described in narrative terms, but it is a narrative void of drama, as it mitigates the freedom of both author and participant. The tendency to deny the concrete unity and individuality of composite substances renders the significance of particular historical events otiose.

Rarely have commentators attended to the dialectical context of the arguments for the ultimate end. If they had attended to the critical path Thomas travels in reaching his conclusion, they would have been greatly assisted. Indeed, the arguments against the Arabic penchant for deducing the ascent from the descent should guide our reading of his own alternative teaching on the ultimate end.

Thus far in the aporetic inquiry into the nature of human happiness, Thomas has considered a number of opinions from the many and the wise. He has argued that no good in this life satisfies the character of the end and hence that the end must be transcendent. The natural appetite for happiness, whose formal notion is fulfilled only in the contemplation of God, constitutes the natural inclination of every human being. As Thomas unambiguously states: "every intellect naturally desires the vision of the divine substance" (III, 57).[28] But we have already seen that the desire for God does not necessarily entail conscious awareness on the part of human beings.

Often unnoticed in the disputes is that Aristotle's definition of happiness underlies Thomas's argument. Yet in the final book of the *Ethics* Aristotle resists the identification of the end as contemplation. From this, Jorge Laporta thinks that Thomas corrects Aristotle.[29] But it is not clear that Thomas does so from within the realm of philosophy. Instead, he underscores the dialectical character of the inquiry and celebrates the inconclusiveness of Aristotle's investigation of human destiny. Given the achievability of some portion of happiness and the limitations to what natural reason can discern about immortality, Aristotle's restraint is warranted. Aristotle's account of the good points to something that unassisted natural reason cannot possess; his acknowledgment of the limits of philosophy should be commended, not chastised. The limitations can be overcome only in Christian revelation, which Aristotle cannot be faulted for ignoring. Aristotle's dialectical account opens the way for the disclosure of the Christian narrative. From that vantage point, Aristotle's entire account becomes one moment in a larger narrative.

The *via negativa* argument for the ultimate end culminates with the claim that felicity cannot be had in this life (III, 48).[30] All who describe happiness speak of stability, continuity, the termination of desire, and the elimination of evil. Yet every form of temporal happiness is imperfect, mutable, and discontinuous. The contingency and vulnerability of human happiness is evident not only in its susceptibility to fortune and forces outside the control of human beings, but also in the temporal and incomplete character of our approach to perfection. The awareness of such phenomena leads Aristotle to assert that we are capable of only imperfect happiness and that we are happy, not absolutely, but in a human mode. Some philosophers even suppose that the weakness of the human intellect precludes the possibility of a transcendent end. Thomas comments: "In which it is sufficiently apparent how even the brilliant minds of these men suffered from narrowness" (III, 48).[31] From what point of view does Thomas overcome the parochial perspective of the greatest philosophical minds?

Thomas responds, "From which narrowness we shall be liberated if we posit, according to the preceding proofs, that the soul is able to reach true felicity after this life, when the soul will exist immortally, in which state it will understand through the mode by which the separate substances do."[32] The passage is problematic for a number of reasons. The use of the term "proofs" (*probationes*) here is at best analogical, perhaps equivocal. Can philosophical psychology determine anything more than the separability of the intellect? Can it say anything about how or whether it will understand once it is separate? As we have already noted, there is a tension in the previous proofs for the immortality of the human soul. The striking assertion that the separated soul will understand just as the angels (II, 81) marks a retreat to the misleading assimilation of souls to angels and renders dubious the painstaking elaboration of arguments for the necessity of the union of soul and body.[33] It seems to render death a natural stage in the perfection of human beings and risks lapsing into the Arabic understanding of the achievement of the ultimate end as the result of a natural process. If the soul needs the body for the perfection of its understanding, then how could its knowledge apart from the body be other than confused and imperfect?[34]

It is difficult, then, to determine what philosophical reflection alone can conclude about the end. As Aertsen notes, there is a "dialectic in the natural desire to know," evident in the use of Aristotle against Aristotle.[35] Thomas's use of Aristotle highlights the incompleteness of, and the dialectical anguish attendant upon, philosophical reflection about the end. While he repeatedly cites Aristotle in support of a transcendent end, he also cites Aristotle's belief that we can attain only imperfect happiness. Thomas does not say that the foregoing proofs establish that we *do* reach beatitude, only that we *can* reach it (*pervenire posse*). Similarly, concerning the ultimate end, philosophy can determine that there is a desire to know the ultimate cause of being, but not whether or how any direct vision is possible. In confirming the existence of such an end, Thomas resorts not to philosophical authority but to our Lord's promise of reward in heaven (III, 48).[36] Appropriately, the chapters defending the possibility of the vision of God contain a plethora of scriptural citations, more than in any other section of the third book (III, 51–53).[37] Scriptural authority counteracts the temptation to despair concerning the highest good, even as it underscores the limits to natural reason.

The exegesis of Aristotle is crucial to the dispute over the ultimate end. The commentators share with Thomas a general conception of the end, yet none of the philosophical attempts to overcome the gap between aspiration and achievement succeed.[38] All distort one or another feature of embodied rationality. An adequate reading of Aristotle—even if it goes beyond the *littera* of his texts—salvages the philosophical basis of the natural desire for, and the possibility of, beatitude, without diminishing the mystery of faith and the supernatural character of the gift of beatitude. The rhetorical strategy of the ultimate end mirrors that of the divine names. Jordan's comments about the names apply equally here: "One must resist . . . both the presumption of a language which seeks to become identical with its referents and the presumption of a language which closes in on itself as its own referent."[39]

Most commentators have resisted one or the other but not both of these presumptions. A persistent question in the debates over the ultimate end is this. Does Aristotle's argument, taken to its logical term, demonstrate that there must be such an end for the rational creature? Does it (to use the language of neoscholastic debate) create an exigency in the creature for such a vision? As Kevin Staley has recently argued, the responses to these questions have too often supposed a univocal conception of the end.[40] On the one hand, those who follow Cajetan's denial of natural desire for God rely upon the premise that natural inclinations correspond to natural capacities. Since there is no natural capacity for the beatific vision, there can be no natural desire for it. On the other hand, the followers of de Lubac insist solely upon the desire for perfect happiness, realizable only in the direct vision of God. They repudiate any notion of incomplete or imperfect happiness as a contradiction in terms. These tendencies can be seen in the most influential readings of the *Contra Gentiles*. Commenting on the two exegetical tendencies, exemplified in the writings of de Broglie and Gauthier, Corbin writes, "de Broglie insists unilaterally on the unity of the end of man and refuses the notion of a supernatural end exterior to a natural end, while Gauthier insists unilaterally on the distinction between natural and supernatural end."[41]

The positions of de Lubac and de Broglie tend either to minimize the gratuity of the vision or to collapse nature into supernature. One might suppose that the rhetoric of Thomas's treatise entirely undermines philosophical reflection about the good and renders human life, apart from the intervention of divine grace, tragic and meaningless. The incomplete character of philosophical inquiry is not a cause of excessive anxiety, however; natural reason can articulate and live in accordance with an imperfect conception of the good. The life of moral and intellectual virtue partly satisfies the human desire for happiness. When human beings operate in accordance with their proper operations, they attain and imitate the divine in the measure appropriate to them and in a way similar to that of the rest of creation. For Thomas, the term "happiness" is analogical. One need abandon neither imperfect happiness nor the natural desire for God.

As Laporta, de Lubac, and others have noted, the natural desire for an end that the creature by its own powers is incapable of realizing is an anomaly. Yet it does not involve contradiction, and, in the *Contra Gentiles*, is not unprecedented. The treatment of human nature in the second book focuses on the peculiar status of human nature, existing on the horizon of the spiritual and material. The location at the juncture of matter and spirit makes human operations complex. Anton Pegis comments,

> Natures qua natures are closed only in the sense that they are not subject to more or less. There are, to be sure, closed natures, but they are closed, not because they are natures, but because they are material. If there are creatures with spiritual natures, then they are open because they are spiritual.[42]

Thomas's emphasis on the peculiar status of human nature provides the basis for a response to Suarez's famous objection: "All other creatures are able to achieve their natural ends through means consonant with their nature: why therefore should human nature be in such a worse condition?"[43] The teaching of the second book on human nature as a microcosm is present here. Thomas speaks of human nature as involving a *complicatio* of the powers of all other creatures and as requiring a more complicated pedagogy to reach its end. The complexity of the means necessary for the attainment of the human good is a sign of its nobility, not its inferiority. Laporta speaks of the rational creature's "disequilibrium," which is a "mark of grandeur."[44]

The objections of Suarez and Cajetan are not conclusive. Conversely, their sharp distinction between natural and supernatural ends and their assertion that human nature has only an obediential potency to the ultimate end are problematic. In the *Contra Gentiles*, Thomas does not deploy the language of obediential potency; moreover, the application of it to the beatific vision is dubious.[45] The argument for the ultimate end follows directly from the natural desire for, and the definition of, happiness, whose formal notion is saved only in the contemplation of God. The univocal conception of end as that which does not exceed the powers of the nature in question is inadequate to Thomas's nuanced language. It fails to capture the aporetic character of the philosophic search for the good and tends to close human nature in upon itself. The most unwelcome consequence of the univocal notion of the end is that it undercuts the intelligibility of a transcendent end. If the end is not naturally desirable to us, would not its pursuit entail the substitution of one nature for another? As Thomas writes, "If something essential should be either subtracted from or added to a nature, immediately it will be another nature" (II, 15).[46] Bereft of some natural openness to the vision of God, the supernatural exalting of our nature would not involve perfection but the destruction of one nature and the reconstruction of another. The tradition of Suarez and Cajetan runs counter to the most famous of all Thomistic dicta: grace does not destroy nature but perfects it. Their view lends credence to Nussbaum's skepticism concerning the suitability and desirability of transcendence.

Thomas's preoccupation with combating objections to the possibility of divine union would be unwarranted if we had merely an obediential potency to the vision of God. Obediential potency requires nothing more than the subordination of the creature to the creator. The objections to the possibility of beatitude suppose a chasm between human and divine natures; such is typically the case where obediential potency is present. Thomas counters that the two natures are "not utterly foreign, as sound is to sight or an immaterial substance is to sense."[47] Instead, the "divine substance is the first intelligible and the principle of all intellectual cognition."[48] The efficacy of the analogies from the first book between human understanding and divine intelligence provides antecedent evidence of some link between the two. The divine intellect, nonetheless, greatly exceeds the human in power; hence, the human intellect needs strengthening (III, 54).

The premise that nature does nothing in vain is prominent in the third book. It does not, however, require that natural ends must be realized, merely that they can be realized. Natural events often frustrate the natural ends of creatures. The natural desire to see God would be in vain only "if it were not possible" (*non esset possibile pervenire*) for it to be satisfied (III, 48, 50). The question is crucial not so much for the philosopher, but for the theologian, who considers philosophical matters from the vantage point of faith.

In spite of the arguments for the natural desire to see God, the text contains no evidence that the natural desire in any way anticipates the gift.[49] Such an anticipation would come dangerously close to the position of Arabic neo-Platonism, which Thomas castigates. Certain views of Thomists threaten to negate the "drama of finite and infinite freedoms" by anticipating grace in transcendental subjectivity. Balthasar notes the similarity between certain modern Thomisms and neo-Platonism: "The merciful aid of God—in Jesus Christ and already in the election of Israel—to the lost world: this arch-dramatic act of the gracious God becomes the undramatic and static conception of a God who is, as with Plato and Plotinus . . . , the 'sun of the Good,' eternally shining."[50]

Thomas argues that human beings can enjoy a vision of the divine essence only by God's imposing a new form onto the soul. By its natural power, no creature can achieve the vision of God (III, 52). The philosophical ascent to a knowledge of the highest cause is inherently limited. As Thomas writes, "what is proper to a superior nature is not able to be achieved by an inferior nature, except through the action of the superior nature to which it is proper. . . . Thus no intellectual substance is able to see God through the divine essence itself unless God is the agent."[51] In the attainment of the vision, God is formal and active, while the soul is material and passive. In this case, God is both what is seen and that whereby it is seen. The argument of the second book indicates that philosophy, too, is made possible by the first gift of God in creation. Receptivity to a further gift makes possible the achievement of the aspiration given in creation. For all its flaws, the argument of *Surnaturel* rightly focuses upon the "twofold gift." There is no basis, then, for the conflation of contemplation with control and power.

The twofold gift fits nicely the twofold mode of truth, both of which are internal to "what we confess about divine things." The connection points the way to a resolution of a problem concerning the structure of the text. As Lafont sees it, "the axis" of the work is found "in the consideration of beatitude," which allows Thomas to "complete the circle," to make the transition from the *exitus* to the *reditus*. But if the arguments for the ultimate end are pivotal in the transition from reason to faith, will reason then give the definitive shape to the work? This would be so only if Thomas had given some indication that natural reason could in any way anticipate the gift, that there could be some sort of deduction of the latter from the former. But he does not. Instead, in the words of Balthasar, there is only the "aporia . . . of finitude."[52] The emphasis, moreover, upon the creature as passive and receptive with respect to that vision is an initial indication of the dramatic reversal that characterizes the shift from reason to faith.

The vision of God fulfills every desire. In that vision, human beings attain in a unified and immediate way what they seek in the world in divergent and indirect ways. Whatever is sought in the pursuit of truth or in civil and private life is even more perfectly possessed in the vision of God (III, 63). The theological response to the question of the ultimate end overcomes the opposition between dominant and inclusive ends. The account of the coincidence and absolute intensification of all goods in God does not result merely from the summation of particular temporal goods. It is rooted in the metaphysics of creation and participation. Creation is an imperfect imitation of the perfections that exist in God in a simple and supereminent manner. Just as descent precedes ascent in the narrative of the universe, so too the vision of God is not an escape from the world but rather a return to its transcendent ground, whose stability and simplicity insure that felicity is more than transient pleasure or the heaping together of diverse goods.

IV. PROBLEMS OF PROVIDENCE

The arguments for God as end provide the foundation for the notion of God's providence: "Whenever certain things are ordered to some end, they are all subordinate to the disposing power of the one to whom the end principally belongs" (III, 64).[53] According to Thomas, the Aristotelian conception of God as unmoved mover entails divine governance, since providence is "nothing other than to move things to an end through understanding."[54] The transition from God as end to God as governor underscores the subordination of all things to the end. Thomas moves from a consideration of the capacities and destiny of human nature to that of creation as the narrative of a divine artisan. The shift introduces a temporal and historical dimension unknown to Aristotle. As Pegis puts it, there is nowhere for an Aristotelian nature to go. From the vantage point of providence, Aristotle's account of the good life is but one moment in the life of a wayfarer. The movement from Aristotle to scripture entails the transformation of naturalism "in a system historical and created."[55] The emphasis upon God as an artist operating through time and history marks the most profound use of narrative in the work thus far. Before the narrative can be explicitly considered, objections to the coherence of the notion of divine providence must be addressed. Dialectic, once again, precedes narrative.

In the discussion of providence, Thomas amplifies the teachings about God's relationship to the world from the first book and about created *esse* from the second book. The reconsideration of topics involves another application of Aristotelian dialectic. We have already shown that the dialectical engagement of received opinions is the key to the method of the text. Dialectic is operative in another way in the repetitious consideration of topics. Thomas typically provides a schematic introductory investigation, which is adequate to initial questions. The account remains open to further clarification and greater resolution in light of other, usually more complex, questions. Here he considers more amply the problems surrounding the notion of divine providence. Previously he argued that God alone is the cause of being and that in every creature there is a composition of being and substance. Here he argues that God preserves things in being. Once an agent has ceased acting, its impression remains in the effect only when "it has been converted into the nature of the effect."[56] But being is not reducible to nature or essence. God continuously conserves every creature (III, 65).

The primacy and irreducibility of being (*esse*) applies not just to the existence but also to the operations of creatures. Actions that do not continue when the causal activity of an agent ceases are due to that agent. But if God's conservation were to cease, so too would the activity of creatures. The reduction of all acts to created *esse* indicates that in every moment of their existence creatures are radically contingent, utterly dependent on God's will. Thomas says,

> The highest in goodness and perfection among those things of which a secondary agent is capable resides in the power of the first agent. For the complement of the power of the second agent is from the first agent. What is most perfect in all effects is being. Any nature or form is perfected through its being in act, and is compared to being in act as potency to act. (III, 66)[57]

Just as God gives and preserves being, so too he gives and preserves the operative powers of creatures.

Thomas counters two principal misinterpretations of divine providence: first, that providence usurps the proper operations of creatures and eliminates freedom and contingency, and, second, that it is beneath God's dignity to have direct providence over singulars and lowly things. He combats various kinds of denials of natural causality: the views that the species of sensible things are separate from, and causes of, sensible things (Plato), or that they flow from an agent intellect (Avicenna), or that they pass actively through passive bodies (Avicebron).[58] In response to the complete reduction of causality to divine operation, Thomas attempts to save the appearances of the structure of ordinary experience from which human reflection about God begins. As he puts it in the commentary on Aristotle's *De Interpretatione*, the goal is "to save the roots of contingency."[59] If God alone operates in things and if his activity introduces no change in him, there would be no diversity of effects. But this is contrary to sense experience. The denial of secondary causality repudiates the position that the "power of a created cause is manifested through its effects." This is contrary to the suppositions and deliverances of the sciences. The view undermines the foundations of human knowing and detracts from the perfection of creatures (III, 69).

Thomas draws upon the Aristotelian view of the proximate intelligibility of natural substances and upon the Dionysian thesis that it befits the divine perfection for creatures to be "coworkers" with God: "from an abundance of perfection" a being is able to communicate perfection to another (III, 69).[60] Thomas holds that God is the cause of operation for all things and that proper actions can be attributed to natural things. He must, then, confront the apparent redundancy involved in claiming that one effect arises simultaneously from two agents. Thomas distinguishes between the thing itself which acts and the power by which it acts. Whenever there is a hierarchical ordering of agents, the lower agent acts through the power of the entire order of higher agents and, ultimately, of the first agent. But an action is nonetheless attributed to the lower agent. Confusion arises from conceiving the action as done partly by one agent and partly by another, as if they constituted a mixture on the same causal plane. He writes,

> The same effect is not thus attributed to the natural cause and to divine power, as if it were partly done by God and partly by a natural agent. Instead, the whole effect is from each in different ways, as the same entire effect is attributed to an instrument and to the principal agent. (III, 70)[61]

Divine causality is not an addition to the cause of the creature; the latter's activity presupposes the causal primacy of God, as intensive and extensive act.[62]

Contemporary philosophers have found Thomas's understanding of divine causality unintelligible or internally contradictory. Between Thomas and some analytic philosophers there is a nearly unbridgeable gap in vocabulary and conceptual scheme. Thomas speaks neither of God's choosing among various possible worlds nor of his actualizing states of affairs.[63] As James Ross has argued, some critics have failed to come to terms with, indeed even to understand adequately, Thomas's metaphysics of created being. In an attempt to articulate Thomas's alternative understanding, according to which the whole act is attributed both to God and to natural causes, but in different modes or orders, Ross speaks of "logically ordered sufficient conditions of different kinds."[64] States of affairs are parasitic upon actually existing entities; God's creative and conservative causality has to do primarily with the latter. He writes,

> Does God's necessary and sufficient causation extend to my whole being, through time, even to my accidents and, therefore, to whatever I do freely? Absolutely. The whole physical universe, all of it, is actively caused to be. Still, to say that freedom or human agency is thereby impeded is absurd. Nothing can be or come about unless caused to be by the creator. So the fact that God's causing is necessary for whatever happens cannot impede liberty; it is a condition for it.[65]

For God not to usurp the proper operations of creatures is consonant with the very nature and purpose of creation. As Thomas argued in the second book, the proper operations of creatures manifest the "beauty of order" (*decor ordinis*, III, 70). The "highest beauty" (*summus decor*) requires the presence of distinct and unequal things. If the universe is to contain all grades of creatures, then there must be free and contingent creatures. If providence were to eliminate freedom and contingency, God would contradict his own act of creation and frustrate his own design (III, 72–3). Numerous characteristics of divine causality indicate that its primacy need not eliminate contingency or freedom. According to Aristotle's *Ethics* III, 1, violence involves the unnatural influence of an external agent. God's influence cannot be understood in such terms, however. He is intimately present to the soul, not through physical contact but through incorporeal power.

The perfection of the universe requires variety and multiplicity and the inclusion of contingent and free beings. "Contrariety and incompatibility," then, are ineliminable. The generation of one thing may well be the occasion for the corruption of another. To eliminate evil entirely, numerous goods would have to be abolished. There is thus a natural, suppositional necessity to the possibility of evil. The presence of evil also serves a pedagogical end. The good is better known by comparison with evil, while the endurance of evil makes our desire for good more ardent (III, 71). Certain virtues, for example, "the patience of the just," are made possible by the presence of evil. Thus Thomas extends his initial remarks concerning the nonbeing of evil and explicitly locates it within the narrative of the good life.

The third book inscribes the account of creation within the rational plan of divine providence, whose goal is to lead creatures to increased participation in divine wisdom. It embodies the principles concerning the theological mode of consideration and is rhetorically ordered to leading readers to see the world and themselves from God's perspective. The intimate connection between providence and the human good requires a reconsideration of the causal relationship of God to creatures, especially human creatures. Problems peculiar to the third book provide the occasion for dialectical refinement of principles adduced in the first book. Thomas eliminates causal determination of the will or intellect by celestial bodies (III, 84–7). He repeats the thesis defended earlier that acts of will are caused not only by the will, but also by God (III, 89), and that these are subject to divine providence (III, 90). To isolate more noble powers, such as intellect and will, from the order of divine providence is to invert the intelligible structure of reality and to demean rational creatures.

The question of the role of intermediate or rival powers in the ordaining of events prompts a discussion of fortune and fate (III, 91–3). Thomas begins with Aristotle's description of fortune as occurring when "something good happens to someone outside the order of his intention" (III, 92).[66] There are three possible sources of the influence of fortune: natural capacities, the influence of the celestial bodies on bodily dispositions, and the persuasion of the intellect by angels. In his discussion of the last influence, Thomas moves away from the language of fortune to that of benevolent governance. All these influences, moreover, are subject to God, in relation to whom "neither in things human, nor in any other thing can there be anything unforeseen and by chance."[67] Although Thomas allows for intermediate influences on human beings, the ultimate determination of all events is traced to God. Thomas will admit the existence of fate so long as it is understood in Boethius' terms as a "disposition inherent in mutable things" at the service of providence. Following Augustine and Gregory, however, Thomas counsels against the use of the term "fate," on account of the penchant among unbelievers to ascribe fate to the controlling power of the stars (III, 93).

In contrast to fate or fortune, providence is rational and certain (III, 94). The certainty of providence raises yet another difficulty. It seems that "either providence is not certain or all things occur from necessity."[68] The objection that the certitude of divine providence necessitates actions arises from an Aristotelian argument: if every effect is directly caused and if the effects of direct causes occur of necessity, then future events will happen of necessity. Aristotle circumvents the difficulty by denying that all causes necessarily bring about their effects; some can fail. This is not an option with respect to divine providence, however. Thomas buttresses the objection by analysis of the proposition, "If God foresees this, this will be." Since the antecedent is necessary, so too is the consequent. But this reduces all events to God's necessary causality.

Thomas addresses these difficulties by showing that they rest on a misunderstanding of God's relationship to the world. First, creation is an ordered whole, containing both necessary and contingent beings. The inclusion of contingent beings in creation does not entail God's distance from them. Divine providence is the "*per se* cause why this effect comes forth contingently."[69] Second, the fallacious interpretation of the conditional proposition, "If God foresees this, this will be," arises from our failure to see that God's foreknowledge has not the relation of present to future, but of present to present. That is, since the "this" of the protasis is present, so too is the "this" of the apodosis. The necessity is not absolute but hypothetical.[70]

Contingency is integral to creation. As an imperfect imitation of God, the order of nature is not absolutely necessary; different orders are conceivable (III, 99). There is nothing contradictory or incoherent about God's producing effects apart from the ordinary course of nature. Such effects reveal that "all of nature is subject to the divine will" and that creatures "proceed from him, by free will, not natural necessity."[71] The events wherein God acts apart from the ordinary course of nature are miracles, for "we marvel at something when, while seeing the effect, we do not know its cause."[72] Since the immediate cause of miracles is utterly hidden, miracles are especially indicative of the way in which the divine essence exceeds the comprehension of mortal minds (III, 101). Miracles thus intensify our sense of wonder, awe, and reverence, which Thomas previously identified as the theological goal of the study of creatures.

From the perspective of Thomas's theocentric metaphysics, a natural form is "nothing other than the divine likeness participated in things" (III, 97).[73] In relation to the first agent, nature is a contingent instrument:

> All creatures are compared to God as products of art to an artist. . . . Whence the whole of nature is like an artifact of divine art. It is not contrary to the essence of an art product for the artist to work on it even after it has been given its first form. (III, 100)[74]

God's providence encompasses both the natural and the supernatural. The contingency of the natural order, in its original foundation and in its openness to the intervention of its maker, indicates that creation is fundamentally a narrative. The possibility of supernatural intervention in the natural order, coupled with the openness of finite intellectual creatures to the infinite, sets the stage for the drama of redemption.

The natural and supernatural communication of God with creatures constitutes two moments in divine pedagogy, corresponding to the two-fold mode of truth. The second mode is not simply placed on top of the first; instead, it makes its appearance felt through concrete and wondrous events within the natural whole of creation. The story of creation is open to unexpected shifts in plot and to dramatic alteration. As exceptions to the common order of nature, supernatural events are akin to the accidents of chance and fortune. They are not posterior to nature and intellect but superior and prior to them. In his eschewal of fortune, Thomas eliminates a chief source of the tragic view of human life, the view either that imperfect intellectual beings control the order of events or that blind fate is the final arbiter.

V. DIVINE PEDAGOGY AND DRAMATIC
REVERSAL IN THE RETURN TO GOD

Some glimpse of the Christian narrative can be gained from the ethical teaching of the *Summa Contra Gentiles*, which is part of the discussion of divine providence. Thomas distinguishes between God's universal rule, which applies to all creatures, and his particular rule, which applies solely to intellectual creatures (III, 113). God cares for and governs these creatures for their own sake. The rational creature has, beyond the inclinations of the species, the ability to deliberate about particulars: "he can perceive how in different ways something may be good or evil, insofar as it is suitable to various individuals, times, and places."[75] External forces cannot directly cause acts of will. Created substances can move the will only by means of a good that is understood, "by persuading" the rational creature that some good ought to be pursued. Since God creates and sustains the rational creature in being, he can directly cause acts of will. The influence of God upon the will is not violent, as God is intimately and internally present to the will (III, 88).

Thomas calls the peculiar guidance given to human beings law, which he defines as a "reason and rule of acting" (III, 114).[76] The prominence of law in the ethics of the *Contra Gentiles* should not be confused with late medieval or classical modern divine command theories. Thomas's conception of law is teleological and pedagogical. The law provides explicit instruction concerning the goods, often only inchoately apprehended, to which human nature is naturally inclined. Law ordains the means to various ends; similarly, the end of the law is said to be love, or the condition of virtue that enables us to cling to the good with firmness and joy. Divine law also orders us in relation to our neighbors; it confirms and reinforces our natural social dispositions (III, 117). The intelligibility of the law is tied to the goods secured by obedience to precepts.

The pedagogical character of the law is clear from its subordination to virtue. Thomas speaks of the twofold manner, internal and external, of impelling to the observation of the precepts of divine law. What is done only from fear of punishment is said to be done from external force. The virtue of charity, however, makes human beings a "law to themselves" (Rom. 2:14). They are "inclined of themselves to do what is just," even

without a law (III, 128).[77] The passage indicates the subordination of
law to virtue. It implies that the influence of divine grace is not violent,
that God is not coercive. Although he does not develop the notion of
natural law in the *Contra Gentiles*, Thomas does argue that certain acts
are right by nature (III, 129).[78] Divine law itself commands us to live
in accordance with reason (III, 128). There is, then, a certain overlap
between what divine law commands and what is naturally right. The
coincidence provides an initial illustration of the congruence of natural
and revealed morality; it reflects the previous assertion that the pedagogy
appropriate to rational creatures is "persuasion" (III, 88).

Central to the consideration of law in the *Contra Gentiles* is the discussion of divine worship. The cult of *latria*, the cult of worship, service,
and sacrifice, is to be offered to God alone, not to any creature. Although
worship itself is properly an internal act, it is appropriate that internal acts
be both initiated by and manifested in external acts (III, 119). Sensible
signs and sacrifices help us to remember God; through them, we order
both soul and body to God from whom they were given in our creation.
Thomas aligns the repudiation of sensible "manifestations" with the
heretical view that God is not the creator of bodies. He accuses his
opponents of forgetting that they are human. In creation, God manifests
his wisdom, goodness, and beauty; so too, in divine worship, there is an
external *manifestatio* of interior devotion:

> External sacrifice represents true, interior sacrifice, according to which the
> human mind offers itself to God. Our mind offers itself to God as the source
> of its creation, the author of its actions, and the end of its happiness. (III,
> 120)[79]

The reference to God as principle, author, and end recalls the division
of the first three books and their dominant themes: the correction of
idolatrous views about the divine nature, of views concerning creation
that detract from the perfection of God and creatures, and of philosophical
misconstruals of the sense in which God is the end of the rational creature.
The correspondence between internal and external in divine worship
presupposes the account of the union of soul and body. Human sacrifice
orders the whole of creation to God. The convergence of these various
themes underscores the importance of worship in the structure of the
whole work.

Despite the apparent continuity in the movement from the discussion
of the good life through the analysis of contemplation to the passages on

the cult of *latria*, Thomas has clearly stretched probable argumentation to its limits. The subsequent consideration of the counsels and the theological virtues exacerbates the problem. Many have objected to the inclusion of such topics in the first three books, in the section of the text that addresses what is accessible to reason. Before proceeding to an analysis of the remainder of the third book, three comments are in order. First, the first three books do not constitute an autonomous philosophy. Faith is not held in abeyance; it is the formality under which the consideration of nature proceeds. Second, in contrast to his commentators, Thomas is much less anxious to determine a precise line of demarcation between the purview of reason and that of faith. He regularly distinguishes between the truths accessible to reason, for example, the existence and simplicity of God, and those known only through revelation, for example, the Trinity and the Incarnation. But he does not provide an exhaustive list of which truths belong where. Still, the list of truths considered in the third book has rightly troubled commentators. Third, as we shall see in what follows, the narrative structure of the work alleviates these difficulties. Thomas does not "deduce" the theological virtues and the counsels from the teaching on the ultimate end, the *reditus* from the *exitus*. The supernatural means to God introduce a dramatic reversal in the narrative of the good life.

The disparity between the account of the good life accessible to philosophy and that open to reason under the tutelage of faith is palpable in the discussion of the counsels of poverty, chastity, and obedience. The counsels free us from the concerns of self, family, and external goods. While the precepts are enjoined upon all who seek salvation, the counsels are "urged" upon those who seek excellence, who wish to withdraw from the concerns of the present life and to renounce lesser goods for the sake of higher goods (III, 130). The counsels do not fit neatly into an Aristotelian account of the virtues. Aquinas is not unaware of the disparity. The principal objections to the life of poverty see it as vitiating natural goods. Among the objections are (a) that it is natural to gather and keep what is necessary to sustain life, (b) that poverty undermines the common good, and (c) that poverty is an excess, departing from the mean of liberality. Thomas's initial response runs thus: Although riches provide for human life and make the virtue of liberality possible, they are not constitutive of the good life. Solicitude for wealth often breeds greed, while success in attaining riches may engender pride. The life of contemplation, which is superior to that of action, has less need of external goods.

The defense of voluntary poverty concentrates upon the objection that it is deleterious to society. Thomas's response draws upon themes from Aristotle's *Politics*. In contrast to Plato, Aristotle holds that the *polis* is naturally a plurality, unified through education and law.[80] Numerous offices and various virtues must complement one another if the common good is to be realized. Thomas follows a similar line of reasoning. He does not propose that all citizens should embrace the counsels. Universal practice of the counsels would countermand the order of nature, which is part of divine providence. Conversely, if all were to care only for their personal possessions, no one would serve the common good (III, 135). Soldiers and rulers receive support from those they serve, so too those who embrace poverty for Christ serve the common good and deserve support.

There is some ground for discussion between Thomas and Aristotle on the question of the place of the counsels in the good life. Yet Thomas's defense hinges upon reason's apprehension of a transcendent end and upon the description of the means to that end in the Gospels. Even though the voluntarily poor succor the common good, their assistance has more to do with the spiritual than the temporal welfare of citizens. Just as Thomas reworks the Aristotelian position on the role of bodily and external goods in the good life, so too he transforms the Aristotelian understanding of the noble, the best, and the beautiful. Right reason no longer takes its bearings from the standard of natural virtue; the standard is the transcendent end of union with God. But where are we to find the means to that end? In keeping with the principle behind the division of the first three books from the fourth, Thomas minimizes the role of scripture in his discussion of the means. It is significant, however, that, among the scriptural citations, there are numerous references to the New Testament. This marks a departure from the typical practice of emphasizing the wisdom literature of the Old Testament. The transformation and surprising reversals that Aristotelian teachings undergo in this section point to scripture and the life of Christ as the model for the discussion.

The response to the objection that poverty is an extreme illustrates Thomas's novel application of Aristotelian teachings. The very indeterminacy of prudence—the impossibility of reducing prudence to unalterable rules—provides an opening for Thomas to transform Aristotle's account. He begins by noting that the objection misconstrues the mean in mathematical terms (III, 134). Thomas counters: the mean is not taken "according to the amount of exterior things," but according to reason, which "measures not only the amount of the thing used, but also the condition of the person, and the intention, as well as the occasions of place and time . . . , which are integral to the acts of the virtues."[81] Provided, then, that one embraces it for the right reason and with due regard to circumstances, voluntary poverty is not excessive. But the formality (*ratio*) under which one embraces poverty is not one known to Aristotle.

From an Aristotelian perspective, the deeper criticism of mendicancy is that it is contemptible. The response is instructive:

> It is obvious that mendicancy is not without a certain humiliation, as it is more ignoble to suffer than to do an action, to receive than to give, and to be ruled and obedient than to govern and command. On account of some added circumstance, however, this may be reversed. (III, 135)[82]

Thomas acknowledges the natural superiority of active power and rule over receptivity and obedience. Virtuous humiliation, however, is not stupidity, the unthinking acceptance of any kind of abjection. One should accept humiliation only when it is a necessary means to virtue. Begging is part of the life of voluntary poverty, a life that frees one to follow Christ, to devote oneself to contemplation, and to serve the poor and the suffering. Thomas's novel application of the Aristotelian mean to the question of the use of bodily and external goods and his advocacy of humiliation with discretion involve nothing less than the articulation of Christian prudence. The descent of humility and charity must precede the ascent to the transcendent good; the Christian narrative thus reverses the expectations of the philosopher.

The counsels are not for the weak but for those who wish to pursue the highest good with greater devotion. The emphasis is neither upon renunciation for its own sake nor upon the discipline of the self as an end in itself; a fervent desire and love for God are the motives for "casting aside" other things. While obedience, chastity, and poverty are means of liberation, they expose men to dangers here below. From the perspective of the natural virtues, the counsels seem to trace a descending, rather than an ascending, path. They introduce a dramatic and unanticipated reversal in the narrative of the good life.

Thomas's integration of contemplation and action in the good life further indicates that the movement from the natural to the supernatural involves transcending Aristotle's view of the moral life. Aristotle does seem to advocate some sort of unification of action and contemplation in his account of happiness (*eudaimonia*). Thomas's peculiarly Christian account of contemplation overcomes the tension between the two claimants.

Christian contemplation arises from and overflows into charity.[83] The followers of Christ enlighten people "by their wisdom, learning, and examples," and strengthen them "by prayer and intercession" (III, 135). The unity of contemplation and action recalls the prologue of the book; what Thomas adds here is that the infused virtues eclipse the Aristotelian duality of contemplation and action.

While Thomas continues to assert that contemplation is *per se* superior to action, the ligature of wisdom and charity complicates the relationship. The active life, which properly disposes the will, is the indispensable condition for contemplative union. According to Aristotle, friendship is constitutive of the natural social life of human beings; it unites love of self and love of other. Thomas concurs that friendship occurs between equals; still, he envisions Christian friendship or charity as equalizing unequals, as drawing the beloved to an ever increasing participation in the life of the lover. Grace establishes "friendship between God and man" (III, 157). Christian friendship has its source in the descent of the superior to the inferior, the strong to the weak. The ethical teaching of the *Contra Gentiles* comports nicely with the metaphysics of creation, which envisions creatures as fundamentally receptive and as communicating to others what they have received from the transcendent source of being and goodness. Thus do the relationships among creatures imitate the relationship of God to the world.

According to Aristotle, exemplary friendships exist among privileged members of the city (*polis*), in whose lives social position, proper education, and virtue fortuitously coincide. With its offer of salvation to all, Christian universalism explodes the limited purview and dubious efficacy of pagan philosophy. One of Thomas's criticisms of philosophy's claim to teach with peremptory authority on the topic of beatitude is that it reaches only the few and even then with an admixture of error (III, 39). Christian revelation reaches the low and the high alike and unites them to that good to which the philosophers aspire. Embracing not just the philosopher's aspiration for the good, but also the longing of the whole "human genus," revelation is more capacious than philosophy.

Thomas ties the pedagogical conception of divine revelation to a fundamental tenet of the *Contra Gentiles*, namely, that God disposes of things in accordance with their natures. He deploys a principle from physics to describe the relationship between the natural and the supernatural:

> Whenever something is moved by an agent toward that which is proper to the agent, in the beginning it is imperfectly subject to the agent's impressions,

which are as yet alien and not proper to the thing moved. But at the end of the motion the impressions become proper to it. (III, 152)[84]

Divine grace does not alter our natural mode of understanding; it places no new powers or operations within the soul. Instead, it perfects and elevates our natural powers so that they might become docile to the promptings of God and be directed toward divine union. Thomas's reference to grace as placing a superadded form onto preexisting nature might seem to obviate this reading. It does not. The superadded form perfects and habituates the powers of the soul so that it performs acts "connaturally, easily, and enjoyably." The transformation of the beloved by the lover is proper to divine love (III, 150).

The gap between belief and vision is a natural consequence of the order of learning. As Aristotle puts it, the "learner must believe." By comparing the life of faith to the student's pursuit of goods internal to crafts or disciplines, Thomas implicitly denies the position that faith is utterly internal, private, and inexplicable. In his description of faith, he develops an analogy between the order of natural knowledge and divine instruction:

> When someone is taught by a teacher, it is necessary at the beginning that he accept the conceptions of the teacher, not as if he understood them through themselves, but by way of belief, since they exceed his capacity. In the end, however, when he has become instructed, he will be able to understand them. (III, 152)[85]

Theological pedagogy certainly accentuates the gap between belief and vision, but the gradual appropriation of revealed wisdom means that the lacuna can be partially eclipsed in this life. The first three books confirm this understanding of divine pedagogy. The believer's descent to reason can be understood in Anselmian terms as faith seeking understanding.

Thomas's hierarchical understanding of the relationship between nature and grace, philosophy and theology, has led many to assume that divine pedagogy directs a unilateral ascent to the good, from the natural to the supernatural. Such a reading supposes that the supernatural begins where the natural ends, that the realm of grace is superimposed upon a complete and autonomous realm of nature. As we have already seen, the picture is too simple. What remains to be seen is precisely how the various considerations of the first three books find their place within a distinctively Christian narrative.

An initial indication of the structure of that narrative can be seen not only in the discussions of the counsels and the theological virtues, but also and more pointedly in the final twenty-four chapters of the third book, which treat of human actions in relation to divine grace, election, and reprobation. Human acts of vice merit punishment, while virtuous acts deserve reward (III, 140). Given the disparity between worldly success and virtue, the reverse might seem to be the case. But this would be so only if bodily goods were our ultimate end. The worst punishment for sin in this life consists in God's granting external goods that are incentives to further evil (III, 141). The disorder consequent upon sin fosters a greater inclination to sin. If not rectified through grace and repentance, serious sins render one unfit for eternal happiness (III, 144). Grace is necessary for salvation and cannot be merited in advance (III, 147 and 149). But grace should not be understood as violent or coercive; it assists, and invites the cooperation of, free choice (III, 148).

Sanctifying grace transforms the powers of the soul so that human beings are internally moved toward the ultimate end (III, 150). The preservation and amelioration of choice under the influence of grace does not eliminate contingency. Since salvation occurs through "successive choices," we are "subject to variation" and need "external government" to persevere in the good (III, 155). The third book culminates with the mysteries of the divine will, of divine predestination, reprobation, and election. Since God offers grace to all, the responsibility for damnation must be ascribed to some obstacle in the individual. Thomas chooses the striking image of someone who keeps his eyes closed while the sun shines to depict our resistance to grace (III, 159). God is not, then, the cause of sin (III, 162). Evil is a defect, the absence of a due perfection. Whatever perfection or being there is in a human action is from God; the defect is in the proximate agent. God frees some, but not all, from the obstacle of sin. No reason can be given for this discrimination on God's part (III, 161). Still, in the words of 1 Tim. 2:4, God "wills all to be saved."

The end of the third book returns us to ourselves, to our natural potencies, our longing for happiness, and our weaknesses and disorders. The turning to oneself is of course only the first step in turning toward God. As Joseph Wawrykow argues, Thomas's mature teaching on grace subordinates the issues of freedom and cooperation to the ordination of divine providence. The consequences are telling: "with his talk of ordination, Thomas has put the human achievement into its proper context; he shifts the focus to God, to what God has done and why God has provided for human beings in this way."[86]

VI. DIALECTIC AND NARRATIVE
IN THE FIRST MODE OF TRUTH

Dialectic figures prominently in three segments of the second and third books. In the opening section of the second book, on creation and the eternity of the world, Thomas argues that reason cannot settle the question of the world's eternal existence. He adds that the best probable argument for the temporal beginning of the world is that it manifests more explicitly the utter transcendence of God. The emphasis upon God as transcendent exemplar and artist, manifesting his wisdom and goodness in creation, and upon the temporal beginning of his artifact, provides the metaphysical foundations for the narrative structure of the universe. The discussion of divine creation from nothing requires an analogical use of the term "making," which involves the negation of key features of natural and human production. The discussion of creation continues the deployment of the dialectical strategies of analyzing the meaning and context of words. As in the first book, so too in the second and third books Thomas attends to the scope and boundaries of various Aristotelian inquiries. The theological appropriation and transposition of terms from their original settings in Aristotle's texts requires exegetical care and dialectical insight.

The most lengthy dialectical sections of the second and third books have to do with human nature and the human good. The study of the order (*ordo*) of creation focuses upon the union of soul and body. The prominence of dialectic indicates the difficulty of achieving clarity about human nature. Yet Thomas does reach positive assertions about the unity of soul and body and about the incorruptibility of the soul. The dialectical defense of Aristotle's position on the unity of soul and body, where the former is to the latter as act to potency, secures the integrity of human nature. Thomas underscores the naturalness of the embodiment of the human soul in a number of ways: by speaking of the soul as a potency that is made actual through interaction with the external world, by contrasting the immediacy of angelic intuition with the temporal character of human knowing, and by arguing that the human body has a dignity appropriate to its form and that bodily operations manifest the splendor of intelligence. The intellect transcends the material conditions of human knowing and is thus separable from the body. The natural embodiment of the soul, however, renders onerous any philosophical attempt to speak about the state of the soul after its separation from the body.

Embodiment is also an important theme in the dialectical discussion of the human end. Thomas eschews the Arabic view that the soul transcends its bodily condition and becomes united with a separated substance through some sort of natural process. Human knowledge does not exceed the scope of Aristotle's metaphysics, which studies substances separate from matter only insofar as they can be known from sense experience. Nonetheless, neither metaphysics nor practical wisdom completely fulfills the human aspiration for happiness. Aristotle is correct in his definition of happiness and in his view that we can attain only imperfect happiness.

Philosophical dialectic looks beyond what is merely said in various opinions to uncover the meaning of things that the opinions seek to explain. Dialectic constructively unites various accounts and finds an explanatory ground for them. It marks the transition from opinion to knowledge. In the *Contra Gentiles,* dialectic is typically constructive; it provides the starting point of numerous demonstrative arguments. Even where it is not constructive, it is instructive. In the cases of the eternity of the world, the state of the soul after death, and the possibility of complete happiness, dialectic is incapable of passing into an apprehension of the truth of the matter. In crucial instances, the positive achievements of dialectic mark the limitations of philosophy.

The progress of philosophical inquiry culminates in darkness concerning the ultimate state of the human person and of human happiness. The negativity and silence in which the best of ancient philosophy terminates distinguishes it from modern, systematic conceptions of philosophy, which encapsulate and usurp reality in theory. Only certain kinds of philosophy, then, are compatible with Christianity. The negativity in which Platonic and Aristotelian philosophy culminates provides a space for revelation. Answering the question of what it would mean to go beyond philosophy presupposes a painstaking elaboration of the achievements of philosophy. The descent to reason in the first three books enables one to recognize what is distinctive about Christianity.

In the Christian context, imperfect happiness is not the last word on human happiness; it is ordered to a vision beyond time and history. What Aristotle calls imperfect happiness is the happiness allotted to us in this life. The pursuit of happiness has a narrative structure that reaches from the here and now into eternity. That narrative is not accessible to the philosopher, however. The complete return to God cannot be discerned in the nature of what has come forth from God. All that can be determined from the order of creation is that creatures seek to imitate God in the measure and mode appropriate to their natures. Human nature exhibits a natural capacity for knowing God from his effects and an openness to some greater vision. But that vision cannot be deduced from human nature. The transcendent *reditus* is not inscribed in the *exitus*. The return is inscribed in divine providence, of which the natural order offers a partial glimpse. Both the supernatural and the natural fall within the scope of providence, which encompasses two modes in one plan. The distinction within unity underscores the view that the "twofold mode of truth" is fundamental only from our vantage point.

The transformation of our vantage point is of course one of the goals of the first three books of the *Contra Gentiles*, which considers creatures under the light of divine revelation and seeks a knowledge that is more like God's knowledge (II, 4). In both the second and third books, Thomas begins with the language of similitude and likeness. While the first book ends with God as the exemplar of the life of wisdom, the second book begins with the statement that the theological study of creatures gives rise to a "certain likeness of divine wisdom" (II, 2). Similarly, the third book opens with a reference to the human person as a "similitude and image" of the divine. The repetition of the language of image and similitude is striking. Taken in conjunction with the assertion that the *Contra Gentiles* studies creatures in relation to God and by the light of revelation, it indicates that the theological reversal of the philosophical order of proceeding is crucial to the structural unity of the work. The second and third books urge us to reappropriate our understanding of our nature and its longing for happiness as part of a metaphysical and narrative whole. The study of God and creatures reflects back to a study of human nature and its teleology. Thomas thus revives the Platonic notion of human inquiry as "mediating between part and whole."[87]

What makes possible the mediating capacity of man is his creation in the likeness of God, as an image of the one according to whom the whole is patterned. The image in human nature can be seen in both static and dynamic terms, in the rational powers of the soul and in their operations. The former is the basis of, and is ordered to, the latter. The third book, with its emphasis on the ways in which creatures *become* like God, highlights the dynamic character of the image. Even in the second book, in the discussion of wisdom as a likeness to God, the dynamism of the image is prominent. The authoritative scriptural text is Corinthians 3:18: those who behold the glory of God are transformed into that which they contemplate. Every reference to similitude and likeness falls under the general Dionysian principle articulated in the first book. In speaking of the similarity between God and creatures, we should say that creatures are like God and not the reverse, because the former underscores receptivity, dependence, and motion toward a model or source (I, 29). The metaphysics of the first two books undergirds the ethics and politics of the third.

The metaphysical reversal in discourse gives rise to the language of image and exemplar and to a narrative conception of creation. Chenu writes that "the metaphysical structure of man entails a radical opening to history and a dependence on history."[88] The accentuation of history is partly traceable to an emphasis on the human body. Of course the emphasis on history in all its amplitude cannot simply be deduced from human nature. Bereft of the perspective of divine providence, the full import of the narrative structure of creation remains unknown to us. The transition in the middle of the third book from what is achievable by us to what the author of the whole is able to do with and for us marks the transition from philosophical dialectic to theological narrative. Participation in the city of God depends upon the cooperation of human and divine freedom. Nonetheless, the accentuation of the hiddenness of the ultimate plan of providence underscores our inability to write the narrative of the good life (III, 161). It also indicates the limitations inherent in Thomas's attempt to write about divine providence. The most striking use of the image of God as artist occurs in Thomas's citation of Paul: "Has not the potter power over the clay, of the same lump to make one vessel unto glory and another unto disgrace?" (Rom. 9:21).[89] The final chapters of the third book thus have the effect typical of Socratic irony or Kierkegaardian humor: they turn us back upon ourselves. What characterizes the "Christian's earthly and temporal pilgrimage . . . is its anxious unfinality: no matter how desperately low you have sunk, no matter how sublimely high you may rise, take care! for your destiny is not yet decided."[90] The narrative shape of salvation befits the human need for divine assistance along the way toward salvation. The final section of the third book is a fitting rhetorical prelude to the treatment of the drama of redemption in the final book.

5

THE DRAMA OF REDEMPTION

I. INTRODUCTION

The fourth book does not move directly to a consideration of revealed teachings. Instead, it opens with a reconsideration of the themes of the original prologue, especially the twofold mode of truth. Thomas reiterates the central teaching of the third book concerning the natural desire for God. Since the end of human nature is to know God, the universe is so constructed that embodied intellects can "progress through gradual ascent" to God:

> Because the perfect good of man is that he might in some way know God, lest such a noble creature seem to exist in vain, incapable of attaining his proper end, there is given to man a certain way through which he can mount to the knowledge of God. Since all perfections of things descend vertically in a certain order from . . . God, man, beginning from lowly things and gradually rising, may progress in the knowledge of God. (IV, 1)[1]

The passage underscores the importance of the natural desire for God, even as it inscribes that desire within the order of creation. The descent of creatures from God precedes, and makes possible, the human ascent to God. Does the restatement of these now familiar themes shed any light on the structure of the work?

Corbin takes the subordination of ascent to descent as an attempt to recover the unity anterior to the *scission* of the twofold mode of truth. As he sees it, the opening chapter of the fourth book seeks to overcome a tension between the twofold mode of truth and an antecedent, encompassing unity. The opening chapters of the second book, which underscore the differences between philosophical and theological modes of consideration, attempted a similar project of unification. According to Corbin, there remains a certain dissonance between the preludes to the second and fourth books, on the one hand, and the prologue to the first, on the other. The work never succeeds in subordinating the *scission* to an encompassing unity.[2] What are we to make of this thesis?

Corbin holds that the original distinction of the twofold mode of truth addresses the "problem of the integration of philosophical authorities in sacred doctrine."[3] How does the initial formulation of this problem stand in relation to the whole? If, as we have argued, the text contains various strategies inviting the reader to double back and reconsider previous statements in light of subsequent developments, then the so-called *scission* may well take on less importance than Corbin thinks.[4] The *scission* is fundamental and insuperable only if a linear reading of the text is satisfactory. How does a nonlinear reading of the *Contra Gentiles* provide a response to Corbin?

Corbin himself notes that the *exitus-reditus* structure involves a reversal of the philosophical order. Precisely that reversal prepares the ground for the remarks on method in the second book. The first book ends with God as goal, exemplar, and source of the life of wisdom; even in the first book, then, the distinction of the twofold mode of truth is shown to be derivative of a primordial unity. The second book begins with a description of the disparity between philosophical and theological modes of consideration. The *Contra Gentiles* studies creatures under the light of revelation. The pattern of inscribing lower within higher, ascent within descent, philosophical dialectic within theological narrative, pervades the work. The pattern is strikingly present in the third book, where Thomas locates the ascent to the highest good within God's providential ordering of the narrative of human life. Thus, the text anticipates in numerous ways the recovery of an anterior unity that Corbin thinks is distinctive of the opening of the fourth book.

As in the prologue, so too in the opening of the fourth book Thomas underscores the limits to philosophy. The threefold negation in our knowledge is an emphatic reminder of the poverty of human intelligence (IV, 1). First, since our knowledge of sensible substances proceeds from external accidents, we know the lowest natures only imperfectly. Second, even were the natures perfectly known, their order would still escape our comprehension. Third, adequate knowledge of the natures and their order would still fall far short of the principle from which things proceed: "If the ways themselves are imperfectly known to us, how shall we be able to reach through them to know perfectly the source of these ways?"[5]

Since negation presupposes affirmation, the threefold negation of natural knowledge presumes a positive apprehension of the telos of reason. Thomas's *philosophia negativa* opposes those who would enclose human nature upon itself. In accentuating the dialectical limits of the contemplative life, Thomas counters any understanding of philosophy as having a peremptory knowledge of the "decisive truth" about the "right way of life."[6] In the very pursuit of what philosophy most esteems, there are egregious gaps. How then could philosophy presume to exclude in advance the possibility of being subsumed in some larger narrative that would satisfy its own teleology? It can do so only by placing greater emphasis upon rational certitude than upon the objects toward which the whole of the philosophical life tends. Christian wisdom opposes the totalitarian pretensions of philosophy. Aristotle himself argues that imperfect knowledge of nobler objects is superior to certain knowledge of less noble objects.

Through his "superabundant goodness," God has provided another way in which we might come to know him, a way that eclipses that of natural reason. God reveals truths that transcend the "feeble" (*debilis*) understanding of man. Revelation addresses human beings according to their condition. Since our embodied intellects cannot "be elevated entirely to gaze" upon intelligible truths, we cannot comprehend them. We can only believe them. With support from a number of scriptural passages, Thomas stresses the sense of hearing over that of sight in the human reception of revelation. The absence of vision and the emphasis on speech highlight the personal, social, and temporal character of the state of belief on the way to God (*in via*).

Since revelation itself is a means to a higher mode of knowing, its mode of teaching fittingly precludes finality. Faith inflames rather than satisfies desire. As if to underscore the intermediate status of revealed teaching, Thomas now speaks, not of a twofold mode of truth, but of a threefold knowledge of divine things: through natural reason, through revelation, and through an elevated and perfect vision. Scriptural speech, which is obscure and replete with similitudes, befits the intermediate status of revelation. Although its basic teaching is stated plainly, its whole teaching is not evident on the surface. Obscurity is designed to exclude infidels and to signify the infinite depth of divine mysteries. The strategy of the divine names is operative in scripture's mixture of presence and absence. Such a strategy is pedagogically suited to moving a finite creature toward union with an infinite good.

Various features of the first three books prepare the reader for explicit consideration of scripture. First, there is Thomas's practice of confirming philosophical argument with quotation from scripture. Just as particular arguments in the first three books pass into the intelligibility of scripture, so too does the first mode of truth pass into the second. But scripture does not simply confirm the conclusions of an autonomous philosophy. The crucial arguments of the first three books do not deploy explicitly theological premises. They do, however, give special attention to those philosophical issues that bear upon the Christian conception of God, his relation to the world, and upon the Christian conception of human destiny. Second, the persistent references to God as exemplar and artist of creation and to the human creature as an image of God set the stage for the dramatic interaction between God and us. The third book insists that such interaction is impossible apart from a divine gift and shows that God's miraculous intervention in the natural order is neither impossible nor unseemly. To the traditional objection that these arguments bestow upon natural reason an ability to anticipate the supernatural, the following response is in order. The first three books do not constitute an autonomous philosophy. Instead, they involve a descent from faith to reason in order to reconsider the order of nature in the light of revelation. Far from being an addendum, the fourth book considers the narrative that informs the structure of the whole and that determines the principles of inclusion and exclusion of particular topics. Full appreciation of the first three books awaits a reading of the fourth.

God's supernatural mode of teaching is the subject of the fourth book, which concentrates on the doctrines of the Trinity and the Incarnation. The common ground of argument in the fourth book is no longer reason but scripture, which provides the principles (*principia*) of theological discourse. The reference to scripture as providing *principia* might seem to endorse a demonstrative model of theological reasoning, one that would minimize the role of narrative. As Chenu has shown, there is no dichotomy here, for Thomas's conception of theological science embraces a rich array of methods of reasoning.[7] Reason is most successful in the realm of revelation when it works to rebut objections to the teachings of the faith. It also seeks principles that give the intellect some analogical basis for contemplating divine mysteries. There is no tension between scriptural discourse and doctrinal teaching, since scripture itself anticipates, and provides correctives to, erroneous doctrines.[8]

As Thomas's willingness to adduce scriptural passages on both sides of a debate indicates, scripture demands reflective, dialectical exegesis. The difficulty of reconciling apparent contradictions in scripture has often been the occasion of misinterpretations. Heresy makes the theological use of philosophy inescapable. The goal, articulated in the prologue, of convincing opponents (*convincere*), is operative here, as it was in the preceding books. The goal is not to persuade skeptics or even heretics; Thomas focuses on the heresies of the first four centuries, not on those of his contemporaries. Interestingly, he traces many of these heresies to the fallacious philosophical principles of the *gentiles*.[9] The refutation of errors manifests the truth of the Catholic faith to reflective believers.

Dialectic is unavoidable in theology; nonetheless, it is subordinate to an authoritative narration. Dialectic is successful insofar as it "saves" the various locutions, apparent inconsistencies, and dramatic structure of scripture. Thomas reads parts of scripture in light of the whole and depicts the whole as a dramatic narrative.[10] The features of the narrative are evident in the many arguments from "suitability" (*convenientia*). These arguments show forth the harmony and splendor of the life of Christ. Thomas devotes the longest section of the fourth book to a consideration of the suitability of the Incarnation, the dramatic centerpiece of the narrative of redemption.

II. TRINITY

The primacy of scriptural authority and its narrative shape are evident in the initial consideration of the "secret of divine generation." The starting point is what we should hold about divine generation "according to the texts of sacred scripture" (IV, 2).[11] While references to generation appear with regularity only in the New Testament, they do appear occasionally in the Old Testament. In response to those who would limit the application of such Old Testament passages to their immediate context, Thomas admits that some passages refer solely to David or Solomon. Others, however, refer figuratively to Christ in whom "all things are fulfilled."[12] Scripture is a narrative whole with the Incarnation as its dramatic centerpiece (IV, 2).

The scriptural affirmation of divine generation has given rise to various interpretations. The encounter with the first opinion, that of Photinus, illustrates Thomas's theological method. Photinus holds that Christ was son not by nature but by adoption. He was made God in time. Thomas does not argue that the position is utterly baseless; indeed, he cites numerous passages that appear to support Photinus's position, passages that speak of Christ as made, predestined, as deserving of merit, and as possessing various defects of body and soul. There are, however, other passages that speak of Christ's divinity preceding his humanity, of the marked difference between Christ and other holy men, and of the divine works attributed to Christ: the sanctification of souls and the remission of sins. Since Photinus cannot adequately account for these passages, he fails to salvage the whole of scriptural discourse. The teaching that there are in Christ two natures resolves the apparent aporia. Throughout the discussion of the Trinity and the Incarnation, Thomas refers to John's prologue as providing the most explicit statement of the origin of the second person. In so doing, he implements the Augustinian principle that obscure passages should be understood in light of clear statements.[13]

The next opinion is that of Sabellius, who proposes that monotheism is incompatible with the Trinity. Accordingly, the Son cannot be a subsisting person. In order to explain the language of generation, he holds that the Son is a property accruing to an already existing person. Thomas argues that the position renders unintelligible Christ's frequent references to himself and the Father in the plural. If the Son is truly begotten, then he must be distinct in supposit. In defense of the Son's existing prior to the Incarnation, Thomas cites John's Gospel: "The Word was with God." The same passage indicates that the Word is distinct from the Father. Distinction within unity is necessary to make sense of numerous scriptural passages, such as the one where Christ states, "The Father and I are one." In the first two encounters with heretical opinions, Thomas introduces the principles concerning the two natures in Christ and the plurality of persons sharing one divine essence. Only these principles save the phenomena of scripture.

Attempting to circumvent the previous two errors, Arius teaches that the Son existed before creation. Arius denies, however, that Christ has existed from eternity. The origin of Arius' view is a correct apprehension of the distinction between Father and Son, coupled with a faulty supposition of the impossibility of two persons sharing one essence or nature (IV, 6). Thus, Christ must be subordinate to the Father, united to him by "a certain union of consent." Thomas concedes that numerous scriptural passages appear to teach subordination, passages that depict

Christ as receptive, being taught, and obeying. For Christ to be the true Son, however, he must be true God, since what is begotten does not differ in species from the one begetting. Scripture speaks of Christ not just as an image but as a perfect representation of the Father. Scripture repeatedly refers the same operations to God and Christ: the operations of creating and conserving all things in being, and of cleansing sins. Thomas adverts to arguments from the first book against the possibility of a plurality of divine beings. Similarity in operation and identity in power entail identity of nature.[14]

The Arians have inverted the proper relationship between authority and reason. Thomas identifies their view as a piece of Platonic, emanationist metaphysics. They adopted the view because "they were not able to understand and were unwilling to believe" (*non enim intelligere poterant, nec credere volebant*) that two persons could have one nature. An erroneous philosophical teaching blinds them to key features of the Christian narrative. They overlook the audacious rhetoric of the Gospels, a rhetoric that occasioned Christ's passion and crucifixion: "This is the narration of the Evangelist whose 'testimony is true' (John 19:13; 21:24): that Christ claimed to be the Son of, and equal to, God and that for this reason the Jews persecuted him" (IV, 7).[15] The castigation of flawed philosophical arguments removes impediments to the acceptance of what ought to be believed on the authority of scripture.

As if to reinforce the primacy of scriptural authority, Thomas concludes the consideration of these opinions in language echoing the creeds. He speaks of scripture instructing the Church.[16] He proceeds to compare the heresies in point of agreement and disagreement with one another and with the teaching of the Church:

> The Catholic faith, holding to the middle way, confesses with Arius and Photinus against Sabellius that the Father and the Son are not the same person, that the Son is begotten, but the Father completely unbegotten. The Catholic faith also confesses with Sabellius against Photinus and Arius that Christ is true and natural God, of the same nature as the Father, but not of the same person. From this, a judgment of the truth of the Catholic faith can be made. As the Philosopher says, even falsehoods testify, for they stand apart not only from truths but also from one another. (IV, 7)[17]

The passage is instructive for two reasons. First, it underscores the dangers of an autonomous dialectic, which exalts part of the truth to the detriment of the whole. Second, and conversely, it shows the salutary role of a retrospective, dialectical presentation of theological truth. The juxtaposition and dialectical sorting out of partial truths provide a path to the integral truth.[18]

Having considered the scriptural bases for the generation of the Son from the Father, Thomas turns to a treatment of "how generation in the divine ought to be received" (*accipienda*).[19] The use of the term *accipienda* is striking; while it is often translated as "understood," its literal meaning is "received" or "held." Clearly any analogies that assist in our understanding of the doctrine are subordinate to "what is said about the Son of God in scripture." The phenomena of scripture can be saved only if certain metaphysical assertions—for example, that God is triune, or that Christ possesses two natures but one supposit—are not impossible. The discussion of the divine names in the first book fostered the expectation that, in reasoning about divine things, language will have to be reworked. The movement to supernatural truths about God exacerbates the difficulty. Since the thesis that many supposita share one divine essence is "especially distant" from creatures, human reason encounters manifold difficulties.

As a foundation for understanding divine generation and for responding to objections against it, Thomas develops an analogy introduced in the first book. He begins with the observation that in nature the higher a creature is, the more intimate to its nature is what emanates from it. In the inanimate, the only emanation is that of accidents, whereas in plants there is a movement from within to an external manifestation of form. Sensitive souls are pivotal in the hierarchy of beings, as they exhibit a movement from exterior, sensible things to the interior possession of sensible forms. In the highest grade of life, intellectual life, there is an interior emanation of an intellectual word. The act of understanding issues in an intention understood, which is the likeness of the thing understood. There are of course differences between the word in us and the Word in God. Our intention that is understood differs from the object of understanding and from the intellect itself. In God, all three are identical and the Word is identical with the divine nature. Our word, moreover, occurs after the mind has moved from potentially understanding to actually understanding. God exists and understands eternally. Our understanding requires numerous words as likenesses of the many things we understand. God understands all things through his own essence, which is the paradigm of all created things. The opening lines of John's Gospel, which invite the audacious comparison of human words with the divine Word, combat various misunderstandings. "In the beginning was the Word" confirms the eternal existence of the Word. "The Word was God" indicates that the Word is not distinct from God, that it is not merely an intention understood, but a subsistent being. "Through him all things were made" shows that the Word is the exemplary source of all created things.

In spite of the disparities between the human and the divine word, the generation of a word in the act of human understanding provides a positive basis for theological doctrine. Thomas explains,

> Since the word of God is of the same nature as God speaking and is his likeness, this natural proceeding is unto a likeness of him from whom he proceeds with identity of nature. But this is true generation in living things. . . . Therefore the word of God is truly begotten in God's speaking; and his procession can be called "generation" or "birth." (IV, 11)[20]

What remains of the analogy to human understanding is its essential meaning: the word proceeds from the one understanding as the term of the act of understanding. The ground of divine generation is God's self-understanding, wherein to be is to understand and to understand is to speak. The Word is related to God as to one from whom he is. It might seem that the procession of the Word would introduce composition in God. Procession does imply a distinction of relation, but relation does not entail composition.

The consideration of relation borrows from Aristotle's discussion in the *Categories* of the nine genera or kinds of accidents. Insofar as each of these is an accident, it must be understood as inhering in a subject. A consideration of what differentiates the accidents from one another, however, brings to light what is peculiar about the category of relation. In its proper meaning, quantity is the measure of a substance, while quality concerns the disposition of a substance. These accidents contain in their proper significations, not just in the meaning common to them as accidents, the notion of composition. Hence, they are not applicable to the divine simplicity. Relation alone among the accidents has a proper meaning, namely, to be referred in itself to another, that is not derived from reference to a subject in which it inheres. The accident of relation can be transferred from the order of accidents and applied to God.

In regard to the analogy between the generation of the human word and that of the divine Word, Thomas addresses objections to revealed teaching. A number of the objections, those which hold that generation entails change or divisibility or loss, confuse material with intellectual

generation. Only in material things does the reception of a nature involve the division or loss of the nature of the one giving. In human
understanding, the proper nature of what is understood does not cease
with the advent of the act of understanding (IV, 14); the generation of the
word proceeds, not from potency to act, but from the act of understanding
to the actualization of the word. God's "whole fullness" is known in his
act of understanding and is expressed in his Word.

A second set of objections has difficulty reconciling the subsistence
of the divine essence with that of the persons. The twofold subsistence
seems to involve one of two unwelcome consequences: either the Son is
something other than God, as Arius taught, or the Son is not distinct from
the Father, as Sabellius argued. There appears to be no way to insist upon
distinguishing the Son from the Father without introducing composition
in God. Thomas denies the premise that the subsistence of the divine
essence excludes the relation of subsistent persons. Since the generation
of the word is from God's speaking and God's speaking is his essence,
there is no first and second in God, but one, "numerically the same,"
essence. Confusion results from focusing upon the first person, rather than
on the essence itself. According to Lonergan, starting from the essence
enables Thomas to circumvent the incoherence of the Father's having to
"generate before being constituted as Father."[21] Since the relation follows
upon the essence, the principle distinguishing the persons need not be
outside of God. Thomas comments, "There are many subsistent things if
the relations be considered; there is, however, one subsistent thing if one
regards the essence" (IV, 14).[22] Since the relations arise from the essence
of God, in whom there are no accidents, the relations need not introduce
something accidental to, or distinct from, God. Given the unity of the
divine essence, how are we to understand the distinction of the Son from
the Father?

The basis for the distinction of persons is the notion of relative opposition. A final set of objections attacks the very possibility of there being
relation in God. Relations entail correlatives, but the divine essence, from
which the relations purportedly arise, is not dependent on any thing.
The relations in God are substantial, not accidental. How then are we
to avoid the awkward consequence of a plurality of gods? More than
one person never shares in the same substance. Socrates and Plato, for
instance, agree in humanity, but they are not one man. Furthermore,
opposing predicates, for example, unbegotten and begotten, resulting
from the relations, cannot both be said of the same substance.

The responses to these objections are based upon the modal disparity between relations in creatures and in God. Thomas recalls the teaching of the first book that the perfections which creatures acquire through many forms exist simply and unitedly in God; indeed, the perfections are not different from the divine essence. The basis of relations in God is other than the basis in creatures, in which relation is compared to substance as accident to subject. Relations presuppose dependence of being only in creatures, where the being of the relation is other than the being of the substance. But this is not true of God. The substantial predication, furthermore, of "God" to both the Father and the Son does not entail a plurality of gods. The analogy to human individuals, upon which the objection is based, does not apply. Numerous individuals do not share numerically one essence, nor does the essence of humanity subsist. Just as nothing obstructs the united presence in God of perfections from different genera, so too nothing impedes the presence in him of opposed relations, which is not possible in creatures.

All the responses rely upon negations of key features of relations as they are found in composite entities. The strategy is similar to that of the treatment of divine simplicity in the first book. In the discussion of the plurality of persons, however, Thomas must do more than deflate the pretensions to speak univocally about creatures and God. He must provide a basis for the positive assertion concerning the plurality of persons. What makes the relations real? Thomas himself puts the objection that they might be merely relations of reason.[23] The difficulty makes the Trinity of persons inaccessible to natural reason.[24] To make the Trinity a datum of reason is to engage in the most egregious presumption. Relations arising from proper operations exist in the thing operating. While we know that God has proper operations, we do not know that relations arise from it. How then do we know that there is procession and thus relation in God? Clearly this is known only from revelation, from Scripture's persistent reference to the Word as coming from the Father, as distinct from, yet one with, the Father.

Yet there is no incompatibility between revelation and reason. Neither absolute properties, such as goodness and wisdom, nor relations introduce composition into God. Since there is no distinction between abstract and concrete in God, the absolute properties cannot introduce opposition in God and are thus indistinguishable. The proper operations of knowing and loving do, however, entail relative opposition. The operations proper to God are knowing and loving; these operations simultaneously "proceed and remain" their "own principle" (IV, 14, and 26).[25] Since the oppositions arise from the very essence of God, which is simple, they do not presuppose the distinction of subject and attribute, but they do introduce real relations. The persons are just these subsistent relations arising from the operations of knowing and loving.

The operations that proceed and remain are knowing and loving. Knowing establishes the generation of the Son. The operation of loving supplies a basis for explicating scriptural references to the Holy Spirit. Some passages speak of the Spirit in subordinate terms; others associate the Father and the Son but make no mention of the Spirit; still others attribute to the Spirit actions appropriate only to creatures. Thomas counters with passages that urge us to adore the Spirit, and that attribute to the Spirit the divine activities of creation, revelation of mysteries, and sanctification (IV, 17). The account of how we are to understand the third person uses an analogy to human volition and its relationship to understanding (IV, 18). Thomas alludes repeatedly to arguments from the first book on the divine will: that God has will, that the object of his will is his essence, and that his act of will is indistinguishable from his being. The "being of God in his will through love is not accidental, as in us, but essential" (IV, 19).[26] In Augustinian language, Thomas draws the crucial consequence:

> Nothing would be loved unless it were known; not only is the beloved's knowledge loved, but also the beloved as good in himself. It is necessary that the love, by which God is in the divine will as one loved is present in a lover, proceeds both from the Word of God and from God whose Word he is.[27]

Love presupposes knowledge, but it is distinct from knowledge.[28] The procession of the will is not by way of likeness but by a movement toward the object loved. Love presupposes a likeness in the intellect of the thing loved. The term of this movement of love is the presence in the lover of an impression of the thing loved. The distinction suggests a way of differentiating the Son from the Spirit. For the same reasons that the operation of divine knowledge generates a Word, the activity of divine love brings forth the Spirit. God's proceeding by love is a "kind of existing spiration."[29]

III. TRINITARIAN IMAGES AND THE UNITY OF THE WORK

The discussion of three persons of the Trinity brings to the fore the personal, communal life of God and the divine invitation to human participation in that life. On behalf of the equality and subsistence of all three persons, Thomas quotes a scriptural passage that incorporates the drama of redemption within the internal life of God: "Our Lord says to his disciples, 'Go and teach all the nations [gentes], baptizing them in the name of the Father, and the Son, and the Holy Spirit'" (IV, 18). The consideration of the Spirit's effects upon creatures evokes the essential themes of the *Contra Gentiles* (IV, 20–22). The Spirit is the "giver of life" (IV, 20). The Spirit bestows charity and makes us friends of God; the mark of friendship is the sharing of secrets and mysteries (IV, 21). Since the love bestowed by the Spirit is the means to knowing God, the Spirit enables us to achieve the end of human life, the contemplation of God. Indeed, the moving of the whole of creation to God is the work proper to the Holy Spirit (IV, 22).

The restoration and elevation of nature will not occur through some smooth ascent to the first principle, however. The adverse effects of sin can be remedied only through cleansing and repentance. By freely submitting in charity to the precepts of God, we can be liberated from our twofold enslavement: the slavery to passion and the servitude involved in obeying the law against our will (IV, 22). The paradox at the heart of the Gospel is that submission liberates, while proud independence enslaves. The danger of an autonomous philosophy is clear: it risks creating a greater distance between itself and the supreme good even as its knowledge of that good increases. The mode under which, and the spirit in which, one considers the highest things is decisive for progress toward the ultimate end.

The second of the two modes of truth presupposes conversion. Preceding the gift of the Spirit, Christ comes into the world "to manifest the truth." As conceived Word, exemplar of creation, and manifestation of light, Christ is the source of all cognition. Those who remain in darkness do so because they have failed to be "converted" to the Word, as is clear from John's Gospel: "the light shines in the darkness and the darkness did not comprehend it." Ignorance is thus traced to sin.[30] The implicit accusation in the prologue to John's Gospel echoes Paul's assertion that the *gentiles* are without excuse, since the invisible things of God are made manifest by the things that are made, a passage Thomas quotes in the opening of the second book.

In the discussion of the *Verbum* as the wisdom of God, Thomas reiterates that the generation of the word is a "communication of understanding" (*communicatio intelligentiae*), a "showing forth" (*demonstratio*), a "speech" (*locutio*), or "teaching" (*doctrina*). The Greek term *logos* can be translated as both "reason" and "speech." The Latin term *verbum*, which captures the latter meaning, accentuates, not the internal conception of reason, but the external manifestation of the divine Word. Numerous scriptural passages refer to Christ as the "wisdom of God." Since wisdom is a kind of intelligible light and the conceived word is a manifestation of wisdom, Christ is especially called "wisdom resplendent," the perfect image of the divine nature and the exemplar of the whole of creation (IV, 12). Thought and action manifest wisdom. The "unfolding" of things in creation is rightly called wisdom, a reflection of the divine artistry.

Thomas ends the discussion of the Trinity by descending to the level of creatures, from which the discussion had initially ascended. The impetus behind the return is the statement in Genesis 1:26: "Let us make man to our image and likeness." The logic of exemplar and image underlies the return to the likeness of the Trinity in human nature. The language of the *imago Dei* is central to the structure of the *Contra Gentiles*. In his study of the development of Thomas's teaching on the image of God, Merriell convincingly argues that Thomas's mature teaching in the *Summa Theologiae* is thoroughly Augustinian. In fact, Merriell shows that Thomas's appreciation of Augustine's *De Trinitate* was unrivaled in the thirteenth century. Augustine prefers the operations, rather than simply the powers, of the human mind, as analogues of the Trinity. Augustine rejects, moreover, the thesis that the immanent powers and operations of the soul constitute the image proper. Only when the soul is ordered to God as exemplar can the powers and operations be said to constitute an *imago Dei*.[31] As we have already seen, Augustinian language is prominent in Thomas's discussion of the generation of the Word and the procession of the Spirit. Like Augustine, Thomas prefers the language of operations rather than that of powers. He highlights the dynamic character of the image, its ordination to its exemplar. In the discussion of how the Spirit provides remedies for sin, Thomas notes that the image is thereby restored and "configured to God" (IV, 22).

The dialectical doubling back to the reflection of the divine image in creatures is a synecdoche for the whole work. From the vantage point of the Trinity, one can reconceive the first three books as treating, respectively, the Father, Son, and Holy Spirit. The Father is the efficient cause and first principle of all things, the bestower of being; the first book treats of God in himself. The Son is called wisdom, the exemplar of the whole of creation; the second book considers God's wisdom as manifest in creatures. Finally, the Holy Spirit is said to order creatures to their proper end, to move them to God, and thus to govern them; the third book treats of divine providence as evident in the movement of all creatures to their natural ends.[32]

IV. INCARNATION

The structure of the fourth book replicates that of the first three; it begins with God's immanent operations and proceeds to a consideration of his transitive operations. Among divine works, the Incarnation is the most "marvelous," for it exceeds reason more than any other and inspires wonder and reverence (IV, 27). Once again, Thomas castigates heretical opinions for neglecting crucial features of the scriptural narrative, for misconstruing its locutions, and for reducing mystery to rational argument.[33] Photinus, for instance, holds that God did not assume flesh, but rather that the human nature merited participation in divine glory. Photinus can explain passages speaking of glorification and ascent but not those referring to Christ's emptying and descent. He salvages only a portion of what scripture testifies concerning Christ. The view "destroys the mystery" of the Incarnation. The project of "understanding" the teachings of scripture becomes misunderstanding when it eliminates mystery. As a corrective to Photinus's view, Thomas presents Christ's statement that he has come from and will go to the Father, a statement which unites human and divine (IV, 28). He also cites passages from John's prologue, for example, "The Word was made flesh," and from Phillipians on Christ's emptying of himself.

In contrast to Photinus's rejection of divine descent stands the Manichean teaching that Christ did not actually unite human nature to himself but assumed a "fantasy body" (IV, 29). This would make the whole Gospel narrative "poetic and fabulous."[34] He concedes that occasionally the Gospels speak equivocally, but never is the "whole story" narrated thus. The intelligibility of the Gospel is ineradicably tied to its veracity. The issue of the historical veracity of scripture is complex, especially given the cramped notions of realism and history in modernity.[35] Scriptural narrative places a singular emphasis on the truth of its story. In numerous ways, it resists consignment to the genre of instructive fiction.[36] Thomas notes numerous passages where scripture explicitly excludes the notion that Christ's physical presence was merely an apparition. The very rhetoric of the narrative, for example, when Christ corrects the disciples' supposition that he is merely an apparition, combats precisely the view the

Manicheans propose. If the Manicheans were correct, the New Testament would not be significantly different from the Old, where God appeared under figures. But this ignores the very point of the Gospel as fulfillment of God's promise to the Jews.

Valentine's belief that Christ received nothing from Mary but brought a body from heaven shares the Manichean supposition that earthly things are evil (IV, 30). The Incarnation presumes and elevates the dignity of the human body. If Christ did not assume human flesh, he would not be united with us. If he descended with a heavenly body, he would have diminished that body, whereas it is appropriate for him to exalt that which he assumes. The language of descent and ascent, which had been deployed sporadically in the first three books and was explicitly considered at the beginning of the fourth, is prominent in the discussion of the Incarnation. While Photinus denies descent and emptying, Valentine and the Manicheans reject ascent and exaltation.

Thomas uses materials from the first book to repudiate the teachings of Apollonarius, who thought that Christ was not assumed from the Virgin, but was actually changed into flesh, and had no human soul (IV, 31). The thesis is contrary to numerous conclusions from the first book: God is immutable, not composite, and not the form of any body. It is also clear from the second book that, where there is no rational soul, there can be no human nature. Without the soul, bodily parts are so named only equivocally. Scriptural exegesis should not render void what natural reason has established, especially when what reason teaches accords with Christian views of the integrity and splendor of creation. The conclusion of this segment is that three things meet in Christ: divinity, the human soul, and the human body. The omission of any of these runs afoul of both the semantics of scripture and the metaphysics of created being.

The inquiry into the manner of union remains (IV, 34). The first thesis is that of Nestorius, who holds that the human soul and body come together to constitute a man of the same species and nature as other men. Through divine indwelling, the human person was then united with, and elevated to, God. Nestorius speaks of a union arising from a most intimate affection. Such indwelling does not, however, constitute Incarnation; whenever two things differ in supposit or person, it is impossible for one to be predicated of the other. But then we could not say that the Word became man. Scripture's manner of speaking evinces the uniqueness of the divinity in Christ and indicates an identity of supposit. The semantics and modes of discourse deployed in scriptural language about Christ run

counter to Nestorius' view, which divides Christ into two: the adopted
son and the natural Son.

A "difficulty" emerges from the insistence upon two natures in one
person. Everything that "subsists in an intellectual or rational nature
fulfills the account of person." But a soul united to a body subsists, as
does the Word of God, independently of the human substance. The
two natures thus seem to be complete, to subsist independently, and to
preclude further union. Hoping to solve the difficulty, Eutyches proposes
that, while Christ was from two natures, he subsisted only in one. But the
Council of Chalcedon condemned this teaching, and with good reason.
The position is antithetical to scripture's custom of attributing both lowly
and exalted, human and divine, activities to the one Christ. Scripture
states, for instance, that Christ, "in the form of God, . . . took the form
of a servant" (Phil. 2:6–7).[37] Eutyches fails to circumvent the original
problem: two independent things can concur in one only through the
corruption of one or both of the constituents. His view reduces to that
of Mani or Apollinarius: either only the humanity remains or only the
divinity.

A related position is Macarius' thesis that there is but one will in Christ.
Thomas quickly reduces it to Eutyches' position. If Christ had but one
will, he would have just one nature; for, proper operation follows upon
and manifests form. Since in Christ there is the union of two perfect
natures and the perfection of each requires will, he must have two wills.
To this brief metaphysical argument, Thomas adds arguments concerning
the pedagogical and redemptive goals of the Incarnation. Once again, a
heretical position isolates a small portion of scripture from its proper
narrative context. If there were no human will, Christ's sufferings would
merit nothing; nor would Christ's life be a model for imitation by us. A
single will would make nonsense of the crucial passage from the Gospel
where Christ states, "not my will but thine be done" (Luke 22:42). The
error arises from a failure to distinguish what is one simply from what is
one by order. On account of the complete subordination of the human
to the divine will in Christ, the human will is "disposed" to will in accord
with the divine will.[38] The union of two wills in Christ makes actions
and suffering salutary. As Dionysius puts it, the human activity of Christ
is "theandric."

On the basis of the assertion of two wills in Christ, Thomas asserts that
there must be two natures in the person of Christ. Since this "appears
foreign to what natural reason experiences," some authorities attempt

to circumvent Nestorius and Eutyches and still save the appearances of scripture. To avoid Nestorius, some hold that soul and body are not united in Christ; to avoid Eutyches, they argue that Christ assumed human nature as someone wears clothing. The result of the former is that Christ would be called a man equivocally, while the consequence of the latter is that the Word would not subsist in two natures. The root of the error can be found in the literal reading of a metaphorical text: "In habit found as a man" (Phil. 2:70).

The failure of the previous attempts leaves one option, that in Christ the two natures are united in one hypostasis: "In this way alone can the things handed down in scripture about the Incarnation be saved."[39] Scriptural discourses are the phenomena to be saved; heretical opinions represent various failed attempts to do just that. Instead of eliminating mystery by omitting an important portion of scriptural speech, Thomas seeks to find a way of resolving the problem of conflicting predications. Without distinction, scripture attributes the "things of God to that man and the things of that man to God." Since opposites cannot be said of the same things in the same way, a distinction must be introduced between the "about which" (*de quo*) and the "what" (*quod*) of predication. The former mode of predicating concerns the one supposit, that is, the one subject of the two natures, while the latter regards the respective natures, which ground distinct sets of defining predicates (IV, 39). Thomas concludes by comparing the logic, based on the distinction between nature and supposit or person, of the two great mysteries of the Christian faith: "As in the Trinity there are many subsistent persons in one nature, so in the mystery of the Incarnation there is one subsistent person in many natures."

Having offered an initial articulation of the union of two natures in one person, Thomas gives an account of how the Incarnation is to be understood (IV, 41). He first distinguishes union in nature from union in person or hypostasis. He concedes the impossibility of adding to a species already established. It is, however, possible to add to an individual member of the species things not integral to that species, as white or dressed can be added to Socrates. Things incapable of being united in nature may be united in person or hypostasis. After restating failed attempts to explain the Incarnation, he writes,

> Let the Word be said to subsist in a human nature, made his own through the Incarnation, so that that body is truly the body of the Word of God, and similarly the soul, and the Word of God is truly man.[40]

Although no adequate explanation of the Incarnation is possible, nothing is "so like" it as the union of soul and body. There is a twofold relationship of body to soul, as matter and as instrument. The former relationship is in no way comparable, since the union of soul and matter constitutes one nature. Instrumental union presents a more promising basis for understanding the Incarnation, especially since the ancient doctors refer to the human nature in Christ as a "certain organ of the divinity."[41] The human nature of Christ is so united to the divinity that instrumentally it performs operations proper to God. It performs the operations of a "proper and conjoined instrument," as the hand is the instrument of the rational soul. Through the intellect as medium, the Word is united to the whole human nature. From this vantage point, the detailed dialectical clarification of the union of soul and body takes on added significance, as does Thomas's frequent use of the neo-Platonic image of the human species as the horizon of matter and spirit. Thomas ends by reminding the reader that the analogies deployed in the chapter are but feeble attempts to understand the mystery of the Incarnation, for the Word is "more sublimely and more intimately" united to human nature than the soul is to its instrument. This is precisely the weakness of the so-called mereological model of the Incarnation.

Thomas is now in a position to respond to objections (IV, 40). In the response, the primary principle has to do with the hierarchical subordination of the human nature to the divine (IV, 49). The divine nature "draws the human nature to its subsistence and person," so that the latter participates in the hypostasis of the former.[42] The assumed nature depends on the divine suppositum for its very existence; it has no being (esse) apart from that of the divine Word. Some objections focus on the adverse effects of the Incarnation upon the divinity. One supposes that Christ's acquisition of a new nature renders divinity mutable. Thomas responds that, just as creation introduces no change or dependence into God, so too the Incarnation effects change only in the nature assumed. Another holds that, since a hypostasis does not extend beyond the nature of which it is the hypostasis, Christ's power would be circumscribed by the human nature. Thomas concedes a revised version of the first premise: a hypostasis does not extend beyond a nature "from which it has subsistence." However, Christ subsists "in the human nature," not through it.[43] A related objection proposes that, since the hypostasis of human nature is constituted by signate matter, Christ will also be so constituted. There is, however, only one nature by which Christ has being; not the being of Christ, but only his being "this," is constituted by signate matter.

Other objections focus on the incongruity between the Incarnation and what we know to be true of natural, especially human, substances. According to one objection, the very notion of substance entails that there be only one quiddity for each. The objection equates human nature with a hypostasis. But the two are not identical; instead, <u>what subsists in a nature is a hypostasis.</u>[44] There is a difference between common natures signified by "man" or "humanity" and supposita or persons. Person and nature should not be conflated. In Christ, the human nature subsists in the hypostasis of the divine Word. Such distinctions enable Thomas to navigate between "the Christological counterparts of Scylla and Charybdis, viz. Nestorianism and Monophysitism."[45] Alfred Freddoso explains,

> Christ is the ultimate but mediate subject of his purely human characteristics. That is, such characteristics have as their immediate subject Christ's individual human nature and as their mediate but ultimate subject the divine person himself. Since they are ultimately the characteristics of the Son of God, the communication of attributes is, pace Nestorianism, upheld. . . . On the other hand, since the purely human characteristics are only mediately the characteristics of the Son of God, Aquinas is able, pace Monophysitism, to preserve the doctrine that the divine and human natures remain integral and unmixed in Christ.[46]

The Incarnation does not constitute a second suppositum, added to that of the person assumed; rather, the human nature, given no hypostasis of itself, is assumed into and subsists through the hypostasis proper to the Word. This soul and this body do not constitute a distinct person but are assumed into the person of the Word. In this way, Thomas rebuts the objection that, since the union of soul and body suffices to constitute a hypostasis, there must be two supposita in Christ. Finally, Thomas addresses the objection that "man" will be said equivocally of Christ, as the understanding of this man will include what is not true of any other man, namely, a divine hypostasis. Difference of form, however, and not merely difference of supposit, is required for equivocation. The term "man" signifies the same form when said of human beings and of Christ.

V. THE FITTINGNESS OF THE INCARNATION
AND THE DRAMA OF REDEMPTION

Having rebutted charges of incoherence, Thomas considers the fittingness (*convenientia*) of the Word's assumption of human nature (IV, 51). The etymological meaning of *convenientia* is "coming together" or "convergence." A Thomistic lexicon notes that the term is synonymous with "consonance" (*consonantia*) and "harmony" (*harmonia*), words prominent in Aquinas's definition of the beautiful.[47] The shift to the suitability and harmony of the Incarnation signals another and more profound movement to narrative. Scriptural narrative envelops the whole of the fourth book. The first stage in understanding its discourse is to clarify its locutions, modes of speaking, and narrative purpose. The attempt to salvage the speech of scripture requires an explication of pertinent metaphysical principles. But all of this is inscribed within, and subordinate to, the mystery of the drama of redemption. The very term *convenientia* underscores the absence of deductive necessity. What sort of intelligibility do arguments from suitability have? Although the fittingness of God's deeds in history cannot be anticipated, it can be pondered retrospectively. The intelligibility of divine revelation is historical in character.

The first consideration of the suitability of the Incarnation is brief. It precedes the response to objections against the possibility of the Incarnation and focuses on the fittingness of the Word's assuming human nature. The Incarnation is ordered to the salvation of human beings, who are made perfect by the contemplation of the "first truth." Salvation is fittingly undertaken by the Word who proceeds from the "Father by an intellectual emanation." The term *logos*, which means "word" and "reason," further indicates the congruence between the Word and human nature, for it is on account of the possession of speech and reason that both the divine Word and the human person are called images of God. Finally, the Word is the exemplar for the artistry of creation; all creatures reflect the Word. Hence the union of the Word with a creature is most fitting (IV, 42).[48]

The references to the artistry of creation and the image/exemplar relationship of our nature and God hint at the dramatic shape of the arguments from suitability. The primacy of dramatic structure is evident in Thomas's chief argument from suitability, which has to do with original sin. The authoritative text is Romans 5:19: "As by the disobedience of one man many were made sinners: so also by the obedience of one many shall be made just." The chief opponent is Pelagius, whom Thomas counters by citing two other texts from Romans and the teaching of Genesis on death as a penalty inflicted on all from the moment of Adam's sin. Supporting evidence for original sin can be garnered from "probable indications," universally observable in the human condition.[49] From the presence of the penalty, we can surmise the fault.

The location of the consideration of original sin is instructive. There is a twofold subordination of the intelligibility of the topic; it is subordinate to revelation and—within revelation—to the topic of the Incarnation. Thomas's favorite source for the doctrine is Romans, where Paul retrospectively identifies a typological relationship between Adam and Christ. The subordination of original sin to the passion, death, and resurrection of Christ makes clear the Christocentric character of the fourth book, indeed of the whole text.

Indications or signs of punishment can be garnered from death and bodily infirmities. The "greatest of the spiritual penalties is the weakness of reason." Might these defects be natural, merely the result of the disposition of matter or a consequence of the soul's union with the body?[50] The metaphysics of created being eliminates the possibility of reducing evil to a primordial conflict between matter and spirit. The schematic depiction of evil in the first three books of the *Contra Gentiles* is an implicit critique of philosophical attempts to comprehend evil. From the perspective of revelation, the deficiencies inherent in philosophical attempts to delimit the cause of evil highlight the primacy of salvation history. The original state of human beings is not one of pure nature. What characterizes the first state of human life is the subjection of reason to God and of the other powers to reason. But this order is consequent upon a grace added to nature, which was to be propagated along with nature. This first gift is utterly unknown to the philosophers. They could not know the cure of evil because they did not know its cause. Only Christ, the true physician of souls, can provide an adequate diagnosis and an efficacious cure.

Original justice is not a state of pure nature, but one of grace.[51] The gift of original justice was "in some sense natural," not that it was caused by principles of nature, but that it was intended to accompany nature. The continued subordination of reason to God would have insured the obedience of inferior powers to reason. The gift, not the nature, is lost in reason's turning away from God. The objections to original sin mistakenly presume the state of original justice to be caused by principles intrinsic to human nature. Some object that the guilt of sin is not communicable.

Thomas responds that other human beings did not sin in Adam by exercising any act, but in his power as original principle. Adam's obedience to God would have safeguarded, and insured the transmission of, the grace of original justice. Others object that sin cannot eradicate goods of nature. Since the defect of original sin is a defect "of a principle added to the principles of the species," the objections are baseless (IV, 52).[52]

The need to satisfy for original sin, then, is the primary argument for the suitability of the Incarnation. Still, satisfaction could have occurred by other means. Neither the fact of salvation nor its means can be determined by reason. The paradoxical elevation and satisfaction of the philosophical desire to know the cause of the whole occur through unanticipated, contingent, historical events. So far above reason is the descent of God that it seems in many respects unbecoming. A general account of the suitability of the Word's assuming human nature is necessary.

Thomas argues that the distance between God and us is precisely a reason for the suitability of the Incarnation. Unless Christ bridged the gap, we might presume that the attainment of union with God were impossible. On account of human ignorance and attachment to bodily pleasures, we have not only sought lower goods but have also worshiped the universe and its parts. As is clear from the detailed analysis of misconceptions of the divine nature in the first book, the practice of limiting God to the imaginable or of construing the divine nature in terms of the grammar of abstract objects has been a habitual tendency among the *gentiles*, a tendency that underlies idolatry. Christ corrects idolatry, not by a negation of created things, but by reordering them to God. Through the Incarnation, God "induces" us to love him, not by an onerous command, but by providing a direct, sensible manifestation of his love for us. The Incarnation makes palpable the dignity of human nature and the nobility of human destiny.

The main reason for the Incarnation is the need to satisfy for sin. The satisfying power of Christ's sacrifice results from his "extraordinary charity" (*propter eximium caritatem*), which unites the human will in perfect obedience to the will of God. The quality and intensity of the loving obedience of Christ, not some quantitative calculation of offenses and penalties, is prominent in Aquinas's discussion of why God became man (*cur Deus homo*).[53]

Thomas also focuses on the pedagogical benefits of the Incarnation. He borrows two Aristotelian theses: that beatitude is the "reward of virtue," which is taught by words and examples, and that friendship presupposes equality. God's descent to us provides concrete examples of virtue and bridges the distance of inequality. The Incarnation thus resolves difficulties from Aristotle's *Ethics*. First, following Aristotle, Thomas holds that the virtuous person is the measure of virtue. Yet, as he also notes, infallible opinion about human beings has never been possible. Second, Aristotle never fully resolves the tensions between the demands of the active life and the life of contemplation. The life of contemplation seems disproportionate to our embodied natures. In the Incarnation, the object of contemplation is in some measure proportioned to our mode of knowing; through the Incarnation, the active life is ordered to, and harmonized with, the life of contemplation. As Thomas puts it, quoting from the Mass of the Nativity: "while we know God visibly, we are seized by a love of things invisible" (*dum visibiliter Deum cognoscimus, in invisibilium amorem rapiamur*, IV, 54). Through contemplation of the deeds and words of Christ, we are made friends with God.

In the longest and richest chapter of the fourth book, Thomas responds to objections to the suitability of the Incarnation. Some objections find God's descent unbecoming; these recall the objections from the first book concerning God's knowledge of, and providential care for, singulars and lowly things. In the Incarnation God's excellence is untainted while the creature's dignity is exalted. Although God's will is by itself sufficient for the salvation of humankind, "divine wisdom" provides for each thing in a mode congruent to that thing. In his defense of the preferability of Christ's union with human nature rather than with a separate substance, Thomas recurs to the dominant motif of the second book, the theme of human nature as microcosm, existing on the boundary (*confinium*) of the realms of spirit and body. He writes,

> It seems fitting that the universal cause of all things should assume that creature into a unity of person in which it shares more with other creatures. . . . Since he is the term of creatures, presupposing all others in the natural order of generation, man is appropriately united to the first principle of things so that, by a certain cycle, the perfection of things might be accomplished. (IV, 55)[54]

The passage points up the intimate connection between the two modes of truth. But there are different ways of interpreting the link. On the one hand, Lafont highlights the role of human nature and human destiny in the arguments for the fittingness of the Incarnation. Since the principle that enables Thomas to "finish the cycle" is reason or human nature, Lafont concludes that the work is insufficiently theological. Anton Pegis,

on the other hand, argues that Thomas orders and subordinates many of
the dominant themes of the first three books to the Incarnation. To which
view should we incline? Recall Thomas's opening comments about the
mystery of the Incarnation:

> If anyone should consider diligently and piously the mystery of the Incar-
> nation, he will find such a profundity of wisdom that it exceeds all human
> knowing. As the Apostle states: The wisdom of men is foolishness before
> God. (IV, 54)[55]

The reference to the profundity of wisdom situates the Incarnation at
the apex of the life of wisdom. From our lowly position, the Incarnation
seems foolish. It is not something that human wisdom would or could
anticipate; divine wisdom exceeds our natural (fallen?) expectations. The
discussion of the circular character of creation in the second and third
books tellingly falls short of establishing the elevation of human nature
to union with God.

Lafont voices another objection to Thomas's emphasis on the role
of Christ as completing a cosmic cycle. The emphasis abstracts from the
concrete historical conditions of human nature and of the deeds of Christ
in the flesh. Yet these themes are by no means absent from the *Contra
Gentiles*. The consideration of the time of the Incarnation is relevant to
Lafont's thesis. In the third book, Thomas noted that divine law ordains
human beings to the love of God. In the fourth book, in the context of
the fittingness of the Incarnation, he returns to the divine law in language
that underscores the personal encounter between human beings and God.
The human condition is now set in the context of salvation history and
its three epochs: before the law, under the law, and under grace. The
pedagogy of the law has the intelligibility of a narrative and the unity
of a drama. Redemption comes only after the human person has been
left alone to gain self-knowledge through an experience (*ut experiretur*)
of insufficiency (*quod ipse sibi non sufficeret ad salutem*). The efficacy of
the arguments from fittingness presuppose an appropriation of one's own
experience of sin and of the trials involved in attempting to live virtuously.

Divine pedagogy engages human beings individually and concretely;
it counteracts the twin vices of the human condition: pride and despair,
presumption and fragility.

> Presuming neither on knowledge nor on virtue, he could be given effec-
> tive assistance against sin through the Incarnation . . . by which he was to

be instructed in doubtful matters, lest he lack knowledge . . . , and made vigorous against the taunting of temptation, lest he be deficient through infirmity. (IV, 55)[56]

In previous books of the *Contra Gentiles*, Thomas has spoken of the temporal character of human knowledge, of the fallibility of human reason, and of the mutability of the will, even of infused habit. The positive correlate of these apparently negative consequences of human temporality is that human mutability provides an opening for "expiation" (IV, 55). The narrative shape of redemption suits the temporal form of the human condition. Faith comes not through vision but through hearing. It works through "promises and testimonies" that dispose us to belief. The ordering of temporal moments to eternity is evident in Thomas's response not only to the question of why Christ came when he did, but also to the question of why Christ did not remain incarnate until the end of the world. After performing wondrous deeds, he withdraws his presence, so that "by his absence" (*per eius absentiam*) souls might be better prepared for spiritual gifts (IV, 55). In its natural and supernatural modes of communication, divine pedagogy intertwines presence and absence. Even the mode of Christ's presence on earth—the hiddenness of his divinity in mortal flesh, his bodily infirmity, suffering, and death—suits the freedom of finite creatures. Christ wants to persuade, not compel.

The centerpiece of the narrative of grace is redemptive suffering. Once again the cosmic and the moral intertwine, as Thomas argues that God permits the existence of natural and moral evil because (a) without contrariety and incompatibility the goods of order and beauty would be eliminated, and (b) the presence of evil enables us to know and desire the good more fully (III, 70). From the perspective of the Christian doctrine of redemption, evil is seen as part of God's providential plan. One of the goals of the passion and death of Christ is to demonstrate God's benevolence and thereby to inflame human hearts with a longing for union with God. Thomas recasts Aristotle's view that virtue is taught by example in terms of redemptive suffering. Enduring bravely and in obedient charity the sufferings of the flesh becomes a key to the good life.

Suffering is in itself evil. God does not will the death of human beings but the "virtue through which man endures death courageously and in charity abandons himself to the dangers of death."[57] The pointless suffering of lowly things is not virtuous. Instead, the virtue of humility is operative when, from necessity and for the sake of some good, someone great suffers something lowly. In this case, "the more exalted the majesty, the more marvelous is the humility" (*humilitas tanto est mirabilior quanto maiestas sublimior*). The humility of Christ is evident not just in his descent to the human order but in his living a "needy and private life," especially in his suffering a lowly and abject death. The good, to which Christ's humility is ordered, is persuasion and conversion:

> Because of pride, men were lovers of earthly glory. In order to change their souls from love of earthly glory to love of divine glory, he wished to endure, not any sort of death whatsoever, but a most ignominious death. (IV, 55)[58]

By "bearing in themselves the marks of the passion of Christ" (*portantes in seipsis insignia passionis Christi*), the followers of Christ replicate in their own lives the aesthetics of a humiliated God. In Christ, sufferings become remedies. The emphasis upon redemptive suffering involves a transformation of Aristotle's understanding of the noble and the beautiful. The philosophical account of human nature and of the human good is now located within a larger historical context, within a more capacious narrative. What the *gentiles* understood to be natural is actually fallen. Conversely, the *gentiles'* understanding of the program of human perfection, which consists in an ascent to the divine life, is simplistic. Instead, the descent of humble obedience precedes any ascent.

Thomas's comments on the efficacy of divine pedagogy capture Christianity's narrative reversal:

> A great portion of humanity, leaving aside the cult of angels, of demons, and all creatures, disdaining fleshly pleasures and all bodily things, have devoted themselves to the worship of God alone, in whom alone they expect the completion of beatitude. (IV, 54)[59]

The exaltation of lowly "idiots," as Thomas calls them in the original prologue, reflects an unexpected twist in the plot of creation. The twist in plot, as MacIntyre shows, introduces a new set of virtues and reshapes the narrative structure of the good life.[60] Humility plays a role unknown to the ancients. The virtue of fortitude is prominent in the discussion of how Christ faced death; yet it is recast as the virtue of the martyr, who suffers death not for worldly honor but out of charity. The chief virtue is no longer magnanimity, at least not as Aristotle depicts it. Friendship, now understood as charity, has been transposed from an auxiliary to a constitutive role in the good life. It is the central and formative virtue. As John Milbank suggests, the "telos is no longer an action remaining in a mover, but rather a surplus overflow."[61] This is the ethical correlate of the metaphysics of divine perfection. Thomas's account of the good life reflects both his revision of the *gentiles'* understanding of divine perfection and his description of the trinitarian life of God.

VI. TIME, ETERNITY, AND THE SACRAMENTAL ETHOS

The remarkably fertile discussion of the fittingness of the Incarnation inscribes the entire created order within salvation history. Apart from that history, creation remains mute concerning the most important things. One can rightly read nature only after having been instructed by the discourse of scripture, where the signs of the natural and human world find ample explication. The divine names, the pinnacle achievement of natural theology, provide both a list of names or signs and a training in how to read them. While some are more informative than others, all fail to deliver what they signify. What is the relationship between the divine names and scriptural speech? The most palpable use of the divine names in the fourth book is as a rule of exclusion; they aid the exegete in determining what expressions must be taken metaphorically and what theological doctrines are impossible. This is not to say that revelation must vindicate itself in the court of philosophy; it is to say that divine revelation does not occur in a vacuum but presupposes, and does not conflict with, God's first mode of teaching in creation.

While the divine names exercise some authority over scriptural discourse, they are subordinate to, and cannot achieve fulfillment apart from, that discourse. But not even the discourse of scripture is an end in itself. The discourse of scripture is, as Erich Auerbach suggests, "fraught with background."[62] The entirety of scripture refers to Christ, in "whom the whole is fulfilled." The Incarnation is the pivotal event in the drama of redemption but it is not the final event. Christ makes us loving exegetes; he teaches us how to read temporal, embodied signs in light of, as ordered to, eternity.

In the time between the Incarnation and the judgment of the world, the sacraments constitute the principal signs of the divine; they continue the sanctification of the temporal, sensible order and anticipate the elevation of the cosmos in the "new heaven and new earth." The contrast between the sacraments of the Old Law and the New Law is instructive. While the former point to salvation, the latter "deliver" it. The difference between the two sacramental modes is explained in terms of God's providential activity in history, an activity that "disposes diverse things in accord with different times." The sacraments order human lives with respect to the center and telos of history: "God fittingly handed on certain sacraments and teachings before the Incarnation to signify future things, and others after the Incarnation to hold forth things present and to recall things past" (IV, 57).[63] The sacramental ethos cultivates a communal memory of contingent historical events.

The discussion of the sacraments, which follows that of the Incarnation, binds together various themes: the critique of idolatry, the embodiment of human nature, the communal orientation of human nature, and its contemplative aspiration. The sacraments curb our tendency to treat physical things as the source of evil. They temper sorrow with joy and mitigate fear and despair through hope. In so doing, the sacraments bridge the gap between time and eternity and anticipate union with the triune God.

The sacramental remedy is congruent with the condition of those who are to be healed and proportionate to the first cause (IV, 56). In accordance with the human mode of knowing and Christ's manner of teaching, the sacraments manifest the power of spiritual and intelligible realities under sensible signs. The sacraments heal the soul and restore our appreciation of the goodness of the sensible order. In the sacraments, the pedagogical use of creatures reaches its pinnacle. But the sacraments do more than provide an occasion for education; they provide the necessary disposition for the embodied, temporal soul to profit from, and live in accordance with, eternal truth.

The sacraments order the whole of time to Christ, upon whose life, death, and resurrection history pivots. They also apply the remedies of the Incarnation to the various stages in the life of each individual and of every community (IV, 58). They extend the redemptive benefits of Christ's death and resurrection through time and history. The sacraments follow the order of the natural, bodily life of human beings. Corresponding to the reception of life, growth, nourishment, and the healing of bodily ailments are the sacraments of baptism, confirmation, the Eucharist, and penance and extreme unction. Among these, the Eucharist, which is both a "memory and a representation of our Lord's passion," is central (IV, 61). The final two sacraments, matrimony and holy orders, correspond to the two principles of rule in the natural order: parents and political leaders.

The grace of the sacraments heals and elevates nature, but it does not eliminate human freedom (IV, 70). Impeccability presupposes an immutable will. After the reception of grace, human beings can sin again. Numerous passages in scripture admonish the converted to resist temptation. Having sinned, they may once again receive grace through penance. Were this not so, despair would prove a path to "sinning freely." Even after Christ and under grace, the life of the believer is one of "struggle and warfare." The struggle ends in death, at which time the will is unalterably fixed with respect to its ultimate end.

The ordering of temporal moments and signs to eternity is accomplished through the sacraments, which have their "efficacy from the passion of Christ" and are intended "for man's assistance along the road to the end."[64] Thomas links the Church, its priesthood, and its hierarchical unity to the sacramental character of the Christian life. Given human nature and divine disposition, the sacramental ethos of the Church requires communal embodiment and public expression. To sever private belief from communal, public expression would be to lapse into some form of pagan dualism. Fittingly, when Christ was about to withdraw his bodily presence, he instituted an order of priests so that the sacraments might be dispensed by visible men with spiritual powers (IV, 74). The notion of the Church as a body, with Christ as its head, pervades the discussion of the sacramental ethos. The episcopal power insures the unity of the Christian people (IV, 76).

We have already argued that creation has a sort of narrative intelligibility, with a beginning, middle, and end. Five of the last six chapters of the fourth book underscore the finality of the end of time; they address the immutability of the wills of the dead (92–95) and speak of the last judgment (96). The chief argument against an infinity of souls is that it is contrary to the notion of an end (97). The thesis of some *gentiles*, according to which there is an unending alteration of life and death, undermines divine purposiveness in the world. From this vantage point, the dialectical arguments in the second book against the eternity of the world take on added significance. They make room for the Christian narrative of creation, fall, redemption, and last judgment.

The last judgment occurs in two stages: first, at the moment of death, the souls of individuals are judged "one by one"; second, at the time of the resurrection, all are judged communally in soul and body. The emphasis on individual judgment at the end of the fourth book recalls the discussion of the significance of the actions of individual human beings at the end of the third book. What we do merits reward or punishment. Each individual will be judged alone. The Christian narrative isolates in order to reincorporate. The second stage of judgment occurs communally after the bodily resurrection. The reunion resulting from the bodily resurrection, which the sacramental community anticipates, is akin to the diversity within unity of the life of the Trinity.[65]

The doctrine of bodily resurrection has two sources. First, scriptural texts depict bodily resurrection as a consequence of Christ's victory over sin and death (IV, 79). Second, the unity of soul and body is natural and perfective. Without the body, the soul is an imperfect part. Once God gives being to the essential principles of human nature, it is not appropriate that these should revert to nothingness (IV, 81). The salvation of the soul does not constitute the salvation of the human person. These comments eliminate any lingering temptation to construe the previous discussion of soul and body in dualistic terms. As Chenu comments: "Man is not a person other than in a body: his 'incarnation' is at once the principle of individuality, sociability, and of historicity."[66] An emphasis on the body underlies Thomas's conception of history and narrative. The prominence of the body is especially evident in the discussion of salvation. Both in this life and the next, the body is the locus of salvation.

The last judgment will be a public, sensible manifestation of the divine mercy and justice. Thomas writes,

> Since in his humanity Christ suffered and rose and thereby merited for us resurrection and eternal life, the general judgment belongs to him. . . . Christ will judge in the form of humanity, which all may see, both the good and the wicked. The sight of his divinity, however, . . . will be seen by the good alone. (IV, 96)[67]

Thomas associates the fittingness of Christ's role as judge to his central, historical role in the economy of divine providence. The words of judgment of Christ, the exemplar of creation and the one in whom the entirety of history is fulfilled, mark the end of time, the end of a human drama written by a divine artist. But the reading of the story presupposes certain dispositions, which can be achieved only through human cooperation with a divine gift.

Just as the significance of Christ's earthly life remained hidden under the flesh, so too his divinity will remain veiled to those whose wills are turned from the good. Turned from God, the "affections" of the souls of the damned will be "carnal." The deformity of their souls will be manifest in the heaviness and darkness of their bodies. Their souls will be "wrenched, completely frustrated in their natural desire for happiness"

(IV, 89).[68] The very disorder of their wills is a punishment unto itself. They will endure condign punishment in their bondage to those lower things in which they erringly sought their ultimate end (IV, 90).

Christ's descent to the human order and his embrace of lowliness and suffering complicate the relationship between the two modes of truth. The second mode does not just supplement nature; rather, it manifests the higher in and through the lower; it corrects, transforms, and elevates nature. Christianity introduces a more complex protreptic than that known to antiquity. The similarities between philosophical protreptic and medicine were not lost upon the ancients. In his analysis of the nature and necessity of penance, Thomas makes ample use of comparisons to medicine (IV, 72). The threefold disorder of sin—the perversion of the mind, the weakening of natural good, and the guilt of punishment—requires correction through contrition, confession, and satisfaction. The healing of the soul restores our ability to see spiritual splendor manifest through the body.

The stages in the narrative of restoration can be seen in Thomas's successive treatments of the human body. In the consideration of creation in the second book, the accent was upon the manifestation of divine wisdom and goodness in the sensible world, especially in the union of soul and body. Original sin, the result of which is the insubordination of bodily powers, disrupts the relationship between higher and lower, spirit and body. Disorder and spiritual deformity ensue. Original sin is the root of our inveterate temptation to disdain the body. The restoration of the order and beauty of soul and body occurs through the virtuous endurance of suffering and death.

The Christian drama of redemptive suffering, which culminates in the exaltation of the human body, resolves the problem of the body, which is closely allied to the problem of evil. The ancients were preoccupied with this question; even Aristotle, whose position on the natural union of soul and body Thomas eagerly embraces, could not avoid the tragic consequences of the sundering of soul and body in death. The Christian view does not denigrate the body, nor does it suppose that the naturalness of the body undermines the possibility of a transcendent good. Instead, grace enables human beings to embrace the infirmity, deformity, and corruptibility of the body. The body is the site of salvation. The bodies of those who suffer in charity merit glorious elevation. Of Christ's body, Thomas writes, "It was necessary that his splendor, which was hidden under the weakness of flesh, be manifested through the glorification of the flesh" (oportebat quod sua claritas, quae sub infirmitate carnis erat occulta, per carnis glorificationem . . . manifestaretur, IV, 8). The use of the term "claritas," which means a manifestation of splendor is central to Thomas's account of beauty, which introduces a notion of beauty unknown to the ancients.

The effects of grace in the human person are especially evident in the relationship of soul and body. The bodies of the risen will be the same in nature as they were in this life, but they will have a different, incorruptible disposition (IV, 84–5). The body will be in complete harmony with the soul. Thomas underscores the height of the exaltation of the body in the following passage:

> Just as the glory to which the human soul is raised exceeds the natural power of the heavenly spirits, . . . so too does the glory of the risen bodies surpass the natural perfection of the heavenly bodies so as to have a greater splendor, a more firm impassibility, a more facile agility, and a more perfect nobility of nature. (IV, 86)[69]

The final chapter of the Summa Contra Gentiles "on the state of the world after judgment" indicates the transformation and elevation of nature by grace, the comprehension of the first mode of truth in the second mode. Bodily things are ordered to human beings. In the resurrection, accordingly, the material world will achieve "a certain glory of splendor" (quandam claritatis gloriam). He ends by quoting the prophecy from Revelation 21:1: "I saw a new heaven and a new earth" (IV, 97).

6

RECAPITULATION: THE SUMMA CONTRA GENTILES AS DIVINE COMEDY

The narrative structure of the *Contra Gentiles* has now been described in some detail. It can be categorized superficially in terms of the neo-Platonic theme of the *exitus-reditus*. Yet the disparity between Thomas's account of creation and the neo-Platonic account introduces complications into the *exitus-reditus* structure. Creation is not the result of a necessary, divine emanation, nor is it to be understood negatively as a fracturing of primordial unity or a lapse into finitude. Instead, creation is rooted in the divine freedom and is a positive reflection of the divine wisdom and beauty. Existing on the horizon of the worlds of matter and spirit, embodied rational creatures occupy a pivotal and unifying place in the order of creation. While they can achieve goods of both the active and the contemplative lives in a mode proportionate to their nature, the human longing for happiness is never fully satisfied by any finite good or activity. Divine providence, of which the natural order is but a partial realization, has ordained human beings to a higher good than their fragile natures are capable of attaining.

In such terms does Thomas describe the narrative of creation in the first three books. In the final book, he describes the drama of redemption, which situates the human condition within a more capacious historical narrative than that available to the *gentiles*. Salvation history, with its stages of creation, fall, redemption, and exaltation, has the unity of a dramatic narrative. In that story, the author of the entire drama enters history and embraces our fallen, fragile, suffering condition in order to reconcile us with God. The drama does not end with the completion of Christ's earthly task; the whole of time is now ordered through Christ to a final transfiguration.

Given that the neo-Platonic motif of *exitus-reditus* is misleading, is there some other way to speak of the narrative of the *Contra Gentiles*? Is it susceptible to further classification? Can it be understood, for instance, in terms of the genres of tragedy and comedy?[1] Before we speculate further on the genre to which the *Contra Gentiles* belongs, two cautionary comments are necessary. First, while numerous strategies and structural features of the work point to its having a narrative structure, Thomas gives no indication of conceiving the work in terms of the genres of tragedy and comedy. Indeed, the scattered references to comedy and tragedy in his writings indicate that he had only a conventional and simplistic understanding of these two genres. Second, notions of tragedy and comedy, even in the Middle Ages, were remarkably fluid and variegated.[2] In speaking of these genres and differentiating them from one another, we can hope to attain only family resemblances, not univocal criteria.

Given the difficulties involved in the notions of tragedy and comedy, why should one suppose that they are relevant to philosophy and theology? At least one Thomist has argued that philosophy embodies a tragic narrative. In a chapter on the "grandeur and misery" of metaphysics, Jacques Maritain writes: "This is the misery of metaphysics (and nonetheless its grandeur): It awakens the desire for a supreme union, for a spiritual possession consummated in the order itself of reality, and not only in idea. Yet it is not able to satisfy it."[3] Maritain's view finds some textual support in Thomas's depiction of the aporetic character of philosophical discourse about the highest things. Thomas does not, however, exaggerate the tragic elements of philosophy; indeed, the life of that portion of humanity that philosophy leaves in "darkest ignorance" seems more aptly described as tragic.

One might object strenuously to the description of philosophy as tragic. Contemporary accounts of tragedy underscore the differences between it and the philosophical life. John Milbank argues that tragic narrative involves the assertion of "ontological violence" at the roots of the natural and moral cosmos.[4] Paul Ricoeur and René Girard make a similar point about tragedy's depiction of "primordial incoherence."[5] Is it not precisely the achievement of Plato's speculative philosophy— in its celebration of the transcendence of the Good—to have eclipsed the vision of the tragic poets? Is not this the outcome of what Socrates calls the ancient quarrel between philosophy and poetry? Aristotle, too, defends speculative philosophy against the charge of *hubris*; he argues that the contemplative happiness enjoyed by God is not utterly foreign to human nature and that God does not jealously exclude humans from participation in that good.[6]

In Aristotle's discussion of tragedy there is little emphasis on themes prominent in contemporary discussions of tragedy as involving moral or metaphysical conflict.[7] Strikingly absent from the *Poetics* is any detailed attention to the role in tragedy of the gods, fate, and necessity.[8] Silence about these matters accords well with Aristotle's criticisms of the notion that a divinity could be jealous. Aristotle highlights the pedagogical value of certain kinds of tragedy, namely, those which underscore the sheer difficulty of gaining self-knowledge, of living in accordance with the requirements of moral virtue, and of hitting the mean in action, of performing an action that is right in every respect. He also celebrates the noble response of persons to bad fortune, to circumstances that are at least to some extent outside of their control.[9] The difficulty of hitting the mean in action and the virtuous response to bad fortune are of course important themes in Aristotle's *Ethics*.[10] Yet tragedy does not focus on characters of complete excellence, on the sort of person the *Ethics* describes. Even in the *Ethics*, the virtues constitutive of excellence are described separately and somewhat abstractly. Once again, Aristotle underscores the distance between human aspiration and human achievement.

From the perspective afforded by the narrative of the *Contra Gentiles*, two things can be said about such an understanding of tragedy. First, tragedy, as conceived by Aristotle, has a clear pedagogical value.[11] The Old Law, as conceived by Aquinas, performs a similar pedagogical function. The law simultaneously teaches moral precepts and reveals our insufficiency to live in full conformity with the precepts. But the law, whose revelation might be said to introduce the possibility of tragedy into the narrative of scripture, is only one moment within a more comprehensive comic narrative. The law cannot be understood apart from the promise of divine assistance; it points to the coming of a redeemer (II, 38). Thus, second, tragedy cannot provide the dominant narrative description of human life. Tragedy is ignorant of the cause of the human condition and the remedy for it. Yet the narrative of redemption is able to account for both the merits of tragedy and its limitations. The relationship between Aristotelian tragedy and Thomistic comedy provides another illustration of the way theology answers philosophical difficulties.

Neither Plato nor Aristotle ally philosophy itself with tragedy. Philosophy's contemplative yearning for the Good, its recognition of its own limitations, and occasionally its hope in the possibility of complete beatitude as a gift or as a vision possible beyond this life—these distinguish the contemplative life (*theoria*) from the tragedy of the poets. They allow Thomas to commend the achievement of philosophy and to deploy philosophy against those notions of tragedy that depict "ontological violence" or "primordial incoherence." In his metaphysics of created being, Thomas draws upon philosophy to repudiate every vestige of Manichean dualism, the view that evil is coextensive with the good, or that finitude somehow entails evil. Creation *ex nihilo* confounds these teachings. Thomas refutes the errors of the natural philosophers who suppose that matter is eternal and that creation is the introduction of order into a preexisting state of chaos, that at the origin of things is conflict and violence (II, 38). In shifting the emphasis from necessity and fate to intelligibility and the good, Plato and Aristotle clearly progress beyond the errors of the natural philosophers. Still, Plato's mythological account in the *Timaeus* of creation as the introduction of order into chaos, and Aristotle's emphasis in the *Physics* upon the eternity of the world, continue to veil the absolute primacy of divine goodness, as Aquinas himself notes (II, 38). Thomas underscores the transcendence of God over all created effects both at the beginning and the end of the work. In between, especially in the third book, he argues that all things naturally tend to the good, that evil is a "privation of the good" (*privatio boni*). In the course of his analysis of the role of tragedy in different myths of creation, Ricoeur states that "guilt must be distinguished from finiteness," and ontology from the historical origins of evil, in order for the tragic vision to be fully eclipsed. Thomas's metaphysics eliminates the possibility of viewing creation in tragic terms. What, then, are we to say about the narrative of the *Contra Gentiles*? Does it belong to the genre of comedy?

A crucial difference between pre-Christian comedies and the Christian narrative is that the former often treat the tragic as innocuous. Indeed, comedy's lack of gravity often underlies the judgment of its inferiority to tragedy. But the Christian narrative does not neglect tragedy. So closely does the life of Christ fit certain themes of tragic drama that one might be inclined to see scripture as tragic, not comic. There are at least two reasons for this inclination. First, scripture celebrates mourning rather than laughing. As St. Thomas More writes, "For to prove that this life is no laughing time, but rather the time of weeping, we find that our savior himself wept twice or thrice, but never find we that he laughed as much as once."[12] Leo Strauss takes the passage as a point of departure for a contrast between religion and philosophy:

> If we compare what More said about Jesus with what Plato tells us about Socrates, we find that "Socrates laughed twice or thrice, but never find we that he wept as much as once." A slight bias in favor of laughing and against weeping seems to be essential to philosophy. For the beginning of philosophy . . . is not the fear of the Lord but wonder.[13]

Second, tragedy and scripture appear to have a common root: sin and atonement through ritual sacrifice. In *Violence and the Sacred*, René Girard traces the catharsis of tragedy to its roots in religious sacrifice:

> Katharsis refers primarily to the mysterious benefits that accrue to the community upon the death of a human katharma or pharmakos. The process is generally seen as a religious purification and takes the form of cleansing or draining away of impurities.[14]

Ritual sacrifice is an integral part of Jewish religious practice, and the passion of Christ is central to the Gospels. Thomas devotes much of the fourth book to Christ's sacrificial offering of himself to the Father and to the ritual atonement offered Christians through the sacraments. Given the apparent alliance between tragedy and religion, how can one argue that the theological structure of the *Contra Gentiles* is comic? The contrast of religion and philosophy in terms of weeping and laughing may well be accurate, but its significance is dubious. In the Middle Ages, comedy often refers to a narrative structure that begins with misery and ends with joy.[15] The *Contra Gentiles* does not of course begin in misery; instead, the focus is upon the sheer actuality and resplendent beauty of God. The metaphysical foundations of Thomas's narrative accentuate the primacy of goodness and truth and the accidental status of evil and unintelligibility.

The comic structure of the *Contra Gentiles* can be seen in the various discussions of God and his providential plan for human beings. Thomas begins by securing the independence and perfection of God, who is best described as *ipsum esse subsistens*. In the dialectical inquiry into God's relationship to the world, Thomas corrects the tendency among Aristotle's commentators to reason from God's perfection to his distance from the world of contingent, singular beings. An insufficient application of negation to language about God underlies the supposition that distance from the world is necessary to safeguard divine perfection.

Purged of anthropomorphism, the notion of divine perfection entails God's immediate and effortless providence over all things. In both its destructive and constructive forms, dialectic prepares the ground for the Christian narrative.

Thomas then secures the absolute contingency in being of the whole of creation. The insolubility of the question of the eternity of the world undermines philosophical objections to the Christian assertions that the world began to be at a certain time and will end at some time, assertions that make possible a narrative construal of creation. The cosmos itself is described as a manifestation of the beauty, wisdom, and goodness of the divine artist. The discussion of providence extends the notions of the contingency of creation and of God as artist. The whole of creation, especially of human history, is subject to God's providential design, which operates both through the order of nature and through miraculous events. Thomas's metaphysics "provides the necessary theological background for a history which both begins and ends beyond time," a history which is an essential feature of Christian comedies.[16]

The connection between providence and history suggests a narrative conception of creation and especially of human destiny. The events of salvation history can be appreciated by us only after their occurrence. The doctrine of original sin, unknown to natural reason, underscores the crucial importance of historical events for understanding the human condition. Christianity's eclipse of tragedy offers the comprehensive vision sought by the philosophers, but it does so by transforming our understanding of that vision and the means to its attainment. By undercutting the proud aspirations of fallen human beings, it invites us to embrace and transform those elements of human life that the philosopher may wish to flee.[17] The ambiguous status of evidence in a fallen world vitiates the philosopher's project of understanding himself in relation to the whole. According to the Christian narrative, even the philosopher suffers from a sort of tragic ignorance. The universal applicability of both diagnosis and cure indicates that the purported gap between the few and many, although is is real, does not extend to what is fundamental about the human condition.[18] The restoration of the whole of humanity occurs through the Incarnation, which manifests the wisdom of God in the foolishness of divine descent.

Other features of comedy are present in the text.[19] Comedies typically end with communion overcoming isolation and with the elevation of persons beyond their expectations and deserts. The themes of restoration and elevation are central to Thomas's conception of divine grace and to his vision of the state of the world after judgment. The work ends with the prophecy from Revelation, 21:1: "I saw a new heaven and a new earth." The narrative structure of comedy, moreover, is allied to a particular view of time. As Northrop Frye puts it, "In comedy time plays a redeeming role: it uncovers and brings to light what is essential to the happy ending."[20] In the *Contra Gentiles*, time has an intelligible order and is a vehicle of redemption, whereas in tragedy it is the enemy of the protagonist. In the Christian narrative, the moment of recognition, which in tragedy occasions the downfall of the protagonist, allows for the acknowledgment of sin, for reconciliation, and for restoration.[21]

The individuation of human persons runs counter to the tragic assimilation of individuals into the whole constructed by myth. Ricoeur speaks of "the deliverance which is not outside the tragic, but within it: an aesthetic transposition of fear and pity by virtue of a tragic myth turned into poetry and by the grace of an ecstasy born of a spectacle."[22] In contrast to tragedy's absorption of the individual in the spectacle, the Christian narrative separates the individual from the mechanism of a fallen social order. Only after the separation can there be a reunion that establishes communal celebration of a divine gift: the restoration of human freedom through obedience to the divine will.

The Christian narrative traces out the "complete pattern" of creation, sin, and redemption, but for each reader the drama is presently incomplete. The reality of sin entails the possibility of damnation as well as redemption. How then can the drama remain comic? The emphasis upon the mutability of the human will and on the individual's inability to secure salvation in advance might seem to represent a reversion to tragedy. Its point, however, is to offer liberation from tragedy. Although the temporal character of human action precludes a peremptory resolution, it also provides opportunity for the expiation of sin. Time need not be a "nemesis."[23] The Gospel invites us to participate with Christ in breaking the chain of sin. The reversal is present in the very structure of biblical narrative. In God's voluntary submission to expulsion and violence we are liberated from the mechanical determinism of sin.[24] The contingency of sin and the possibility of redemption repudiate the identification of sin with finitude. Salvation is not equated with a knowing (*gnosis*) that annuls time. The Incarnation occurs in the fullness of time (*ex consummatione temporis*). The Christian conception of time and providence renders tragedy an inappropriate vehicle for describing the structure of reality.

The Christian strategy is to render the "complete pattern" "so appealing that it . . . leaves the audience wishing to live their incomplete and as yet potentially tragic lives in the light of the enacted ideal."[25] Might this provide a clue to the distinctively Christian character of the protreptic of the *Contra Gentiles*? Even for a Christian audience, salvation remains a hope and a promise, not something already achieved. Indeed, Thomas devotes the final twenty-four chapters of the third book to the connection between acts performed in time and punishment or reward in eternity. Divinely infused habits "do not take away free choice" (III, 155). These chapters immediately precede the treatment of the central mysteries of the Trinity and the Incarnation. In the last of these chapters, he argues that the rationale of salvation is hidden in the divine will; hence, the final structure of the narrative, as incorporating each person, is not ours to write (III, 163). The *Contra Gentiles* is a divine, not a human, comedy.

The inclusion of topics such as final judgment and predestination in the third book has troubled commentators. These topics, along with those concerning the theological virtues and the counsels, are properly theological; it would seem appropriate for Thomas to postpone consideration of them until the fourth book. The comic structure of the work suggests a response to this objection; for it is precisely in the latter part of the third book that comic features come to the fore. In this section, Thomas subordinates the order of nature to the plan of divine providence and shows that it is not unbecoming of God to intervene within an order he has already established. While God does not contradict his original creation, he may reveal something that will lead us to rethink our understanding of, and our place within, the whole. The discussion of the role of miracles in divine providence paves the way for explicit consideration of the comic reversal introduced by the Incarnation. Anticipations of that reversal can be seen in the treatment of the theological virtues and especially of the counsels. Poverty, chastity, and obedience are means to the life of perfection. Yet they involve something of a reversal of human expectation, since they lead only indirectly to that which is intrinsically desirable. What they directly involve is a life of suffering, self-abnegation, and submission. Even if Thomas includes certain properly theological topics in the third book, he does not fail to underscore the disparity between the Christian narrative and that of Aristotle's *Ethics*.

The fourth book articulates the central dramatic events in that divine narrative and issues an invitation to a more complete participation in that mystery. After he has discussed redemption through Christ and the sacraments, Thomas reiterates that revelation does not eliminate temporality, contingency, or freedom. There is no impeccability where there is no immutability of will (IV, 70). The temporality and contingency of the Christian life, captured nicely in the medieval notion of the *homo viator*, make narrative an apt vehicle for the expression of the ordering of time to eternity.

The possibility of tragedy and the reality of sin and suffering persist in the Christian narrative. Tragedy is not so much refuted as embraced, comprehended, and transformed. Stanley Hauerwas puts the relationship between tragedy and the Gospel thus:

> We believe, on the basis of the cross, that our lives are sustained by a God who has taken the tragic into his own life . . . we are thus freed from the obsession of securing our significance against death.[26]

The *Contra Gentiles* affirms the reality and inescapability of suffering, after the advent of sin. Nearly all the references to suffering occur in sections of the text devoted to theological, particularly trinitarian, themes. In the Christian narrative, the significance of human suffering is tied to a divine gift, inviting human beings to participate in the internal life of God. In the life of Christ, tragedy is embraced and overcome precisely through suffering and humility. Christ's enduring a "death abject in the extreme" is ordered to instruction and conversion. As Ricoeur observes, the "divine abasement completes and annihilates tragedy." The suffering servant transforms the symbolism of evil so that the "evil undergone is an action redeeming the evil committed."[27] Thomas has similar things to say about the meritorious sufferings of Christ and his followers. Through grace, "penalties become medicinal"; through charity, a believer "suffers with a suffering friend" (*patienti amico compatitur*, III, 158).

The prominence of suffering in the Christian life is of course what leads Thomas More to speak of this life as a "time of weeping" and Strauss to align Christianity with tragedy. Yet, according to Northrop Frye, there is a "kind of comedy where the complications in front of the happy ending become tragic, so that the comedy contains a tragedy instead of avoiding one."[28] He even speaks of scripture as a "'divine comedy' in which the two greatest tragedies, the fall of man and the Crucifixion, are episodes."[29] It is important, furthermore, to see that the comic features of Christianity are not postponed until after death; instead, there is continuity between this life and the next. Through Christ, who is both sign and signified, we can experience anticipations of the comic denouement here and now. The discussion of the sacraments exhibits not only the ordering of time to eternity, but also the transformation of human life available in time. The receptivity of the Christian narrative, moreover, to speculative inquiry indicates that the gap between belief and knowledge can be partially bridged in this life. Authentic faith is always in search of understanding.

There is another contrast between tragedy and comedy. Comedies typically make conscious and public use of artifice and readily refer to their authors, at times going so far as to make the author part of the drama. Tragedy, on the other hand, tends to conceal its artificiality and to remain silent about its author. We have already noted the prominence in the *Contra Gentiles* of descriptions of God as an artist whose wisdom and goodness is manifest in creation. The narrative structure of nature, in its going forth from, and returning to, its source, is intended and directed by the divine artist. Throughout the *Contra Gentiles*, Thomas underscores the artificial character of the entire cosmos, of human history, and of time. The author of the narrative of the universe does not remain outside the drama; instead, he is the agent upon whom the internal movement of the narrative pivots.

The Incarnation, in which the author enters his own narrative and contrives to bring the story to a happy ending, involves comic reversal. The Gospel is not of course a typical comedy. Eric Auerbach has observed its unique combination of lowly and grand styles. Thomas' discussion of the Incarnation confirms Auerbach's observation:

> Just as sublime things can be said of that man by reason of the union: that he is God, that he raises the dead, so lowly things can be said of God: that he was born of a Virgin, suffered, died, and was buried. (IV, 34)[30]

The combination of servile and noble themes enables the divine comedy of redemption to engage directly the motifs characteristic of tragedy. Redemption is not simply restoration, but elevation beyond human desert, capacity, or expectation.

A comic narrative thus encompasses, corrects, satisfies, and elevates the philosophic pursuit of wisdom described in the prologue. Christianity's comic narrative is not inimical to the life of inquiry. Some portion of revelation is susceptible to rational confirmation; moreover, revelation has a remarkably sophisticated understanding of the human condition. One of the suppositions of the *Contra Gentiles* is that theology can answer questions that philosophy finds irresolvable. The obvious objection is that the term "answer" is being used equivocally in philosophy and theology. In its reference to the "foolishness" of Christian wisdom, scripture anticipates, even celebrates, the objection. Just as one who is not situated appropriately with respect to the arguments of metaphysics will fail to apprehend their truth and may even deem the entire pursuit so much nonsense, so too those lacking the requisite dispositions cannot but see Christian wisdom as foolish. The appropriate disposition is not, however, one of resignation to an inscrutable fate, but one supplied by divine grace through the mediation of a comic narrative that restores the self to itself and enlivens one's sense of wonder. The result is not laughter, but joy, an exultation that renders the philosopher's knowledge a paltry mediocrity. As Louise Cowan puts it, "the high point in comedy lies not in knowing, but in being shown, being led into the harmony of the cosmos to receive better than one deserves."[31]

APOLOGETICS AND THE SUMMA CONTRA GENTILES

The arguments, some of which we have already discussed, against the view that the *Contra Gentiles* was a missionary text are numerous. By Dominican standards, the *Contra Gentiles* is an enormous failure as a missionary work. The Dominicans had exacting rules for debating rivals from other religious traditions. Raymond of Penafort, at whose request the work was purportedly composed, articulates and practices the "strategy of refutation from within the opposing tradition."[1] Thomas, too, follows such a pattern in his own polemical works, for example, in the *Contra errores Graecorum* and the *De rationibus fidei contra Saracenos, Graecos, et Armenos*. Aside from some passing references to Muhammad in the prologue of the *Contra Gentiles*, Thomas does not address the Muslim religion. He avails himself of none of the religious texts of the Muslims. The references, scattered through the work, to the *gentiles*, lend no support to the missionary thesis, while the book's complex manner of argument renders its usefulness for missionary work negligible. Having dismissed the possibilities that the *Contra Gentiles* was intended to be "placed in the hands of potential converts" or to be used as a "manual for detailed training of missionaries," Mark Jordan entertains the possibility of a qualified apologetic intent:

> The Contra Gentiles . . . was intended to provide a reference book of philo-sophical arguments against the conceptual errors instanced in unbelievers, to be read by Christians who live in contact with them. . . . He wrote a foundational work that would undergird any detailed missionary attack.[2]

Even if such an indirect and qualified apologetic intent can be attributed to the *Contra Gentiles*, the work fails to provide strategies or recipes for translating its conclusions into apologetic capital. As Jordan notes, Thomas seems more intent on fostering intellectual virtue in believers. Of course a by-product of such an education would be that they could give reasons for at least a certain portion of their beliefs and counter objections to the remainder. But this is clearly secondary. As Jordan concludes, what little evidence there is of a missionary intent is subsumed within a larger project.

On that note, there is an instructive parallel between the *Contra Gentiles* and the *Summa Theologiae*. On the basis of numerous similarities between the second part of the *Summa* and Dominican manuals for confessors, Leonard Boyle argues that Thomas's intention in writing the *Summa* was to "break out of the narrow tradition of practical theology."[3] By subordinating the discussion of particular moral questions to an ample treatment of the virtues and vices and by linking these discussions to the Christian conception of human nature, Thomas would locate the study of moral matters "in a full theological context."[4] As Boyle's study of the printing and circulation of the manuscripts of the *Summa* indicates, Thomas's intentions were systematically ignored: the second half of the second part, which treats of moral matters in detail, regularly circulated separately. The practical needs of the care of souls obscured from view Thomas's larger pedagogical project. An even less glorious fate befell the *Contra Gentiles* in its deployment as an apologetic instrument. One might suppose that a work as fertile in argument as the *Contra Gentiles* could have provided ample material for apologetics, even if the material had to be reworked for concrete application. Yet the text was never directly used by missionaries. There are, admittedly, some citations of it in Raymundus Martinus's *Pugio Fidei adversus Mauros et Judaeos*.[5] But these are limited to Thomas's refutations of the early natural philosophers.[6] Among the many problems surrounding the legend of the missionary intent of the *Contra Gentiles*, perhaps the gravest concerns Peter Marisilio's claim that the *Contra Gentiles* is deemed to be without equal for missionary purposes.[7]

A comparison of Thomas's two greatest works reveals important differences between the role of the manuals in the *Summa* and the purported role of apologetics in the *Contra Gentiles*. No section of the latter work is directly and immediately applicable to apologetics; at least the *secunda secundae* of the *Summa* addresses moral questions in a way that, according to Thomas, is "useful." Finally, the *Contra Gentiles* shows no reliance on missionary manuals, while the *Summa* does appropriate material from a number of confessors' manuals.[8]

If one sets aside the possibility that the *Contra Gentiles* is a missionary manual, might it not still be feasible to see the work as an apologetic of some sort? Perhaps the strongest description of the work as an apology would run thus. In the first three books, Thomas sets aside faith and operates within the realm of pure reason. His goal is to convince those who do not accept revelation, who may not even be theists, that God exists and that what can be known by reason about God and his relationship to the world is perfectly compatible with what Christian revelation teaches. Having established a theistic foundation on the common ground of pure reason, Thomas proceeds to explicate the supernatural portion of Christian revelation and to defend it against objections. While the first three books would establish a positive correspondence between reason and a portion of revelation, the last book would remove impediments to the reception of faith by showing that, where it exceeds reason, revelation is not contrary to reason. The thesis is not void of textual support. Thomas speaks of convincing opponents and argues that doing so may require believers to descend from faith to the common ground of reason. Certainly the work exhibits the compatibility of faith and reason.

The thesis just outlined is more than an abstract possibility. As influential a writer as Anthony Kenny adopts something very like this view. He states,

> The *Summa Contra Gentiles* is meant as a philosophical work; it is directed to people who are not Christians, who may be Muslims or Jews or atheists. It aims to present them with reasons—reasons that any human being of good will can see to be good reasons—for believing that there is a God, that the soul is immortal and so on.[9]

Kenny's view accords well both with the received view of the *Contra Gentiles* and with a popular view of the traditional project of natural theology. In *Church Dogmatics*, Karl Barth describes natural theology as abandoning "its own standpoint" and feigning to adopt the perspective of "unbelief."[10] There are, however, insuperable difficulties with this reading, not the least of which has to do with the troublesome phrase "pure reason." The very wording echoes the notion of disengaged reason in Descartes and Kant more than it does Thomas's understanding of intellectual virtue. As we have seen, the understanding of the first three books as philosophy is violent and unfounded. The *Contra Gentiles*, moreover, is not addressed to beginners; it presupposes both erudition and a training in the philosophical sciences. "Good will," as Kenny calls it, is hardly sufficient. The work does indeed begin with a somewhat detailed proof of the existence of God. Yet the complete absence of dialectic in this section suggests that Thomas expects his audience to assent readily to the existence of God. This seems to rule out the possibility that the work is an apology in the modern sense; it is not an attempt to persuade skeptics or atheists. If we narrow the focus of the work to theistic traditions, for example, that of the Muslims, other problems arise. Dominican practice and the dialectical method of the work stipulate that the refutation of an interlocutor requires careful analysis of his position. How, then, could the work be effective in refuting other religions, when it contains no citations of the texts of other religious traditions?

If Thomas were engaging in an apologetic of pure reason, he would more likely have adopted a different order of proceeding. He does not begin where it would be most effective for him to begin. Even if he descends to reason in the first three books, he does not adopt the order of teaching appropriate to philosophy. Rather, the structure of the work is theological: it begins, not from what is first in our experience, but from what is first in the order of being. Suspicions about the apologetic thesis increase when one reads in the opening of the second book that the utility of the study of the natural order has to do with fostering reverence for the creator among Christians. Thomas makes no reference here to the apologetic usefulness of the study of creatures and speaks as if his intended audience is the Christian community.

Were it not for these kinds of remarks at the opening of the second book, one might be inclined to adopt a version of Bouyges' thesis, wherein the twofold mode of truth is seen to demarcate two audiences.[11] Both modes would address Christians, while the first mode would also address non-Christians. Bouyges' thesis is an improvement upon the strong apologetic thesis, wherein the first three books appeal solely to pure reason, while the fourth defends revelation against objections from reason. The fourth book does counter some objections from reason, but it begins by stipulating that probable arguments on behalf of revealed truths not be presented before non-Christians, since they may be misled into thinking that faith rests on such feeble arguments from reason. In most of the dialectical sections of the fourth book, the errors of reason merit only incidental attention, insofar as they underlie the heresies condemned in the first centuries of Christianity.

Some have supposed that the refutation of errors, which is one goal of the *Contra Gentiles*, serves an apologetic end. Such a supposition explains the unwillingness of many commentators to dispense with the apologetic hypothesis.[12] Yet there is another possibility. The refutation of errors is intrinsic to the dialectical method of the work and also to the articulation of Christian wisdom. The teaching of the first mode concerns primarily those truths that we should have been able to see if our inquiry were not impeded by intellectual or moral vice. Under the tutelage of faith, we are able to reappropriate the natural intellectual virtues and to see the compatibility of reason and faith. Another goal of the first mode is to articulate in their amplitude the truths of the natural order that the intelligibility of revelation presupposes. Hence the distinction between the two modes need not be motivated by apologetic concerns, but by the thesis at the heart of Thomas's thought: grace does not destroy nature; rather grace presupposes nature, restores, perfects, and elevates it.

If we set aside anachronistic modern understandings of apologetics, might the work be seen as an apology addressed to an intellectual elite, well-trained in the teaching of Aristotle and his commentators? This is more likely, especially since the work addresses erroneous interpretations of Aristotle among Jews and Muslims. Even here, however, the underlying supposition is that the work, at least in the first three books, is a sort of compendium, structurally determined by a catalogue of errors. Such a supposition cannot but impede the reading of the work as a structural unity. Behind this supposition seems to be a further assumption that reason has primarily, or at least for the most part, a hostile relationship to faith and hence faith must adopt a defensive posture toward reason. Nicholas Wolterstorff aptly describes the project of modern evidentialist apologetics:

> Evidentialist apologetics is a strategy not for the believer's ascent toward fulfillment in contemplation but for the construction of supports beneath his feet. It is a movement not within faith but beneath faith. Its concern is not to promote the fulfillment of faith but to assure the legitimacy of faith.[13]

The very term "apology" denotes a response or a defense; too often Christian apologists have adopted a defensive posture toward rational argument or have allowed opponents to set the terms of debate. Thomas does neither. The whole point of the prologue is to underscore the compatibility of Christian and philosophical wisdom. The structure of the work, moreover, is theological; the order of questions, and the principles of exclusion and inclusion of topics, even in the first three books, are theological. Thomas thus subsumes philosophical disputation within a theological pursuit of wisdom. He puts human wisdom at the service of Christian wisdom.

What "apologetic" there is in the text seems to be addressed to Christians with philosophical training. This of course is far from an apologetic of pure reason. Given the intellectual milieu in which Thomas was working, the correction of philosophical errors was a pressing concern. While Bonaventure and others largely accepted the view of Aristotle handed on by his Arabic and Jewish commentators, Thomas seeks to disengage Aristotle from his commentators and to show that, properly understood, there is no incompatibility between Aristotle and Christianity. In that sense, the *Contra Gentiles* is more closely allied to Thomas's extended project of commenting on Aristotle's texts than is the other *Summa,* and hence it is more revealing concerning Thomas's view of philosophy. The dialectical method of the *Contra Gentiles* suits the end of engaging the philosophical tradition. The emphasis upon latent *aporiai* in Aristotle's texts allows Thomas to go beyond what Aristotle says without necessarily contradicting him.

In this way, believers can contribute to philosophical inquiry. The various dialectical strategies of the work provide ample opportunity for the inculcation of intellectual virtue in readers. The philosophical conception of dialogue as the turning of souls through discourse to the highest things is intrinsic to reflective Christian belief. Of course the believer is not a philosopher. It is striking that Thomas does not refer to any Christian teacher as a philosopher.[14] As the prologue indicates, the two sorts of wisdom, philosophical and Christian, distinguish two ways of life, two ways of construing the practice of authoritative teaching about the highest good. The philosophy that Thomas receives from the best of the *gentiles,* Plato and Aristotle, is not an exhaustive system. Philosophy signifies the love of wisdom, not its possession. Its internally acknowledged limitations, its culmination in negativity and silence, provide a space within which Being might manifest itself.

The philosophy of Plato and Aristotle counteracts the temptation to transmute human wisdom into a comprehensive system. This apparently negative counterpart to their positive recognition of the aspiration for contemplative happiness is for Thomas one of their great achievements. There is, then, yet another way in which the *Contra Gentiles* is not an apology in the modern sense. Modern Christian apologists often embrace a novel philosophy and seek to show how faith can be articulated in its terms. But Thomas does not embrace Aristotle because of his currency. He attends to Aristotle's positions because he believes them to be largely true and because they exhibit both the achievements of, and the limitations to, philosophy.

The correction of misreadings of Aristotle restores a certain dialectical integrity to philosophy. Since the vantage point from which Thomas appraises philosophy transcends philosophy, he is able to put the question of what it would mean to go beyond Plato and Aristotle. He is also able to judge philosophy by the light of the Gospel. Is this not the significance of the phrase *contra gentiles* that appears in the title? Thomas's "descent to reason" never forgets its source of inspiration: a gift, unknown to philosophy, of participation in the wisdom proper to the divine Word, the source, measure, and end of the whole. Instead of conforming faith to the neutral standpoint of evidentialist reason, Thomas incorporates "extra-biblical thought, experience, and reality into the true world of scripture."[15] Through participation in the Word, human beings love the whole in a way superior to that of the philosopher. As reason, splendor, and discourse, the Word issues an invitation to participation in the wisdom and discourse that is the life of God. The intimate connection in Christian wisdom between contemplation and teaching mirrors the relationship between the Word and creation. Our inveterate tendency to construe Thomas's pedagogy in terms of an apologetics of pure reason reveals how far we have lapsed from his understanding of Christian wisdom.

NOTES

1. PEDOGOGY AND THE ART OF WRITING

1. *Summa Theologiae*, I, 1, 9, objection 1.

2. *Summa Theologiae*, I, 1, 9, ad 2.

3. Leo Strauss is one of those responsible for the renewed appreciation of the art of writing. His focus, however, is upon "persecution and the art of writing," which he derives at least in part from his reading of the esoteric teaching of Maimonides. See *Persecution and the Art of Writing* (Glencoe, Ill.: The Free Press, 1952) and "The Literary Character of the Guide for the Perplexed," in *Maimonides: A Collection of Critical Essays*, ed. J. A. Biuys (Notre Dame: University of Notre Dame Press, 1988), pp. 59–70. There is, as Mark Jordan notes, a crucial rhetorical difference between Mamonides' *Guide* and Thomas's *Contra Gentiles*: "Mamonides writes obscurely for the just; Thomas writes publicly for the community of believers" (p. 197). See Jordan, "The Protreptic Structure of the Summa Contra Gentiles," *The Thomist* 50 (1986), pp. 173–209.

4. The high regard in which the *Summa Theologiae* is held has numerous sources. It is not just that this is the last major work of Thomas's life, but that the clarity and economy of its expression, as well as its orchestration of varied philosophical and theological sources, mark a kind of perfection in theological discourse that eclipses anything else Thomas wrote, perhaps anything else ever written by a Christian. On numerous questions, Thomas seems to have achieved in the *Summa* a lucidity unrivalled in his previous compositions. Although the work is written for beginners, its manner of presentation is not pedantic or simplistic. The structure of the work mirrors quite closely the method of public disputation of the nascent universities; indeed, the *Summa Theologiae* realizes the possibilities of that genre more than other medieval texts. The intention of the present study is certainly not to diminish the importance of the *Summa*.

5. So influential is the received view that it deserves independent treatment; hence, a brief appendix will be devoted to the question of apologetics in the work.

6. See R. A. Gauthier's *Introduction*, Collection Philosophie Européenne dirigée par Henri Hude (Paris: Editions Universitaires, 1993), pp. 109 and 146–47.

7. See Clément Suermond's *Tabulae schematicae . . . Summae Theologiae et Summae contra Gentiles S. Thomae Aquinatis* (Rome: 1943), pp. 8–9; reprinted in the *Opera Omnia*, Leonine edition, vol. 16 (Rome: 1948), p. 287. See Gauthier's discussion of this matter in his *Introduction* (1993), pp. 146–47.

8. On the dates of composition, the manuscript tradition, the sources, and the strengths and weaknesses of the Leonine edition of the *Contra Gentiles*, see Gauthier's *Introduction* (1993). This new introduction supersedes Gauthier's *Introduction historique au tome I de l'édition bilingue de la Summa contra Gentiles* (Paris: P. Lethielleux, 1961), pp. 7–123. The most important additions in the latest introduction are a list of corrections to the Leonine edition (pp. 45–57) and a table of sources (pp. 183–204). Also see Weisheipl's *Friar Thomas D'Aquino: His Life, Thought, and Works* (Washington D.C.: Catholic University of America Press, 1983), pp. 130–32 and 359–60. Pierre Marc argues strenuously but unconvincingly for moving the composition of the *Contra Gentiles* to Thomas's second Paris residence in the early 1270s. See his introduction to *Summa Contra Gentiles*, I (Turin: Marietti, 1967). The work would thus be contemporaneous with the *Summa Theologiae*. For criticisms of Marc's thesis, see Weisheipl, *Friar Thomas*, p. 428, n. 86, and the reviews by Clemens Vansteenkiste in *Angelicum* 45 (1986), pp. 353–55, and by an anonymous author in *Rassegna di letteratura tomistica* 2 (1970) no. 67, pp. 51–56.

9. M. D. Chenu, *Introduction à l'étude de Saint Thomas d'Aquin* (Paris: Vrin, 1954), p. 247. Unless otherwise noted, the translations of French texts are my own.

10. Étienne Gilson, *The Elements of Christian Philosophy* (Garden City: Doubleday, 1960), p. 5. Gilson thinks that the use of such an array of arguments and sources befits the apologetic intent of the work.

11. Jordan, "The Protreptic Structure," p. 184. For a list of the references to the *gentiles* in the work, see Gauthier's *Introduction* (1993), p. 111, n. 2.

12. Omnium autem ordinatorum ad finem gubernationis et ordinis regulam ex fine sumi necesse est: tunc enim unaquaeque res optime disponitur cum ad suum finem convenienter ordinatur; finis enim est bonum uniuscuiusque. Unde videmus in artibus unam alterius esse gubernativam et quasi principem, ad quam pertinet eius finis. . . . Quae quidem artes aliis principantes architectonicae nominantur, quasi principales artes: unde et earum artifices, qui architectores vocantur, nomen sibi vindicant sapientum.

All references to the *Contra Gentiles* are from the edition of C. Pera, P. Marc, and P. Caramello (Turin: Marietti, 1961). I have also made use of the corrigenda to the Leonine edition in Gauthier's recent *Introduction* (1993), pp. 45–57. Except where noted, the translations are my own. I have profited from reading the English translations of the *Contra Gentiles* published by the University of Notre Dame Press in 1975: Book I, translated by Anton Pegis; Book II, translated by James Anderson; Book III; translated by Vernon Bourke; Book IV, translated by Charles O'Neill.

13. Mark Jordan makes this argument at length in "The Protreptic Structure."

14. *In decem libros Ethicorum Aristotelis ad Nichomachum expositio*, ed. R. Spiazzi (Turin and Rome: Marietti, 1964), Book VI, lectio 7.

15. Jacob Klein, *A Commentary on Plato's Meno* (Chapel Hill: University of North Carolina Press, 1965), p. 6.

16. See G. E. L. Owen's essay "Tithenai ta phainomena," in *Aristote et les problèmes de méthode* (Louvain, 1961), pp. 83–103.

17. Docens . . . incipit docere sicut inveniens incipit invenire. . . . Exterior operatio docentis nihil operaretur nisi adesset principium intrinsecum scientiae . . . sicut et medicus dicitur naturae minister in sanando. Sic igitur causatur scientia in discipulo per magistrum, non modo naturalis actionis, sed artificialis.

18. John Sallis, *Being and Logos: The Way of the Platonic Dialogue* (Atlantic Highlands, N.J.: Humanities Press International), p. 21.

19. See John Sallis's reading of the doctrine of recollection in the *Meno* in terms of the mediation of part and whole (*Being and Logos*, pp. 64–103). Also see Klein's *Commentary*, as well as Robert Wood, "Image, Structure, and Content: On a Passage in Plato's Republic," *Review of Metaphysics* 40 (1987), pp. 495–514.

20. *Summa Theologiae*, I, 1, 10.

21. Gauthier, *Introduction* (1993), p. 159.

22. Augustine, *De Doctrina Christiana*, II, 28.

23. Chenu, *Introduction à l'étude de Saint Thomas d'Aquin*, pp. 247–48. While Chenu thinks that the work is unintelligible apart from its historical context, he argues that it goes far beyond what contemporaries would have expected from a missionary manual (247–48). The testimony is that of Peter Marsilio, who writes that Raymond, "conversionem etiam infidelium ardenter desiderans, rogavit, eximium doctorem sacrae paginae, magistrum in theologia fratrem Thomam de Aquino eiusdem ordinis . . . ut opus aliquod magister ille quod tanti patris humilis deprecatio requirebat, et Summam, quae contra gentiles intitulatur, condidit." In *Raymundiana seu Documenta quae pertinent ad S. Raymundi de Pennaforti vitam et scripta*, Monumenta ordinis Fr. Praed. historica, VI, 1, ed. Balme and Paban (Rome: 1898), p. 12. See Gauthier's discussion of the text and the "missionary legend" in *Introduction* (1993), pp. 165–76. The passage cited goes on to claim of the *Contra Gentiles* that "for such material it is esteemed to have no equal." Given

that the work did not itself serve as a missionary manual and did not significantly influence contemporary missionary writing, this is an odd assertion. Citing the presence of passages from the *Contra Gentiles* in the *Pugio Fidei adversos Mauros et Judaeos*, a contemporary Dominican missionary work, some have argued that it did in fact have an impact. But, as Jordan notes, the meager appropriation of the *Contra Gentiles* that does occur in the *Pugio* occurs in the strictly philosophical portion of the latter work ("The Protreptic Structure," p. 179).

24. M. M. Gorce, "La lutte 'contre Gentiles' à Paris," in *Mélanges Mandonnet* (Paris: J. Vrin, 1930), I, 230–43, and *Bulletin Thomiste*, v. 3 (1930), nos. 1203–6, pp. 179–87. See also the criticisms of Gorce in David Salman's "Sur la lutte contra Gentiles de S. Thomas," *Divus Thomas* (Piacenza), 40 (1937), pp. 488–509.

25. Gauthier, *Introduction historique*, p. 70, as well as the discussion in the *Introduction* (1993), pp. 128–30.

26. Salman's response to Gorce contains detailed analysis of Thomas's usage of the word "gentiles," analysis which reveals that it always refers to the "pagani." "Sur la lutte . . . ," pp. 488–509.

27. . . . quia quidam eorum, ut Mahumetistae et pagani, non conveniunt nobiscum in auctoritate alicuius scripturae, per quam possint convinci. . . . necesse est ad naturalem rationem recurrere, cui omnes assentire coguntur; quae tamen in rebus divinis deficiens est.

28. See the difficulties raised by Gauthier, *Introduction historique*, pp. 60–87, M. Corbin, *Le chemin de la théologie chez Thomas d'Aquin* (Paris: Beauchesne, 1972), pp. 478–89, and M. Jordan, "The Protreptic Structure," pp. 174–91.

29. In his "Le Somme contre les Gentils and la polémique islamo-chrétienne," Van Riet sugggests that the work was indirectly missionary, intended "for the use of persons destined to make contact with the intellectual milieux of the 'infidels,' principally in Muslim countries" (p. 159). But this does little to circumvent the previously mentioned objections to a direct missionary thesis. Van Riet sees Thomas's hasty and vituperative criticisms of the religion of Mohammad as lending support to the crusades. But the thesis rests upon what is at best circumstantial evidence and makes no attempt to broaden his reading beyond the prologue. In a related article in the same volume of *St. Thomas and the Problems of His Time*, ed. G. Verbeke and R. Verhelst (Louvain: Publications Universitaires, 1974), Gardet argues that Thomas had little knowledge of "the Islamic world." He, too, sees Thomas's motive as primarily philosophical. "Rather than an encounter between the Christian and Islamic worlds, this is an encounter between Christian thought and Arabic-Muslim philosophy of hellenistic inspiration" (p. 149). See "La connaissance que Thomas d'Aquin put avoir du monde islamique," pp. 139–49.

30. *Introduction* (1993), pp. 122–23 and 128. As Gauthier also points out, Latin editions of the Koran were available in Thomas's time.

31. "The Protreptic Structure," p. 184. Jordan's essay begins by rehearsing and rebutting the various traditional claims concerning the historical context

and missionary intent of the *Contra Gentiles*. See also the study by Grégoire and Orgeils, *Paganus: Étude de sémantique et d'histoire*, in *Mélanges Georges Smets* (Brussels, 1952), pp. 363–400. By Thomas's day, the term *gentiles* no longer typically referred to *pagani*, but to the noble. Thus, Thomas deploys the ancient usage of the first four centuries.

32. Hoc enim modo usi sunt antiqui doctores in destructionem errorum gentilium, quorum positiones scire poterant quia et ipsi gentiles fuerant, vel saltem inter gentiles conversati et in eorum doctrinis eruditi.

33. Iam non ambuletis sicut et gentes ambulant, in vanitate sensus sui, tenebris obscuratum habentes intellectum.

34. In the fourth book, Thomas focuses upon the heresies identified in the early Church. Corbin thus rightly speaks of the "two great preoccupations, Aristotelian philosophy and the heresies of the first centuries." *Le chemin*, p. 486.

35. Gauthier, *Introduction* (1993), p. 142.

36. *Bulletin Thomiste*, 3 (1930–33), pp. 105–12. Feret himself follows Gorce's interpretation.

37. M. Blanche, "Note," *Revue de philosophie* 24 (1924), 444–49. R. Mulard, "Désir naturel de connaître et vision béatifique," *Revue des sciences philosophiques et théologiques* 14 (1925), 5–19, and review in *Bulletin Thomiste*, v. 1 (1925), nos. 195–96, pp. 192–95.

38. Guy de Broglie, "De la place du surnaturel dans la philosophie de saint Thomas," *Recherches de science religieuse*, 14 (1924), pp. 193–246 and pp. 481–96; 15 (1925), pp. 5–53.

39. For a balanced assessment of the difficulties with Gilson's view of Christian philosophy, see John Wippel, "Thomas Aquinas and the Problem of Christian Philosophy," chap. 1 of *Metaphysical Themes in Thomas Aquinas* (Washington, D.C.: Catholic University of America Press, 1984), pp. 1–33. For a response to Wippel, see Thomas D'Andrea, "Rethinking the Christian Philosophy Debate: An Old Puzzle and Some New Points of Orientation," *Acta Philosophica* 1 (1992), pp. 191–214.

40. Corbin, *Le chemin*, p. 621.

41. Gauthier, *Introduction historique*, p. 119.

42. Maurice Bouyges, "Le plan du Contra Gentiles de S. Thomas," *Archives de Philosophie*, 3 (1925), pp. 176–97.

43. In "Le plan de la Somme contre les Gentiles de saint Thomas d'Aquin," in *Revue néo-scolastique de philosophie* 32 (1930), pp. 183–214, N. Balthasar and A. Simonet adopt Bouyges's basic thesis concerning the structure and intent of the work. They take as their point of departure Thomas's admonition in the prologue that one must encounter interlocutors on some common ground. His goal, then, is "to convince his adversaries by using their own rational theories" (p. 202). Concerning the problematic inclusion in the first three books of matters apparently beyond the pale of rational investigation, they hold that Aquinas

justifiably includes them here, since these are matters on which he and his interlocutors share a common ground. On matters peculiarly Christian, such as the Trinity and the Incarnation, there is no common ground; hence these matters are appropriately segregated.

44. Bouyges, "Le plan du Contra Gentiles de S. Thomas," p. 191.

45. See, for instance I, 2 where Thomas writes "our intention is to manifest the truth which our Catholic faith professes by eliminating the contrary errors."

46. Gauthier, *Introduction historique*, p. 122. Gauthier's assertion must of course be qualified. Other authorities, especially pseudo-Dionysius, figure prominently in various segments of the book.

47. Jordan, "The Protreptic Structure," p. 181.

48. A possible non-Christian source of the view that contemplation guides action may well be Maimonides, whose account of Moses as ruling the Jewish people on the basis of his vision of God eclipses Aristotle's discussion of the best life. See Daniel H. Frank, "The End of the Guide: Maimonides on the Best Life for Man," *Judaism* 34 (1985), pp. 485–95.

49. Finis autem ultimus uniuscuiusque rei est qui intenditur a primo auctore vel motore ipsius.

50. . . . ad veritatis manifestationem divina Sapientia carne induta se venisse in mundum testatur.

51. Inter omnia vero hominum studia sapientiae studium est perfectius, sublimius, utilius et jucundius.

52. In his commentary on this passage, Thomas is careful to qualify the scope of Aristotle's critique (Liber I, lectio VI, 79).

53. . . . quod inducitur in animam discipuli a docente, doctoris scientia continet. . . . Principiorum autem naturaliter notorum cognitio nobis divinitus est indita: cum ipse Deus sit nostrae auctor naturae.

54. Corbin, *Le chemin*, pp. 626–27. Corbin has this to say about the focus of the debate: "The totality of commentators is blocked by, and limited to, an examination of a solitary difficulty: how is Saint Thomas able to locate among the demonstrative and probable arguments, among the truths accessible to natural reason, . . . those which are manifestly accessible only on the presupposition of revelation? A problem posed in this immediate manner does not allow for any solution and obliges the commentators to engage in an indefinite debate for or against the fidelity of Saint Thomas to his declared intention" (p. 637).

55. . . . non ex parte ipsius Dei, qui est una et simplex veritas; sed ex parte cognitionis nostrae, quae ad divina cognoscenda diversimode se habet.

56. Jacques Maritain, *Distinguer pour unir ou les degrés du savoir* (Paris: Desclée de Brouwer, 1946), p. 15.

57. Joseph Pieper, *Philosophia Negativa: Zwei Versuche Über Thomas von Aquin* (Munich: Kösel-Verlag, 1953), p. 68.

58. Sallis, *Being and Logos*, p. 64.

59. Remaneret igitur humanum genus, si sola rationis via ad Deum cognoscendum pateret, in maximis ignorantiae tenebris.

Does Thomas here concede, even as he circumscribes, Strauss's point concerning the philosophical difficulty of resolving the tensions between the few and the many? Thomas circumscribes Strauss's point not only by limiting it to philosophical wisdom, but also by his differing interpretation of that wisdom. Following Aristotle, Thomas holds that the best life available to human beings apart from grace involves the integration of contemplation and practice. There are various degrees of participation in happiness, not fundamentally different kinds of happiness. See Strauss's "The Problem of Socrates: Five Lectures," and "How to Begin to Study Medieval Philosophy," in *The Rebirth of Classical Political Rationalism*, ed. Thomas L. Pangle (Chicago: University of Chicago Press, 1989), pp. 103–83, and pp. 207–26.

60. . . . ad altius bonum, quam experiri in praesenti vita possit humana fragilitas.

61. Salubriter ergo divina providit clementia ut ea etiam quae ratio investigare potest, fide tenenda praeciperet.

62. Nullus enim desiderio et studio in aliquid tendit nisi sit ei praecognitum.

63. . . . quando ipsum esse credimus supra omne id quod de Deo cogitari ab homine possibile est.

64. . . . ut totam naturam rerum se reputent suo intellectu posse metiri, aestimantes scilicet totum esse verum quod eis videtur, et falsum quod eis non videtur.

65. Sapientis est veritatem praecipue de primo principio meditari et aliis disserere, ita eius est falsitatem contrarium impugnare.

66. Ego hoc vel praecipuum vitae meae officium debere me Deo conscius sum, ut eum omnis sermo meus et sensus loquatur.

67. See Simon Tugwell's introduction to *Early Dominicans: Selected Writings*, in the Classics of Western Spirituality (New York: Paulist Press, 1982), pp. 1–47.

68. See *De Doctrina Christiana*, I, 14.

69. Haec credendo incipe, procurre, persiste: etsi non perventurum sciam, gratulabor tamen profesturum. Qui enim pie infinita prosequitur, etsi non contingat aliquando, semper tamen proficiet prodeundo. Sed ne te inferas in illud secretum, et in arcanem interminabilis veritatis non te immergas, summam intelligentiae comprehendere praesumens; sed intellige incomprehensibilia esse.

70. Jordan, "The Protreptic Structure," p. 192.

71. Ibid., p. 207.

72. Ibid., p. 206. Jordan and others note that the formal structure of the *Contra Gentiles* shows little of the procedures of formal debate dominant in the universities and in nearly all of Thomas's other works. Yet few have focused explicitly on the literary vehicle of the work. Jordan's essay is an exception, as is Guy H. Allard's "formal perspective." In "Le 'Contra Gentiles' et le modèle

rhétorique," *Laval Théologique et Philosophique* 30 (1974), pp. 237–50, Allard argues that, when one looks to Aristotle for assistance on the method of the *Contra Gentiles*, one should look not to the demonstrative ideal of the *Analytics* but to the models of rhetorical argument found in the *Topics* and the *Rhetoric*, and, beyond Aristotle, to the writings of Cicero. Allard classifies the work as a piece of deliberative oratory. Following Aristotle's emphasis on the future-oriented character of deliberative oratory, Allard sees the work as urging the adoption of a certain way of life on the basis of its promise to secure the ultimate good of human life, happiness (p. 241). While acknowledging the rhetorical character of the work, Jordan differs from Allard in seeing the intended audience as Christian and in accentuating the speculative rather than the political.

73. R. Guindon, *Béatitude et théologie morale chez Saint Thomas d'Aquin* (Montreal: Éditions de l'Université d'Ottawa, 1956), pp. 243–47. For a more extensive study of the theme of circulation in Aquinas, see Jan Aertsen, *Nature and Creature: St. Thomas Aquinas's Way of Thought*, trans. H. D. Morton (Leiden: E. J. Brill, 1988).

74. Ghislain Lafont, *Structures et méthode dans la Somme théologie de saint Thomas d'Aquin* (Paris: Desclée de Brouwer, 1961), p. 138. Lafont argues against the position that Thomas's deployment of causal language in his division of both the *Contra Gentiles* and *Summa Theologiae* entails a preference for Greek over Semitic manners of speaking about God.

75. Ibid., p. 139.

76. The reversal in the relationship between philosophy and theology is not entertained by Lafont, who argues that, since the *Contra Gentiles* excludes from its purview the deeds of Christ *in carne*, it is insufficiently Christocentric (ibid., p. 140).

77. Anton Pegis writes, "The doctrine of the Incarnation is the capital truth of the S.C.G. . . . The supreme abasement of God to man . . . , the Incarnation, is the conclusion to which the whole of the S.C.G. tends, in so far as it is theology. But this is the conclusion to which Saint Thomas has undertaken to steer the aristotelianism of the first part of his work" (p. 174). See Pegis, "Qu'est-ce que la Summa contra Gentiles," in *L'Homme devant Dieu: Mélanges . . . de Lubac* (Paris: Aubier, 1964).

78. The influence of pseudo-Dionysius permeates the first book. For a study of the role of Dionysius in Aquinas, see Fran O'Rourke, *Pseudo-Dionysius and the Metaphysics of Aquinas* (Leiden: E. J. Brill, 1992).

79. Pegis, "Qu'est-ce que la Summa contra Gentiles," p. 173.

80. Ibid., p. 180. Even if one grants the central thesis of Pegis's reading, the precise relationship of Thomas to Aristotle remains to be seen.

81. Corbin, *Le chemin*, p. 615.

82. Ibid.

83. Lafont and Corbin are primarily interested in the *Contra Gentiles* as a moment in what the latter calls "le chemin de la théologie" of Aquinas. Both see the *Summa Contra Gentiles* as striving to overcome the limits of previous theological expositions, for instance, the commentaries on the *Sentences* and on Boethius's *De Trinitate*, and as containing the germs of what would come to fruition in the *Summa Theologiae*. Lafont insists that "the formula . . . in this work is imperfect" (*Structures et méthode*, p. 139), and echoes Gauthier's sentiment concerning the dangers of the location of certain theological doctrines in the realm of those truths accessible to natural reason. Corbin sees the second, vertical division of the text as anticipating the more coherent structure of the *Summa Theologiae*. But the *Contra Gentiles* is an ineliminable stage in the "chemin." For it replaces the less satisfactory ordering of the *Sentences* commentary— divine government/sin and grace/the moral life/theological virtues/and the beatific vision—with the elegant and more intelligible grounding of the structure upon the twin doctrines of God as end and beatitude, upon which follow the discussions of divine governance and law and grace (*Le chemin*, p. 635).

84. Pegis thinks that the first three books transform, respectively, the *Physics*, *De Anima*, and *Ethics* of Aristotle. What, then, is one to make of Thomas's pervasive claim to have offered a correct interpretation of the *littera* of Aristotle's texts? The intent, according to Pegis, is "the wish to dismantle Averroism as an interpretation" ("Qu'est ce que la Summa contra Gentiles," p. 173). Whether Pegis is correct about the character and goal of Thomas's exegesis of Aristotle remains to be seen. At least one recent commentator sees a slightly different ordering in the appeal to Aristotelian texts. Corbin suggests that the first three books engage, respectively, Aristotle's *Metaphysics*, *Physics*, and *Ethics*. Given that Aristotle treats the *De Anima* as a continuation of natural philosophy, the only substantive difference between Pegis and Corbin concerns the Aristotelian source of the first book. If Corbin is correct, Pegis's thesis about the distance that separates Aristotle's materialism and Aquinas's metaphysics of pure actuality may have to be modified somewhat, as the *Metaphysics* has a fundamentally different mode of proceeding from that followed in the *Physics* and as the former text contains a more ample conception of the first cause. See Corbin, *Le chemin*, p. 636. The thesis that Thomas carries forward a dialectical project begun by Aristotle mitigates the purported opposition, upon which Pegis, Gilson, and others insist, between Aristotle and Aquinas. Pegis does at times speak of Thomas as fulfilling Aristotle's own project, but he does not provide the grounds for seeing the dialectical fulfillment in anything other than Hegelian terms.

85. Corbin resolves the apparent tension between "a theological project *ad intra*" and "an apologetic project *ad extra*" in the following way: "the errors are neither epiphenomena exterior to a disinterested contemplation nor a unique object of attack, no longer in need of inquiry after truth. . . . The response to

the question of truth is identically the response to the problem posed by the errors that he knows, the response for him [ad intra] is identically the response for the others [ad extra]" (p. 516).

86. R. A. Gauthier, Préface to *Sententia libri de anima* (Paris: J. Vrin, 1984). pp. 289–94. See also Gauthier's *Introduction* (1993), pp. 147–56.

87. Gauthier, Préface, p. 293.

88. Aristotle, *Topics*, I, 2. The turn to dialectic was at least partly motivated by the desire to resolve Jonathan Barnes's famous dilemma concerning the apparent disparity between the model of demonstration in the Analytics and the practice of the scientific treatises. See Barnes, "Aristotle's Theory of Demonstration," *Phronesis* 14 (1969), pp. 123–52, and idem, "Proof and Syllogism," in *Aristotle on Science: The Posterior Analytics* (Padua: Editrice Antenore, 1981), pp. 17–59. For a corrective to Barnes's reading, see James Lesher, "The Meaning of NOUS in the Posterior Analytics," *Phronesis* 18 (1973), pp. 44–68, and, more recently, William Wians, "Aristotle, Demonstration, and Teaching," *Ancient Philosophy* 9 (1989), pp. 245–53.

89. See Martha Nussbaum's "Saving Aristotle's Appearances" in her *The Fragility of Goodness: Luck and Ethics in Greek Tragedy and Philosophy* (Cambridge: Cambridge University Press, 1986), pp. 240–63. Nussbaum seems excessively influenced by a Kantian opposition between appearances and things in themselves. More recently, Terence Irwin has argued for a much stronger view of dialectic in Aristotle, based upon a distinction between "pure" and "strong" dialectic. The former places no restrictions upon the *endoxa*, while the latter begins from a limited set of *endoxa* and is thus able to yield numerous sorts of scientific conclusions. See Irwin, *Aristotle's First Principles* (Oxford: Clarendon Press, 1988).

90. I have profited from the reading of Kurt Pritzl's, "Aristotle: Ways of Truth and Ways of Opinion," PACPA 67 (1993), pp. 241–52. Pritzl notes that while Aristotle seeks to explain and reconcile various *endoxa*, he may explain them in ways divergent from the account given by their original authors. It may also be the case that *endoxa* lack an appropriate "dimension of depth," that is, they may lack a "why" (*dioti*). In this case, they are dropped as false. Aristotle does not simply receive opinions passively.

91. My reading of *Physics* I, as well as my understanding of the various uses of dialectic in Aristotle, has been influenced by an unpublished paper by Arthur Madigan, S.J., "Varieties of Aristotelian Dialectic."

92. Thomas Aquinas, *In octo libros Physicorum Aristotelis*, ed. by P. M. Maggiolo (Turin and Rome: Marietti, 1965).

93. For the origins of these views, see Amos Funkenstein, *Theology and Scientific Imagination* (Princeton: Princeton University Press, 1986), pp. 22–31, and throughout.

94. Gauthier, *Introduction*, p. 121.

95. Alasdair MacIntyre, *Whose Justice? Which Rationality?* (Notre Dame: University of Notre Dame Press, 1988), pp. 165–208 and 349–88.

96. Thomas himself often refers to dialectic as yielding only probable knowledge. See, for example, the proemium to the *Sententia super Posteriora Analytica* (Turin and Rome: Marietti, 1955).

97. Aristotle speaks of induction in *Topics* I, 12.

98. The operation of the agent intellect, whose function is to apprehend universals in particulars, requires the proper disposition of the sensitive powers and practice (*Summa Theologiae*, I, 79, 4, ad 3).

99. Aertsen, *Nature and Creature*, p, 217.

100. Ex quo etiam judicium veritatis catholicae sumi potest; nam vero, ut Philosophus dicit, etiam falsa testantur; falsa vero non solum a veris, sed etiam ab invicem distant.

101. In *Metaphysics* XII, 7, 1072b13–29, Aristotle also describes the life of God as a model of the contemplative life.

102. Divinae virtutes nostrarum exemplares dicuntur. Nam quae sunt contracta et particulata similitudines quaedam absolutorum entium sunt, sicut lumen candelae se habet ad lumen solis.

103. Omnes creaturae comparantur ad Deum sicut artificiata ad artificem. . . . Unde tota natura est sicut quoddam artificiatum divinae artis. Non est autem contra rationem artificii si artifex aliter aliquid operetur in suo artificio, etiam postquam ei primam formam dedit. Neque ergo est contra naturam si Deus in rebus naturalibus aliquid operetur aliter quam consuetus cursus naturae habet.

104. See the treatment of these notions in pagan and Christian neo-Platonism in Stephen Gersh's *From Iamblichus to Eriugena: An Investigation of the Prehistory and Evolution of the Pseudo-Dionysian Tradition* (Leiden: E. J. Brill, 1978), pp. 27–57, 152–90, and 204–43.

105. Hoc autem modo mirabilis rerum connexio considerari potest.

106. . . . ut experiretur quod ipse sibi non sufficiret ad salutem, neque per scientiam naturalem, . . . neque per virtutem propriam.

107. . . . tantum sapientiae profunditatem quod omnem humanum cognitionem excedat.

2. GOD: SUMMIT, SOURCE, AND EXEMPLAR OF THE LIFE OF WISDOM

1. See Louis Mackey, "Entreatments of God: Reflections on Aquinas's Five Ways," in *Franciscan Studies* 37 (1977), pp. 105–19.

2. For a careful study of the stages of the argument in the *Contra Gentiles*, see Joseph Owens, *St. Thomas Aquinas on the Existence of God: The Collected Papers of Joseph Owens*, ed. John R. Catan (Albany: SUNY Press, 1980), pp. 154–56 and 166–68. Owens's treatment is burdened by the dubious thesis that our under-

standing of *esse* arises from judgment. The thesis is central to both existential and transcendental Thomism, yet it finds little support in Thomas's texts. Judgment reaches only the fact of existence, not *esse* as intensive actuality. See G. Lindbeck, "Participation and Existence in the Interpretation of St. Thomas Aquinas," *Franciscan Studies* 17 (1957), pp. 1–22, 107–25. The proof has been subject to much scrutiny. The most influential critique can be had in Anthony Kenny's *The Five Ways* (London: Routledge and Kegan Paul, 1969). For a response to Kenny, see Robert J. Fogelin, "A Reading of Aquinas's Five Ways," in *American Philosophical Quarterly* 27 (1990), pp. 305–13.

3. See Aristotle, *Physics*, VI, 4, 234b10–20.

4. Ibid., VII, 1, 242a17–243a2.

5. The part of a self-moving being could of course move accidentally in virtue of the motion of the self-mover.

6. See Joseph Owens, "Immobility and Existence," in *St. Thomas Aquinas on the Existence of God* (Albany: SUNY Press, 1980), pp. 222–26.

7. Est autem via remotionis utendum praecipue in consideratione diviniae substantiae. Nam divina substantia omnem formam quam intellectus noster attingit sua immensitate excedit.

8. The bulk of the chapter focuses upon the thesis that no infinite power can be in a magnitude. Thomas reproduces the following Aristotelian argument. A greater power produces an equal effect in a shorter time than does a lesser power. An infinite power would thus produce an equal effect in a time less than any finite power. Thus, "to move, to be moved, and motion" would occur instantaneously, which is impossible. Such a power would not be a magnitude but an intellect which would move by will.

9. Essentia in compositis significatur per modum partis, ut humanitas in homine.

10. David Burrell, *Knowing the Unknowable God: Ibn-Sina, Maimonides, and Aquinas* (Notre Dame: University of Notre Dame Press, 1986), p. 46. For a recent defense of the notion of divine simplicity, see Stump and Kretzman, "Absolute Simplicity," in *Faith and Philosophy* 2 (1985), pp. 353–82. Also see James Ross's comments on their article in the same issue. These treatments do not quite find the right language to capture Thomas's view, but they are far superior to Alvin Plantinga's *Does God Have a Nature?* (Milwaukee: Marquette University Press, 1980). For a response to Plantinga, see Burrell's *Knowing the Unknowable God*, pp. 35–50.

11. He thus overcomes the "opposition between Platonic participation and Aristotelian causality" that had "rendered impossible an adequate explanation of the foundation of the real." See "The Intensive Hermeneutics of Thomistic Philosophy: The Notion of Participation," *Review of Metaphysics* 27 (1974), p. 457.

12. Hanc autem sublimem veritatem Moyses a Domino est edoctus: qui cum quaereret a Domino, Exod. III, 13–14, dicens: *Si dixerint ad me filii Israel, Quod*

nomen eius? Quid dicam eis? Dominus respondit: *Ego sum qui sum. Sic dices filiis Israel: Qui est misit me ad vos,* ostendens suum proprium nomen esse Qui Est. Quodlibet autem nomen est institutum ad significandum naturam seu essentiam alicuius rei.

13. The compatibility of the philosophical notion of God as subsistent being with scriptural authority was for Gilson a singular instance of Christian philosophy. See his discussion of "Haec Sublimis Veritas" in *Le Thomisme: Introduction à la philosophie de saint Thomas d'Aquin* (Paris: J. Vrin, 1944), pp. 123–39. Through a historical analysis of various descriptions of God, Gilson shows the novelty of Thomas's position, even if in his discussion of Aristotle's "l'ontologie . . . de la substance" (p. 135), he overlooks the importance of Aristotle's conception of actuality in Thomas's natural theology. The importance of the passage for Christian thinkers has a long history. See, for example, C. J. de Vogel's " 'Ego sum qui sum' et sa signification pour une philosophie chrétienne," *Revue des Sciences Religieuses* 35 (1961), pp. 346–53.

14. In the commentary on the *Sentences,* Thomas enumerates the reasons for the fittingness of this name (In I *Sent.* d. 8., q. 1, a. 1). For a broad textual treatment of the topic, see Armand Maurer, "St. Thomas on the Sacred Name 'Tetragrammaton'," *Mediaeval Studies* 34 (1972), pp. 275–86.

15. In *Knowing the Unkowable God,* Burrell shows how Thomas corrects and perfects the language in Avicenna and Mamonides about God as being. For a study of the divine nature in the *Contra Gentiles,* especially of Thomas's transformation of neo-Platonic teachings on God's transcendence of being, see Anton Pegis, "Penitus manet ignotum," *Mediaeval Studies* 27 (1965), pp. 212–26.

16. Christopher Hughes, *On a Complex Theory of a Simple God: An Investigation in Aquinas' Philosophical Theology* (Ithaca: Cornell University Press, 1989), p. 5.

17. Ibid., p. 20. As Norman Kretzman and Timothy O'Connor point out, Hughes's misreading of Aquinas on God as subsistent being underlies most of the book's criticisms of divine simplicity (*Faith and Philosophy* 9 [1992], pp. 526–34). As is often the case in analytic work in philosophical theology, little attention is paid to the great care medieval thinkers, especially Thomas, exercise in speaking about God. There are indeed antecedents for a conceptually naive approach to God, but Thomas is not among them. Borrowing from Gilson, Burrell writes, "One may indeed, with the help of Gilson, trace a lineage through medieval platonism from Avicenna to Duns Scotus, which secured conceptual realism by a theory of knowledge and a philosophical method which presumed our formulations to be congruent with the essences of things. No second thoughts here about how we might use the languages and concepts available to us; with clear formulation went simple application" (*Knowing the Unknowable God,* p. 38).

18. . . . . oporteret omnia simpliciter esse unum.

19. Esse omnium est super-essentialis divinitas.

20. O'Rourke, *Pseudo-Dionysius and the Metaphysics of Aquinas*, p. 152. His explication of *esse commune* is helpful: "The concept of *esse commune* neither includes nor excludes any further specification; otherwise nothing could be understood as existing, since in reality *esse* requires a specific determination." Also pertinent is Joseph Owens, "Diversity and Community of Being," in *St. Thomas Aquinas on the Existence of God*, pp. 97–131.

21. Divinum autem esse est absque additione non solum in cogitatione, sed etiam in rerum natura: nec solum absque additione, sed etiam absque receptabilitate additionis. Unde . . . concludi potest quod Deus non sit esse commune sed proprium: etenim ex hoc ipso suum esse ab omnibus aliis distinguitur quod nihil ei addi potest.

22. . . . in nobis simplicissimum invenitur, non tam rem completam, quam rei aliquid esse.

23. . . . dicentes totum mundum esse Deum, non ratione corporis, sed ratione animae.

24. In "Eternity, Awareness, and Action," Stump and Kretzman show that naive assumptions of the theological usefulness of ordinary modes of discourse vitiate many recent criticisms of divine eternity and simplicity. They comment: "An insistence on interpreting 'duration,' 'persistent,' 'life,' and 'present' in their ordinary temporal senses would effortlessly render the concept of eternity incoherent." They trace numerous recent criticisms to such assumptions. See Stump and Kretzman, *Faith and Philosophy* 9 (1992), pp. 463–82.

25. In genere autem causae efficientis fit reductio ad unam causam, . . . a quo sunt omnes res, ut in sequentibus ostendetur.

26. . . . non solum fiendo pervenit ad actum completum, sed id etiam quod est in actu completo absque omni factione,

27. E. Corsini has shown that Dionysius transforms the traditional neo-Platonic practice of applying only negative predicates to God by adding affirmative predicates. See his *Il trattato "De Divinis nominibus" dello Pseudo-Dionigi e i commenti neoplatonici al Parmenide* (Torino, 1962), p. 42.

28. Eadem similia sunt Deo et dissimilia: similia quidem, secundum imitationem eius qui non est perfecte imitabilis qualem in eis contingit esse; dissimilia autem, secundum quod causata habent minus suis causis.

29. In *Aquinas: God and Action* (Notre Dame: University of Notre Dame Press, 1979), David Burrell provides an instructive discussion of the grammatical character of Thomas's discourse about God.

30. Quia enim omnem perfectionem creaturae est in Deo invenire sed per alium modum eminentiorem, quaecumque nomina absolute perfectionem absque defectu designant, de Deo praedicantur et de aliis rebus: sicut est bonitas, sapientia, esse, et alia huiusmodi. . . . Quae vero huiusmodi perfectiones exprimunt cum supereminentiae modo quo Deo conveniunt, de solo Deo dicuntur: sicut summum bonum, primum ens, et alia huiusmodi.

31. See Battista Mondin, "Il principio 'omne agens simile sibi' e l'analogia dei nomi divini nel pensiero di S. Tomasso D'Aquino," *Divus Thomas* (Piacenza) 63 (1960), pp. 336–48.

32. The best treatment of analogous naming in Aquinas remains Ralph McInerny, *The Logic of Analogy: An Interpretation of St. Thomas* (The Hague: M. Nijhoff, 1961).

33. "The Names of God and the Being of Names," pp. 182 and 180, in *The Existence and Nature of God* ed. Alfred Freddoso (Notre Dame: University of Notre Dame Press, 1983), pp. 161–90.

34. René Roques, *La Hiérarchie Céleste*, (Paris: Éditions du Cerf, 1970), pp. xxvi–vii.

35. See the fascinating study of Dionysius by Jean-Luc Marion, *L'idole et la distance: Cinq études* (Paris: Bernard Grasset, 1977). Marion does not seem to realize that a conception of divine being such as that developed by Aquinas is intended precisely to guard against idolatry.

36. In die illa erit Dominus unus et nomen eius unum.

37. See Julien Péghaire, "L'axiome Bonum est diffusivum sui dans le néoplatonisme et le thomisme," *Revue de l'Université d'Ottawa* 1 (1932), Section Spéciale, pp. 5–30. Thomas's most explicit statement of the principle is in *De Veritate* 21, 1, ad 4: "Cum autem dicitur quod bonum est diffusivum secundum sui rationem, non est intelligenda effusio secundum quod importat operationem casuae efficientis, sed secundum quod importat habitudinem causae finalis."

38. Signum perfectionis est alicuius quod *simile possit producere*, ut patet per Philosophum, in IV Meteororum.

39. O'Rourke, *Pseudo-Dionysius and the Metaphysics of Aquinas*, pp. 248–49.

40. In his commenatary on the passage in the *Ethics* where Aristotle rejects the relevance to moral philosophy of the idea of the Good, Thomas is careful to circumscribe the scope of Aristotle's critique: "Aristotle does not intend to refute the opinion of Plato in so far as he posits one good, separate from the whole universe, on which all goods depend." According to Thomas, what Aristotle finds objectionable is that Plato "holds the separate good to be a certain idea common to all goods" (liber I, lectio VI, 79). Thomas refers us to the *Metaphysics* for Aristotle's affirmation of the claim that God is a good, separate from the whole universe. For Thomas's commentary on the pertinent passage, see *Sententia super Metaphysicam* (Turin and Rome: Marietti, 1950), liber XII, lectio 12, 2627–62.

41. Nihil eorum quae conveniunt huic signato inquantum est hoc signatum, possibile est alii convenire.

42. In *On a Complex Theory*, Christopher Hughes rejects the notion that all attributes are identical in God: "If God's goodness is an attribute He shares with creatures, it cannot be an insular attribute, and thus cannot be identical to God" (pp. 67–68). He anticipates the Thomistic rejoinder that the attributes are said

analogically of God and creatures and that the latter doctrine is partly grounded in the claim that God is identical to his existence. Since Hughes denies the latter, he thinks Thomas has no grounds for the former. But, as we have seen, his denial reposes upon a misreading.

43. Omnis actus alteri inhaerens terminationem recipit ex eo in quo est.

44. Omne quod habet aliquam perfectionem, tanto est perfectius quanto illam perfectionem plenius participat. Sed non potest esse aliquis modus, nec etiam cogitari, quo plenius habeatur aliqua perfectio quam ab eo quod per suam essentiam est perfectum et cuius essentia est sua bonitas.

45. Id quod omnino non est infinite distat ab actu.

46. Huic etiam veritati attestantur antiquissimorum philosophorum dicta, qui omnes infinitum posuerunt primum rerum principium, quasi ab ipsa veritate coacti.

47. Cum omne movens moveat per aliqum formam quam intendit in movendo, quod forma per quam movet primum movens, sit universalis forma et universale bonum.

48. . . . intellectus, per speciem rei formatus, intelligendo format in seipso quandam intentionem rei intellectae, quae est ratio ipsius, quam significat definitio.

49. . . . conceptio intellectus divini, prout seipsum intelligit, qui est verbum ipsius, non solum sit similitudo ipsius Dei intellecti, sed etiam omnium quorum est divina essentia similitudo. Sic ergo per unam speciem intelligibilem, quae est divina essentia, et per unam intentionem intellectam, quae est verbum divinum, multa possunt a Deo intelligi.

50. Igitur divina sapientia, seipsam cognoscens, cognoscit omnia, et materialia immaterialiter, et indivisibiliter divisibilia, et multa unitive.

51. There is no strict segregation of topics. Chapter 48 argues that God primarily knows only himself, while 49 introduces the consideration of God's knowledge of other things. With some exceptions, notably in the chapters on God as truth (61–63) and on the presence of will in God (72–74), chapters 49–87 focus on God's relationship to the world.

52. Knowing the Unknowable God, pp. 72–108.

53. Seipso autem cognito, cognoscit quod ab ipso immediate est. Quo cognito, cognoscit iterum quod ab illo immediate est: et sic de omnibus causis mediis usque ad ultimum effectum. Ergo Deus cognoscit quicquid est in re.

54. . . . ultimae perfectiones, quibus perficitur proprium esse eius.

55. Intellectus igitur divinus id quod est proprium unicuique in essentia sua comprehendere potest, intelligendo in quo eius essentiam imitetur, et in quo ab eius perfectione deficit unumquodque.

56. Fran O'Rourke has shown that Thomas's sympathy for Platonic ideas is made possible by Dionysius's correction of Platonic assertions of transcendent pluralism and of separately existing universal causes. O'Rourke, Pseudo-Dionysius and the Metaphysics of Aquinas, pp. 123 and 129.

57. For a comparison of Aquinas with Avicenna and Maimonides, see Burrell, *Knowing the Unknowable God*, pp. 80–91.

58. Deus causat res, inquantum facit eas esse in actu: universalia autem non sunt res subsistentes, sed habent esse solum in singularibus.

59. Artifex autem suae artis cognitione etiam ea quae nondum sunt artificiata cognoscit.

60. Temporis duratio successione prioris et posterius extenditur. Translation by Anton Pegis, *Summa Contra Gentiles*, I (Notre Dame: University of Notre Dame Press, 1977).

61. . . . cum res quaelibet operetur per suam formam, a qua est aliquod esse rei, oportet fontale principium totius esse, a quo est etiam omnis forma, omnis operationis principium esse; cum effectus casuarum secundarum in causas primas principalius reducantur.

62. Dominium autem quod habet voluntas supra suos actos, per quod in eius est potestate velle vel non velle, excludit determinationem virtutis ad unum, et violentiam causae exterius agentis.

63. Obviously, Thomas's introductory comments do not resolve all difficulties concerning contingency, human freedom, and God's apparent complicity in the evil deeds of rational creatures. Following Thomas, we will address these in subsequent chapters.

64. . . . ita sit in re sicut intellectus dicit.

65. . . . inquantum propriam sui rationem quae est in mente divina, imitatur.

66. Intellectus autem divinus per suam scientiam est causa rerum. Unde oportet quod scientia eius sit mensura rerum: sicut ars est mensura artificiatorum, quorum unumquodque in tantum perfectum est inquantum arti concordat. Talis igitur est comparatio intellectus divini ad res qualis rerum ad intellectum humanum.

67. The departure from Aristotle on the question of the divine will may be traced to a disagreement over the very notion of will. Many commentators have argued that the notion of will is absent from Aristotle. Still, will in Aquinas is closer to Aristotle's conception of rational appetite than it is to many modern doctrines of will. For a discussion of how the necessity of God's willing his own goodness does not impugn his freedom and of how he can will other things freely, see Stump and Kretzman, "Absolute Necessity," pp. 359–74. The latter issue will be treated in more detail in the next chapter.

68. Sic igitur procedere possumus in assignando divinae voluntatis rationem. Deus vult hominem habere rationem ad hoc quod homo sit; vult autem hominem esse ad hoc quod completio universi sit; vult autem bonum universi esse quia decet bonitatem ipsius.

69. The possible-worlds metaphysics, so popular among analytic philosophers of religion, has no basis in Thomas's texts.

70. Peter Geach has raised questions about Thomas's account of divine omnipotence. See his "Omnipotence," in *Providence and Evil* (Cambridge:

Cambridge University Press, 1977), pp. 3–28. For responses to Geach, see Ralph McInerny, "Aquinas on Divine Omnipotence," in *L'Homme et son univers au moyen âge. Actes du septième congrès international de philosophie medievale*, ed. C. Wenin (Louvain-la-Neuve: Institut Superieur de Philosophie, 1986), pp. 440–44 and Stephen Brock, "The 'ratio omnipotentiae' in Aquinas," *Acta Philosophica* I (1993), pp. 17–42. Brock partly bases his rejoinder to Geach on Thomas's discussion in *Contra Gentiles*, II, 26–27.

71. . . . gaudium et delectatio est quaedam quietatio voluntatis in suo volito.

72. . . . quanto id ex quo est unio est magis intimum amanti, tanto amor fit firmior. . . . Id autem unde omnia Deo uniuntur, scilicet eius bonitas, quam omnia imitantur, est maximum et intimum Deo: cum ipse sit sua bonitas.

73. Unde et divinae virtutes nostrarum exemplares dicuntur: nam quae sunt contracta et particulata, similitudines quaedam absolutorum entium sunt.

74. . . . status omnium bonorum congregatione perfectus.

3. DIVINE ARTISTRY: THE METAPHYSICS AND AESTHETICS OF CREATION

1. Translation by Anderson, adjusted slightly. See *Summa Contra Gentiles*, vol. 2 (Notre Dame: University of Notre Dame Press, 1975). Cum igitur Christiana fides hominem de Deo principaliter instruit, et per lumen divinae revelationis eum creaturarum cognitorem facit, fit in homine quaedam divinae sapientiae similitudo. Hinc est quod dicitur II Cor., III, 18: *Nos vero omnes, revelata facie gloriam Domini speculantes, in eandem imaginem transformamur.*

2. James Weisheipl's thesis in *Friar Thomas* that the structure of the second book "adheres strictly to the needs of the Moslem mission" needs revision (p. 133). His related thesis, that the treatment of creatures in the *Contra Gentiles* is metaphysical, is correct but does not go far enough. It fails to capture Thomas's insistence that the entire discussion occurs under the light of revelation.

3. Pieper understands Aquinas's positive appraisal of the teaching of Aristotle in terms of the doctrine of creation, in *The Silence of St. Thomas: Three Essays*, trans. J. Murray and D. O'Connor (New York: Pantheon Books, 1957), p. 48. Recently Jan Aertsen in *Nature and Creature* and Oliva Blanchette in *The Perfection of the Universe According to Aquinas: A Teleological Cosmology* (University Park: Pennsylvania State University, 1992) have emphasized the importance of creation for Aquinas.

4. . . . Dei cognitioni similior, qui seipsum cognoscens alia intuetur.

5. Relativa sunt quae secundum suum esse ad aliud quodammodo se habent.

6. . . . non quia ipsum referatur, sed quia aliquid aliud refertur ad ipsum.

7. Excessus autem divinae bonitatis supra creaturam per hoc maxime exprimitur quod creaturae non semper fuerunt. Ex hoc enim apparet expresse quod omnia alia praeter ipsum eum habent sui esse auctorem; et quod virtus

eius non obligatur ad huiusmodi effectus producendos, sicut natura ad effectus naturales; et per consequens quod est voluntate agens et intelligens.

8. . . . ens commune et ea quae sunt separata a motu.

9. Fabro brings out the disparity between predicamental or finite causality and transcendental or divine causality in a list of contrasts: agens intrinsecum vs. agens extrinsecum, causa esse vs. causa motus, causa universalis vs. causa particularis. See his *Participation et causalité selon St. Thomas D'Aquin* (Paris: Éditions Béatrice Nauwelaerts, 1961), pp. 381–97.

10. Ex his autem quae praedicta sunt, vitare possumus diversos errores gentilium philosophorum. Quorum quidam posuerunt mundum aeternum. Quidam materiam mundi aeternam, ex qua ex aliquo tempore mundus coepit generari: vel a casu; vel ab aliquo intellectu; aut etiam amore aut lite.

11. Cornelio, Fabro, "The Problem of Being and the Destiny of Man," *International Philosophical Quarterly* 1 (1961), p. 431.

12. Ibid., p. 420. Fabro compares the Thomistic understanding of nothingness with that of Hegel and Heidegger.

13. John Milbank's thesis in *Theology and Social Theory: Beyond Secular Reason* (Oxford: Basil Blackwell, 1990) is compatible with Gilson's view that creation is a doctrine peculiar to Christian philosophy (*Spirit of Medieval Philosophy*, trans. A. H. C. Downes [London: Sheed and Ward, 1936], p. 439). Yet, pace Gilson, Thomas does indeed hold that creation is at least implicit in the texts of Plato and Aristotle. This is not of course creation in time, but creation understood as causal dependence or, in Platonic terms, participation. See Mark Johnson, "Did St. Thomas Attribute a Doctrine of Creation to Aristotle?" *New Scholasticism* 63 (1989), pp. 129–55. In *The Doctrine of Being in the Aristotelian Metaphysics*, 2d ed. (Toronto: PIMS, 1963), Owens argues that Aristotle's God was only a final, not an efficient, cause (p. 13). For a reconsideration and criticism of Owens's position, see Lawrence Dewan, O.P. "St. Thomas, Aristotle, and Creation," *Dionysius* 15 (1991), pp. 81–90.

14. Laura Garcia, "Divine Freedom and Creation," *Philosophical Quarterly* 42 (1992), pp. 191–213. Garcia also rejects functionalist accounts. She concludes, "In Aquinas's account, we find the metaphor of an artist, freely choosing the forms and materials that suitably realize his design. Surely this artistic metaphor, what has guided theological commentary on creation for centuries, is a far more congenial image of God's activity than either the Leibnizian metaphor of a divine calculator or the functionalist metaphor of a divine automaton" (pp. 212–13). The essay is principally a response to the works of two contemporary philosophers: Paul Helm, *Eternal God* (Oxford: Clarendon, 1988), and William Alston, "Divine and Human Action," in *Divine and Human Action*, ed. T. Morris (Ithaca: Cornell University Press, 1988), pp. 257–80, and idem, "Functionalism and Theological Language," *American Philosophical Quarterly*, 22 (1985), pp. 221–30.

15. See, for example, "debitum per modum cuiusdam condecentiae," and "quantum naturae creatae convenit," (II, 28); "potissime . . . manifestatur divina virtus et bonitas," and "hoc igitur convenientissimum fuit diviniae bonitatis" (II, 38); "summo bono competit facere quod melius est" and "Deus instituit secundum convenientem modum suae naturae" (II, 83).

16. In *Heidegger and Aquinas: An Essay on the Overcoming of Metaphysics* (New York: Fordham University Press, 1982), John Caputo asserts, for instance, that Thomas could not have captured the aletheic character of Aristotle's thought because of the vast etymological differences between Greek and Latin terminology. Yet he offers meager textual support for such theses and rarely bothers to determine how Thomas defines and employs crucial terms. In fact, he passively assents to Heidegger's sweeping generalizations about the differences between Greek and Roman culture. Caputo is correct, nonetheless, to criticize Thomists who seek to defend Thomas as an exception to all of Heidegger's criticisms of Western metaphysics. Having acknowledged the opposition between the two, Caputo might have begun a dialogue. Instead, he "creatively" interprets Thomas's reference to his work as straw as a valediction inviting deconstruction. It would be better, initially at least, to read Thomas on his own terms and to avoid importing into that reading alien categories which set production and beauty, causality and manifestation in necessary opposition to one another. It is becoming increasingly evident that the postmodern critique of reason is itself dubious. See, for instance, Alasdair MacIntyre's exchange between the Thomistic conception of philosophy and genealogy in *Three Rival Versions of Moral Enquiry* (Notre Dame: University of Notre Dame Press, 1990), and John Milbank's Augustinian critique of the "ontological violence" inherent in deconstruction, in *Theology and Social Theory: Beyond Secular Reason*, pp. 278–325.

17. Fabro, "The Problem of Being," p. 435.

18. . . . idem sit esse in quo subsistit compositum et forma ipsa.

19. Since the angels cannot be individuated by matter, each angel constitutes a distinct species. In composite creatures, there are terminated and terminating parts. The matter or genus is terminated, while the form or species terminates. But a simple nature does not possess terminating and terminated parts. Species of angels are distinguished according to their grades of being (II, 95).

20. Substantiae autem intellectuali secundum suum genus convenit quod sit per se subsistens, cum habeat per se operationem. . . . De ratione autem rei per se subsistentis non est quod alteri uniatur. Non est igitur de ratione substantiae intellectualis secundum suum genus quod sit corpori unita: etsi sit hoc de ratione alicuius intellectualis substantiae, quae est anima.

21. *Summa Theologiae*, I, 88, 2, ad 4.

22. It is instructive to compare the common account of angels and souls in the *Summa Contra Gentiles* with the separate treatment of them in the *Summa*

Theologiae, wherein the very order of questions underscores the disanalogies between angels and souls (I, 50–58 and 75–89).

23. See Deborah Modrak, "The Nous-Body Problem in Aristotle," *Review of Metaphysics*, 44 (1991), pp. 755–74.

24. . . . nec materia nec forma potest dici ipsum quod est, nec etiam ipsum esse . . . tota substantia est ipsum quod est.

25. Fabro, "Intensive Hermeneutics," pp. 470–71.

26. Ibid., p. 466, and Gilson, *Being and Some Philosophers* (Toronto: PIMS, 1952).

27. Gilson, *Being and Some Philosophers*, p. 163.

28. . . . de necessitate et semper et inseparabiliter ei inest.

29. Anton Pegis, *At the Origins of the Thomistic Notion of Man*, St. Augustine Lecture, 1963 (New York: Macmillan, 1963), p. 57 and p. 37.

30. Support for this view comes from surprising quarters. See Nussbaum and Putnam, "Changing Aristotle's Mind," in *Essays on Aristotle's De Anima*, ed. A. Rorty and M. Nussbaum (Oxford: Clarendon Press, 1992), pp. 51–55.

31. Pieper, *The Silence of St. Thomas*, p. 58.

32. In his "The Inseparability of the Soul from Existence" (*New Scholasticism* 1987 [61], pp. 249–70), Joseph Owens argues that Thomas proves "only the soul's indestructibility," not its "vital activity" (p. 269). As we shall see, Pegis came to adopt a similar position.

33. MacIntyre, *Whose Justice? Which Rationality?*, pp. 165–208 and 349–88.

34. For an excellent comparison of the methods operative in Euclid's geometry and in the work of Descartes, see David Lachtermann's *Ethics of Geometry: A Genealogy of Modernity* (New York: Routledge, 1989). The points of divergence also apply to the division between Aristotle and Aquinas on the one hand, and Descartes on the other.

35. See Miles Burnyeat, "Is an Aristotelian Philosophy of Mind Still Credible?" in *Essays on Aristotle's De Anima*, ed. A. Rorty and M. Nussbaum (Oxford: Clarendon Press, 1992), chap. 2.

36. Nussbaum and Putnam, "Changing Aristotle's Mind," pp. 28–29.

37. Thomas Aquinas, *In Aristotelis De Anima Commentarium*, ed. Angelus Pirotta , 4th ed. (Turin and Rome: Marietti, 1965), liber I, lectio I, 7.

38. . . . quod est subiectum quoddam illius formae intellectae.

39. . . . habens enim intellectum est intelligens.

40. Operationes enim vitae comparantur ad animam ut actus secundi ad primum. . . . In quocumque igitur invenitur aliqua operatio vitae, oportet in eo ponere aliquam partem animae quae comparetur ad illam operationem sicut actus primus ad secundum. Sed homo habet propriam operationem supra alia animalia, scilicet intelligere et ratiocinari. . . . Ergo oportet in homine ponere aliquod principium quod proprie dat speciem homini. . . . Hoc autem

non potest esse intellectus passivus . . . quia principium praedictae operationis oportet esse *impassibile et non mixtum corpori*, ut Philosophus probat.

41. Bernard Lonergan, *Verbum: Word and Idea in Aquinas* (Notre Dame: University of Notre Dame Press, 1967), p. 218.

42. . . . materiae corporalis ut recipientis et subiecti ad aliquid altius elevati: substantiae autem intellectualis ut principii, et secundum propriae naturae congruentiam.

43. In the *Commentary on the De Anima*, Thomas frequently recurs to the fact that the study of the soul is part of natural philosophy. As a consequence, questions about the intellect are the last to be investigated in an inquiry that begins from what is common to all principles of animate life and only later turns to what is peculiar to humans. When he does comment on Aristotle's discussion of the separability of the intellect, he is careful to circumscribe the scope of the inquiry. He notes, for instance, that the question of whether and how a separated soul might understand is beyond the scope of natural philosophy (Book III, lc. 10, 745).

44. Modrak, "The Nous-Body Problem in Aristotle," p. 758. For Modrak's general view of Aristotle's theory of human knowledge, a view which seeks to provide a unified account of various teachings, see her *Aristotle: The Power of Perception* (Chicago: University of Chicago Press, 1987). The opening chapter of the work rehearses and criticizes recent attempts to understand Aristotle's psychology in terms of the functionalist, dualist, and materialist models of mind.

45. At issue here is the debate between Thomas and Averroës over whether Aristotle's definition of the soul as the form and act of the body applies univocally to all souls. In *Averroës' Doctrine of Immortality* (Waterloo: Wilfred Laurier University Press, 1984), Ovey N. Mohammed articulates and defends Averroës' argument that soul is equivocal. For a response to the Averroistic position, see the interpretive essays by Ralph McInerny in his *Aquinas Against the Averroists: On There Being Only One Intellect* (West Lafayette: Purdue University Press, 1993), pp. 188–204.

46. Anthony Kenny, *Aquinas on Mind* (London: Routledge, 1993), and Gregory Coulter, "Aquinas on the Identity of Mind and Substantial Form," *American Catholic Philosophical Quarterly* 64 (1990), pp. 161–79. Thomas does not identify soul and mind. If he were to do so, he would collapse the distinction between first and second act, between form and power. He does regularly speak of any soul as being named from the highest power in it, but this is not to identify soul and mind *simpliciter*. Thus, soul is subsistent in virtue of the *mens*.

47. Nussbaum and Putnam, "Changing Aristotle's Mind," p. 54.

48. Coulter, "Aquinas on the Identity of Mind and Substantial Form," p. 174.

49. Kenny, *Aquinas on Mind*, pp. 150–51.

50. Hic autem effectus, qui est abstrahere formas universales a phantasmatibus, est in intentione nostra.

51. . . . addiscere nihil aliud est quam *acquirere perfectam habitudinem coniungendi se intelligentiae agenti ad recipiendum ab eo formam intelligibilem.*

52. John Cleary, "On the Terminology 'Abstraction' in Aristotle," *Phronesis* 32 (1985), pp. 13–45. Cleary's reading is an alternative to that of Charles de Koninck, "Abstraction from Matter," *Laval Théologique et Philosophique*, 13 (1957), pp. 133–96, and 16 (1960), pp. 53–69, 169–88. De Koninck's interpretation is inspired by Aquinas's exegesis of Aristotle.

53. Licet natura generis et speciei nunquam sit nisi in his individuis, intelligit tamen intellectus naturam speciei et generis non intelligendo principia individuata: et hoc est intelligere universalia.

54. . . . id quod repugnat intelligibilitati est materialitas.

55. In his *Expositio super librum Boethii De Trinitate* (Leiden: Brill, 1955), Thomas states that the objects of the sciences share in common their universality and immateriality, which they receive from the intellect (V, 1). The different sorts of abstraction, for instance, that of form from matter or whole from part, distinguish mathematical from physical science and are determined by peculiar modes of defining (V, 2–4). The explanation of what abstraction means is compatible with Cleary's "method of finding the primary subject of attributes." The natural philosopher considers physical body qua physical, that is, as including common, sensible matter, and leaves behind or abstracts from particular, signate matter. The mathematician, on the other hand, studies substance as subject to quantity and considers substance without considering, or by abstracting from, signate or common matter. As Cleary notes, mathematics does not abstract from all matter, since its mode of defining includes intelligible matter.

56. . . . ex sensu fit memoria, ex multis memoriis unum experimentum; ex multis experimentis universalis acceptio, quae est principium scientiae et artis.

57. . . . divina sapientia coniungit fines superiorum principiis inferiorum.

58. Umberto Eco, *The Aesthetics of Thomas Aquinas* (Cambridge: Harvard University Press, 1988), p. 48. Previously published as *Il problema estetico in Tomasso d'Aquino* (Milan: 1956 and 1970).

59. . . . erit quidem necessarium multiplicari formam secundum multiplicationem materiae, id est simul cum materia, et proportionem ipsius: non autem ita quod dependeat unitas vel multitudo ipsius formae a materia.

60. Cum anima humana . . . sit *in confinio corporum et incorporearum substantiarum, quasi in horizonte existens aeternitatis et temporis,* recedens ab infimo, appropinquat ad summum.

61. Anton Pegis brings out the difficulties with this argument and the resolution of them in the later *Summa.* See his "The Separated Soul and Its Nature in St. Thomas," in *St. Thomas Aquinas 1274–1974: Commemorative Studies* (Toronto: PIMS, 1974), vol. 1, pp. 131–59. Also see *Summa Theologiae,* I, 89, 1. Yet Pegis does not note that this particular argument is anomalous in the dialectical segment of the second book of the *Contra Gentiles.*

62. Unumquodque enim Deus instituit secundum convenientem modum suae naturae.

63. Among the more important studies of Aquinas's aesthetics are: Francis J. Kovach, *Die Aesthetik von Aquin* (Berlin, 1961); Armand A. Maurer, *About Beauty* (Houston: The Center for Thomistic Studies, 1983); Umberto Eco, *The Aesthetics of Thomas Aquinas*; Mark Jordan "The Evidence of the Transcendentals and the Place of Beauty in Thomas Aquinas," *International Philosophical Quarterly* 29 (1989), pp. 393–406.

64. . . . idem in subiecto, quia tam claritas quam consonantia sub ratione boni continentur. See Aquinas, *Expositio super Dionysiam De divinis nominibus*, IV, 5 (Turin and Rome: Marietti, 1950), and *Summa Theologiae*, II-II, 27, 1, ad 3).

65. Translation by Anderson.

66. . . . ratione differunt: nam pulchra addit supra bonum, ordinem ad vim cogniscitivam (*Expositio . . . de divinis nominibus*, IV, 5.)

67. *Summa Theologiae*, I-II, 33, 1.

68. Sallis, *Being and Logos*, p. 422.

69. As Thomas puts it in the other *Summa*: "from love of God one is inflamed to behold his beauty." *Summa Theologiae*, II-II, 180, 1 and 180, 7 ad 1.

70. Si igitur creaturarum bonitas, pulchritudo et suavitas sic animos hominum allicit, ipsius Dei fontana bonitas, rivulis bonitatum in singulis creaturis repertis diligenter comparata, animas hominum inflammatas totaliter ad se trahet. Unde in Psalmos . . . dicitur: Inebriabuntur ab ubertate domus tuae, . . . et sicut torrente voluptatis tuae potabis eos: quoniam apud te est fons vitae.

4. THE DIALECTIC OF HUMAN INQUIRY AND THE NARRATIVE OF DIVINE PROVIDENCE

1. Final causality has not been well received since the seventeenth century, yet recent texts have shown many modern criticisms to be misguided. See, for instance, Harre and Madden, *Causal Powers: A Theory of Natural Necessity* (Oxford: Blackwell, 1975), and Martha Nussbaum's *De Motu Animalium: text with translation and interpretive essays* (Princeton: Princeton University Press, 1978).

2. Paul Ricoeur, *The Symbolism of Evil* trans. E. Buchanan (New York: Harper, 1967), p. 233.

3. An act is moral only if it is voluntary. Yet moral evil does not reside in an autonomous will. The will is free because it participates in reason, which is able to apprehend and deliberate about a multiplicity of goods. The defect of ordering in reason precedes fault in the will. Error is more likely to occur in moral deliberation than in speculative reasoning since the former has to do with sensible particulars, which are variable, require careful negotiation, and easily distract vagrant appetites (I, 9). An elaborate account—such as the one in the *Summa*

Theologiae—of moral error would develop the connection between perception, passion, habit, and choice. What Thomas insists upon in this context is that, even though the intellectual error precedes volition, moral evil is nonetheless voluntary. After reason's presentation of a particular, apparent good, the will remains capable of willing or not willing.

4. Malum non habet causam efficientem, sed deficientem (*De civitate Dei*, XII, 7).

5. Bernard Lonergan, *Grace and Freedom: Operative Grace in the Thought of St. Thomas Aquinas*, ed. J. Patout Burns (New York: Herder and Herder, 1971), p. 113.

6. As we noted earlier, the argument for an unmoved in the *Physics* need not reach God, but the argument of the *Metaphysics*, which perfects the inquiry of the *Physics*, does reach God.

7. . . . formae quae sunt in materia, venerunt a formis quae sunt sine materia.

8. . . . aliquid prae-existens obtinendum.

9. Chenu argues that Thomas's understanding of creation as an intelligible *ordo* makes possible a positive appraisal of the intelligibility of history. See his "Création et histoire," in *Saint Thomas Aquinas, 1274–1974: Commemorative Studies* (Toronto: PIMS, 1974), vol. 2, p. 393.

10. Ultimus igitur finis generationis totius est anima humana, et in hanc tendit materia sicut in ultimam formam.

11. . . . omnium divinius est Dei cooperatorem fieri.

12. Ex bonitate autem Dei est quod aliis esse largitur; unumquodque enim agit in quantum est actu perfectum.

13. . . . maxime perfectum est unum quodque quando potest alterum sibi simile facere.

14. For an extensive bibliography, see M. Matthys, O.P. "Quid ratio naturalis doceat de possibilitate visionis beatae secundum S. Thomam in summa contra gentiles," *Divus Thomas* (Piacenza) 39 (1936), p. 305. The better-known debate, which focused only incidentally on the *Contra Gentiles*, over the ultimate end in Aquinas was sparked by Henri de Lubac's *Surnaturel* (Paris: Aubier, 1946). For a discussion of the initial responses to that work, see Phillip J. Donnelly, "Discussions on the Supernatural Order," *Theological Studies* 9 (1948), pp. 213–49.

15. . . . relinquitur quod ultima hominis felicitas sit in contemplatione veritatis.

16. Si autem aliqui fuerunt qui sic de divinis veritatem invenerunt demonstrationis via quod eorum aestimationi nulla falsitas adiungeretur, patet eos fuisse paucissimos.

17. John Finnis, "Practical Reasoning, Human Goods, and the End of Man," *Proceedings of the American Catholic Philosophical Association*, ed. Daniel O. Dahlstrom 58 (1987), pp. 99–151. Also see Finnis's *Natural Law and Natural Rights*

(Oxford: Clarendon Press, 1980). For a contrary view, see Ernest Fortin's review of Finnis's book *Natural Law and Natural Rights* in the *Review of Politics* 44 (1982), pp. 590–612.

18. Hannah Arendt, *The Human Condition* (Chicago: The University of Chicago Press, 1958), p. 220. Nussbaum speaks similarly of the "aspiration to rational self-sufficiency," in her *The Fragility of Goodness*, p. 3. For a brief but suggestive comparison of their views, see Joseph Dunne, *Back to the Rough Ground* (Notre Dame: University of Notre Dame Press, 1993), pp. 102–3.

19. Josef Pieper, *Happiness and Contemplation*, trans. Richard and Clara Winston (New York: Pantheon, 1958), p. 71. For an excellent discussion of various contemporary views of happiness and their relationship to the conversation among Thomists, see Deal W. Hudson, "Contemporary Views of Happiness," in *The Great Ideas Today* (Chicago: Encyclopaedia Britannica, 1992), pp. 170–216.

20. Some of the texts in question here are mathematical and scientific; yet little attention is given to these in recent arguments over the relationship between *theoria*, *techne*, *poesis*, and *praxis*. A rare exception—one that spells out in detail the contrast between ancient and modern conceptions of the intellect—is David Lachterman's *The Ethics of Geometry: A Genealogy of Modernity*. The introductory chapter, "Construction as the Mark of the Modern" (pp. 1–24) locates the project within the context of postmodern debates.

21. It seems more likely that the life of action would be allied to making. If, as MacIntyre argues in *After Virtue* (Notre Dame: University of Notre Dame Press, 1984), pp. 190–209, action cannot be understood apart from narrative, then the question of whether narratives are not constructs is unavoidable. In the Christian cosmos, there is no gap between the narratives of scripture and creation, on the one hand, and the real being of things, on the other. But even these, as Thomas tirelessly points out, are constructs. Their being is derivative and their goal is to lead beyond themselves to the author of the whole. As we shall see, one of the chief strategies of scriptural narrative is to undermine the idolatry of narrative.

22. Some have deployed developmental arguments to show that the passages praising contemplation are but pieces of immature Platonism in Aristotle's texts. So Nussbaum argues (*The Fragility of Goodness*, pp. 373–77). A similar approach is adopted by R. A. Gauthier in his *La morale d'Aristote* (Paris, 1958), where he argues that the *Ethics* was written prior to the *De Anima* and hence did not benefit from the mature teaching on the unity of soul and body. If it had been written later, the passages on contemplation would have been excised. See the response of Anton Pegis, "St. Thomas and the Nichomachean Ethics," *Mediaeval Studies* 25 (1963), pp. 1–25.

23. Nussbaum, "Transcending Humanity," in *Love's Knowledge* (Oxford: Oxford University Press, 1990), p. 379.

24. . . . . videndo ipsas substantias separatas, participabit modum illius cognitionis quo substantia separata, intelligens se, intelligit Deum.

25. . . . ad cognoscendum quidditatem . . . non habentem aliquam quidditatem.

26. Cornelio Fabro, "The Transcendentality of Ens-Esse and the Ground of Metaphysics," *International Philosophical Quarterly* 6 (1966), pp. 389–427.

27. Aristotle, *Physics*, II, 2, 193b31–35.

28. . . . omnis intellectus naturaliter desiderat divinae substantiae visionem.

29. Jorge Laporta, *La destinée de la nature humaine selon Thomas d'Aquin* (Paris: J. Vrin, 1965), p. 58.

30. The dialectical engagement of *auctoritates* continues in chapters 46 and 47, where Thomas repudiates the views that the soul can understand itself through itself and that in this life the soul can see God through his essence. Thomas adduces a number of Augustinian passages that appear to affirm the position Thomas rejects. In each case Aquinas argues that Augustine cannot be held to mean what he seems to say. Hence he interprets an Augustinian passage on the immediacy of the soul's self-knowledge as claiming that through itself the soul knows only that it is, not what it is, and proceeds to cite the Aristotelian thesis that the soul knows itself in the same manner as it knows other things. The Augustinian passages on self-knowledge might well be read as reformulations of certain Arabic theses concerning the possibility of a natural, immediate knowledge of God. If we know God through knowing separate substances, might we not know separate substances through knowing our own soul? Thomas agrees that the soul is the starting point for our knowledge of separate substances, but he argues that the soul is not known directly and that it affords knowledge only of the remote genus of separate substances. In a number of other passages, Augustine appears to hold that the soul has a direct apprehension of God in this life, indeed that such an apprehension is the ground of all human knowledge. Understood Platonically, these passages will not bear scrutiny. Thomas attempts to save Augustine's texts by salvaging some formulation of a relationship between immutable truth and human judgment. He identifies the immutable truth with the knowledge of first principles that we apprehend not in, but through or by means of, the light of the first truth. He then cites successively the Apostle's statement that we see now in a mirror and Aristotle's thesis that human knowing never exceeds the senses, even in self-knowledge.

31. In quo satis apparet quantum angustiam patiebantur hinc inde eorum praeclara ingenia.

32. . . . a quibus angustiis liberabimus si ponamus, secundum probationes praemissas, hominem ad veram felicitatem post hanc vitam pervenire posse, anima hominis immortali existente, in quo statu anima intelliget per modum quo intelligunt substantiae separatae.

33. It also runs counter to the principles operative in the arguments for the resurrection of the body in the fourth book, which hold that the salvation of the person requires the body.

34. See Pegis, "The Separated Soul and Its Nature in St. Thomas." See also *Summa Theologiae*, I, 89, 1.

35. Aertsen, *Nature and Creature*, p. 217.

36. Dominus "mercedem nobis in caelis" promittit, Matt. 5:12.

37. Of all the sections in the second and third books, those that focus on the dialectical engagement of philosophical authors contain the fewest references to scripture. The prominence of scriptural passages in the discussion of the vision of God is thus quite significant.

38. McInerny shows that Aristotle acknowledged the "gap between what we aspire to and what we can attain in the matter of happiness." See the *Question of Christian Ethics* (Washington, D.C.: Catholic University of America Press, 1993), p. 38. McInerny is responding to Gauthier's claim that Thomas's ethics is a distortion of that of Aristotle.

39. Jordan, "The Names of God and the Being of Names," p. 172.

40. Kevin Staley, "Happiness: The Natural End of Man?" *The Thomist* 53 (1989), pp. 215–34.

41. Corbin, *Le chemin*, p. 624.

42. "Nature and Spirit: Some Reflections on the Problem of the End of Man," *Proceedings of the American Catholic Philosophical Association* 23 (1949), p. 69.

43. Omnes aliae naturae possunt assequi suos fines naturales per media consentanes naturae: cur ergo natura humana erit in hoc peioris conditionis? *De ultimo fine hominis* (disput. 15, sectio 2, note 6), as quoted in Laporta, *La destinée de la nature humaine*.

44. Laporta, *La destinée de la nature humaine*, p. 127.

45. See ibid., pp. 77–89.

46. Si enim naturae aliquid essentiale subtrahitur vel additur, iam altera natura erit.

47. Divina substantia non sic est extra facultatem creati intellectus quasi aliquid omnino extraneum ab ipso, sicut sonus a visu, vel substantia immaterialis a sensu.

48. Divina substantia est primum intelligibile, et totius intellectualis cognitionis principium.

49. The danger, as Oeullet puts it, is that "everything is already in place before the Savior and the Church come concretely onto the scene. Grace hovers transcendentally over events." Thus, human self-transcendence encroaches upon the "domain proper to divine freedom alone." See Oeullet, "Paradox and/or Supernatural Existential," *Communio*, 18 (1991), p. 271. This was the persistent criticism of de Lubac's position. See the remarks of Donnelly, "Discussions on the Supernatural Order," pp. 241–49. The objection that de Lubac's view would undermine Aquinas's conception of the intelligibility of natures was put by Gerard Smith in "Philosophy and the Unity of Man's Ultimate End," *Proceedings of the ACPA* 27 (1953), pp. 60–83.

50. Hans Urs von Balthasar, *Theodramatik III: Die Handlung*, pp. 71–72, as quoted by Marc Oeullet in "Paradox and/or Supernatural Existential," p. 261. Balthasar has Rahner in mind.

51. Quod enim est superioris naturae proprium, non potest consequi natura inferior nisi per actionem superioris naturae cuius est proprium. . . . Nulla igitur intellectualis substantia potest videre Deum per ipsam divinam essentiam nisi Deo hoc faciente.

52. "Paradox and/or Supernatural Existential," Ouellet, p. 270.

53. Quandocumque enim aliqua ordinantur ad aliquem finem, omnia dispositioni illius subiacent ad quem principaliter pertinet ille finis.

54. Nihil est aliud regere et gubernare per providentiam quam movere per intellectum aliqua ad finem.

55. Pegis, "Qu'est-ce que la Summa contra Gentiles," p. 173.

56. . . . impressio agentis non remanet in effectu, cessante actione agentis, nisi vertatur in naturam effectus.

57. Ultimum in bonitate et perfectione inter ea in quae potest agens secundum, est illud quod potest ex virtute agentis primi. Nam complementum virtutis agentis secundi est ex agente primo. Quod autem est in omnibus effectibus perfectissimum, est esse. Quaelibet enim natura vel forma perficitur per hoc quod est actu; et comparatur ad esse in actu sicut potentia ad actum ipsum. Igitur esse est quod agentia secunda agunt in virtute agentis primi.

58. For a discussion of the philosophical and theological roots of this tradition, see Alfred J. Freddoso, "Medieval Aristotelianism and the Case Against Secondary Causation in Nature," in *Divine and Human Action*, ed. Thomas V. Morris (Ithaca: Cornell University Press, 1988), pp. 74–118.

59. Thomas Aquinas, *Sententia super Peri Hermeneias* (Turin and Rome: Marietti, 1955), liber I, lectio 14.

60. Ex abundantia perfectionis . . . possit alteri communicare.

61. . . . non sic idem effectus causae naturali et divinae virtuti attribuitur quasi partim a Deo, et partim a naturali agente fiat, sed totus ab utroque secundum alium modum: sicut idem effectus totus attribuitur instrumento, et principali agenti etiam totus.

62. Fabro, *Participation*, p. 503. Thomas's account of what Fabro calls "transcendental causality" follows from the first thesis of the neo-Platonic *Liber de Causis*: "Therefore nothing is caused by a secondary cause unless through the power of the first cause" (Et non fit igitur causatum causae secundae nisi per virtutem causae primae).

63. For a corrective, see Ross, "Creation II," in *Divine and Human Action*, pp. 115–40 and Burrell, *Knowing the Unknowable God*, pp. 66, 99, and 102–3. To speak of God's knowing propositions is to indulge in unhelpful anthropomorphism, while the model of possible worlds extends human speculation far beyond

its capacity. In a generally lucid and illuminating piece on Thomist and Molinist accounts of providence, Thomas Flint sees a weakness in the Thomist's inability to account for evil. He writes, "For given the Thomist account of providence, the existence of evil . . . would seem to be all but inexplicable. Surely there are possible worlds that contain free beings but no evil. . . ." The audacious use of possible-worlds logic is baffling. Is logical possibility the real issue here? How could we possibly know what might actually happen in various worlds? Flint, "Two Accounts of Providence," in *Divine and Human Action*, pp. 147–81.

64. "Creation II," p. 132.

65. Ibid., p. 131.

66. . . . quando aliquid bonum accidit sibi praeter intentionem, *Magna Moralia*, II, 8.

67. Ad ipsum, non solum in rebus humanis, sed nec in aliqua re potest esse aliquid casuale et improvisum.

68. Oportet . . . vel providentiam non esse certam, vel omnia ex necessitate contingere.

69. Est enim divina providentia per se causa quod his effectus contingenter proveniat.

70. See Lonergan, *Grace and Freedom*, pp. 105–6.

71. Nullo enim modo melius manifestari potest quod tota natura divinae subiecta est voluntati. . . . Ex hoc enim apparet quod ordo rerum processit ab eo et non per necessitatem naturae, sed per liberam voluntatem.

72. Admiramur enim aliquid cum, effectum videntes, causam ignoramus.

73. Forma nihil sit aliud quam divina similitudo participata in rebus.

74. Omnes creaturae comparantur ad Deum sicut artificiata ad artificem. . . . Unde tota natura est sicut quoddam artificiatum divinae artis. Non est autem contra rationem artifici si artifex aliter aliquid operetur in suo artificio, etiam postquam ei primam formam dedit.

75. . . . percipere potest quomodo diversimode sit aliquid bonum vel malum secundum quod congruit diversis individuis, temporibus, et locis.

76. . . . lex nihil est aliud sit quam quaedam ratio et regula operandi.

77. . . . isti inclinantur ex seipsis ad iustitiam faciendum.

78. Sunt igitur aliquae operationes naturaliter homini convenientes, quae sunt secundum se rectae, et non solum quasi lege positae.

79. Exterius autem sacrificium repraesentativum est interioris veri sacrificii, secundum quod mens humana seipsam Deo offert. Offert autem se mens nostra Deo quasi suae creationis principio, quasi suae operationis auctori, quasi suae beatitudinis fini.

80. Aristotle, *Politics*, II, 5, 1263b36–40.

81. . . . non solum metitur quantitatem rei quae in usum venit, sed conditionem personae, et intentionem eius, opportunitatem loci et temporis . . . , quae in actibus virtutum requiruntur.

82. Manifestum est autem quod mendicitas cum quadam abiectione est. Sicut enim pati ignobilius est quam agere, accipere quam dare, et regi et obedire quam gubernare et imperare: quamvis, propter aliquid adiunctum, possit recompensatio fieri.

83. See the discussion of the gift of wisdom and the infused virtue of charity in the *Summa Theologiae*, II-II, 45, 2–3, where the former is rooted in the latter.

84. Quandocumque ab aliquo agente movetur aliquid ad id quod est proprium illi agenti, oportet quod a principio ipsum mobile subdatur impressionibus agentis imperfecte, quasi alienis et non propriis sibi, quousque fiant ei propriae in termino motus.

85. Cum aliquis a magistro docetur, oportet quod a principio conceptiones magistri recipiat non quasi eas per se intelligens, sed per modum credulitatis, quasi supra capacitatem existentes: in fine autem, quando iam edoctus fuerit, eas poterit intelligere.

86. Joseph Wawrykow, " 'Merit' in the Theology of Thomas Aquinas," *Medieval Philosophy and Theology* 2 (1992), pp. 97–116. Wawrykow's thesis confirms the Augustinian character of Thomas's mature teaching on grace. See Henri Bouillard, *Conversion et grâce chez Thomas d'Aquin* (Paris: Aubier, 1944).

87. Sallis, *Being and Logos*, p. 14.

88. Chenu, "Création et histoire," p. 394.

89. An non habet potestatem figulis luti ex eadem massa facere aliud quidem vas in honorem, aliud vero in contumeliam?

90. Louis Mackey, *Kierkegaard: A Kind of Poet* (Philadelphia: University of Pennsylvania Press, 1971), p. 273. Between Thomas and Kierkegaard, there are of course many differences, perhaps chief among which is the latter's emphasis on the "free election of existential possibility" (p. 274). Still, the ending of the third book does underscore the ultimate possibilities and the need for human cooperation with grace.

5. THE DRAMA OF REDEMPTION

1. . . . quia perfectum hominis bonum est ut quoquo modo Deum cognoscat, ne tam nobilis creatura omnino in vanum esse videretur, velut finem proprium attingere non valens, datur homini quaedam via per quam in Dei cognitionem ascendere possit: ut scilicet, quia omnes rerum perfectiones quodam ordine a summo rerum vertice Deo descendunt, ipse, ab inferioribus incipiens et gradatim ascendens, in Dei cognitionem proficiat.

2. Corbin, *Le chemin*, p. 680.

3. Ibid., p. 645.

4. Corbin's preoccupation with the "chemin" of Thomas's theology lends itself to a linear reading of the text. But is it evident that all of Thomas's major works are attempts at achieving the same goal? Is the unified life of wisdom more

adequately characterized in the *Summa Theologiae?* That does not even seem to be the point of the latter work.

5. Si igitur ipsae viae imperfecte cognoscuntur a nobis, quomodo per eas ad perfecte cognoscendum ipsarum viarum principium poterimus pervenire?

6. Leo Strauss, "The Mutual Influence of Philosophy and Theology," *Independent Journal of Philosophy*, 3 (1979), pp. 113–14.

7. *La théologie comme science au XIII siècle*, 3d ed. (Paris: J. Vrin, 1957). Also see his essay, "Les Magistri: La "science" théologique," in *La théologie au douzieme siècle*, Études de philosophie Médiévale, 3d ed. (Paris: J. Vrin, 1976).

8. See Thomas's commentary on the prologue to John's Gospel, where he interprets the various sections of the prologue as combatting misconceptions of the Incarnation. The order of John's narration "proceeds according to the order of teaching" (*secundum ordinem doctrinae congruentissime sequitur*). See *Lectura super Johannem* (Rome: Marietti, 1952), I, lc. 2, 53.

9. In the commentary on John's Gospel, Thomas argues that the prologue rebuts the gentiles' assertion of a plurality of first principles, the view of the ancient natural philosophers that the world arose from chance, Plato's supposition of intelligences distinct from God, and Aristotle's theory of the eternity of the world (I, lc. 1, 60–67).

10. On the relationship between tradition and theological discourse, see Etienne Ménard, *La tradition: Révélation, Ecriture, Eglise selon saint Thomas d'Aquin*, Studia 18 (Paris: Desclée de Brouwer, 1964).

11. . . . quid de ea secundum Sacrae Scripturae documenta teneri debeat.

12. . . . de David et Salomone haec verba dicantur, secundum morem Scripturae, in alterius figuram, in quo universa compleantur.

13. Augustine, *De Doctrina Christiana*, I, 6.

14. See Aquinas, *Lectura Super Johannem* (Rome: Marietti, 1952) (I, lc. 1, 60–7) for a discussion of Arius, Photinus, and Sabellius.

15. Haec est autem Evangelistae narratio, *cuius testimonium verum est* [Joan. XIX, 35; XXI, 24], quod Christus Filium Dei se dicebat et Deo aeqalem, et propterea eum Judaei persequebantur.

16. Taught by . . . the documents of sacred scripture, the Catholic Church confesses Christ to be the true and natural son of God, eternal, equal to the Father, true God, of the same essence and nature with the Father, begotten, and not made but created.

17. Fides ergo Catholica, media via incedens, confitetur, cum Ario et Photino, contra Sabellium, aliam personam Patris et Filii, et Filium genitum, Patrem vero omnino ingenitum: cum Sabello vero, contra Photinum et Arium, Christum verum et naturalem Deum et eiusdem naturae cum Patre, licet non eiusdem personae. Ex quo etiam iudicium veritatis Catholicae sumi potest: nam vero, ut Philosophus dicit . . . etiam falsa attestantur: falsa vero non solum a veris, sed etiam ab invicem distant.

18. MacIntyre's conception of the rationality of traditions and of the role of translation in tradition applies here. See his _Whose Justice? Which Rationality?_ pp. 349–88. Of course, the Christian tradition is not reversible in the way philosophical traditions are.

19. Quomodo accipienda sit generatio in divinis.

20. Et cum Verbum Dei sit eiusdem naturae cum Deo dicente, et sit similitudo ipsius; sequitur quod hic naturalis processus sit in similitudinem eius a quo est processio cum identitate naturae. Haec est autem verae generationis in rebus viventibus. . . . Est ergo Verbum Dei _genitum_ vere a Deo dicente: et eius processio _generatio vel nativitas_ dici potest.

21. Lonergan, _Verbum,_ p. 206.

22. Sunt igitur plures res subsistentes, si relationes considerentur: est autem una res subsistens, si consideretur essentia.

23. In _De Veritate_ IV, 2, Thomas states the difficulty thus, "It is not immediately evident whether this name 'verbum' implies a real procession; and so it is difficult to determine whether it should be named essentially or personally" (Non statim fit evidens utrum hoc nomen verbum processum realem importet . . . ; et ita difficile est videre utrum essentialiter vel personaliter dicatur).

24. Missing this point, some have supposed that, while Thomas explicitly repudiates Anselm's project of providing necessary reasons for the existence of the Trinity, in practice he gives a rational proof. See Cyprian Vagaggini, "Le hatise des rationes necessariae de saint Anselme dans la théologie des processions trinitaires de saint Thomas," trans. J. Evrad, _Spicilegium Beccense. Congrès International du ix centenaire de l'arrivée d'Anselme au Bec_ (Paris: J. Vrin, 1959), pp. 103–39. For an extended response to Vagaggini, see Robert L. Richard, S.J., _The Problem of an Apologetical Perspective in the Trinitarian Theology of St. Thomas Aquinas_ (Rome: Gregorian University Press, 1963).

25. . . . quod autem procedat intra suum principium, invenitur solum in operatione intellectus et voluntatis.

26. Esse igitur Dei in voluntate sua per modum amoris, non est esse accidentale, sicut in nobis, sed essentiale.

27. Non enim amaretur aliquid nisi aliquo modo cognosceretur; nec solum amati cognitio amatur, sed secundum quod in se bonum est. Necesse est igitur quod amor quo Deus est in voluntate divina ut amatum in amante, et a Verbo Dei, et a Deo cuius est Verbum, procedat.

28. D. Juvenal Merriell shows that Thomas's mature teaching on the Trinity is chiefly indebted to Augustine's _De Trinitate._ See his _To the Image of the Trinity_ (Toronto: PIMS, 1990). Also see John E. Sullivan, _The Image of God: The Doctrine of St. Augustine and Its Influence_ (Dubuque: Priory Press, 1963).

29. Thomas will soon argue in detail that the Holy Spirit proceeds both from the Father and the Son (IV, 24–25). The chief opponent to this position is the Eastern Church. Accordingly, Thomas cites the Church Fathers and the

councils more here than he does in any other section of the fourth book. The task of trinitarian theology is to discern some principle whereby the Son can be distinguished from the Spirit. For a study of Thomas's teaching and his use of sources, see Jaroslav Pelikan, "The Doctrine of the Filioque in Thomas Aquinas and Its Patristic Antecedents: An Analysis of Summa Theologiae, Part I, Question 36," in *St. Thomas Aquinas 1274–1974: Commemorative Studies*, vol. 1 (Toronto: PIMS, 1974), pp. 315–36.

30. In the commentary on John's Gospel, Thomas equates the "darkness" with the penalties of sin, demons, and error or ignorance. He adds that the verb "comprehend" means both "understand" and "conquer." The darkness did not conquer the light, "since his splendor shines through the whole world" (quia eius claritas per totum mundum fulgeret, I, lc. 3, 105–7).

31. In separate inquiries, Lafont and Geiger argue that the centrality of the *imago Dei* to the structure of the *Summa Theologiae* is testimony to Thomas's fidelity to the Church Fathers. See Lafont, *Structures et Méthode*, pp. 265–66, and Louis B. Geiger, "L'homme, image de Dieu: À propos Summa Theologiae, Ia, 93, 4," *Rivista di Filosofia Neo-Scolastica* 60 (1974), pp. 511–32.

32. See Jean Châtillon, "Unitas, Aequalitas, Concordia vel Connexio," in *St. Thomas Aquinas, 1274–1974: Commemorative Studies*, vol. 1 (Toronto: PIMS, 1974), pp. 337–79.

33. For a recent attempt to salvage scriptural locutions about Christ, see Thomas V. Morris, *The Logic of God Incarnate* (Ithaca: Cornell University Press, 1986). For reservations about Morris's project, especially about his understanding of becoming in the Incarnation, see the review by Thomas Weinandy, O.P., in *The Thomist* 51 (1987), pp. 367–72.

34. Esset praeterea tota evangelica narratio poetica et fabularis.

35. If what biblical narrators are claiming is not true, then biblical narrators would have to be conscious and pernicious liars. Indeed, the authoritative claims of their teaching require that we judge them by such standards. As Erich Auerbach puts it, the biblical narrator can be no "harmless liar like Homer." Instead, he would be a political liar, who deceives in the "interest of a claim to absolute authority" (*Mimesis: The Representation of Reality in Western Literature*, trans. Willard R. Trask [Princeton: Princeton University Press, 1953], p. 14).

36. See Hans Frei, *The Eclipse of Biblical Narrative: A Study of Eighteenth and Nineteenth Century Hermeneutics* (New Haven: Yale University Press, 1974). According to Frei, the Bible strives to "incorporate extra-biblical thought, experience, and reality into the true world" of scripture (p. 365). The eclipse occurs when commentators begin to do the reverse.

37. Thomas enumerates the ways in which two things can be made one: by order, composition, or mixture. The first two ways do not suit "the constitution of one nature from a plurality," while union through mixture destroys the previous natures and makes a new, third nature.

38. Directly relevant to this discussion are the previous discussions of the subordination of every human act of will to the divine will, the account of how both wills are operative yet not in the same way, and the claim that the subordination in no way impinges upon human freedom.

39. Hoc enim solummodo salvari possunt ea quae in Scripturis circa Incarnationem traduntur.

40. . . . Verbum in humana natura sicut in sibi propria facta per incarnationem subsistere ponatur; ut et corpus illud vere sit corpus Verbi Dei; et similiter anima; et Verbum Dei vere sit homo.

41. . . . organum quoddam divinitatis.

42. . . . naturam humanam ad suam subsistentiam vel personalitatem trahit.

43. . . . non enim per illam, sed in illa subsistit.

44. Nam humana natura . . . non est hypostasis, id quod in ea subsistit hypostasis est.

45. Alfred J. Freddoso, "Logic, Ontology, and Ockham's Christology," *The New Scholasticism* 57 (1983), p. 293–330.

46. Ibid., pp. 304–5.

47. *A Lexicon of St. Thomas Aquinas based on the Summa Theologiae and Selected Passages of His Other Works*, ed. Deferrari et al. (Baltimore: Catholic University of America Press, 1948).

48. Thomas proceeds to argue that the human nature in Christ did not preexist assumption by the Word but was assumed in the conception itself (IV, 43) and that the human nature was from conception perfect in body and soul (IV, 44). Otherwise, the assumption would form a second hypostasis or take up what was not yet fully human. He then clarifies certain issues concerning the role of the Holy Spirit and Mary in Christ's conception (IV, 45–48).

49. . . . probabiliter quaedam signa apparent.

50. The suggestion that the manifold evil of human life is a result of natural necessity was taken quite seriously among the *gentiles*. In the Platonic tradition, the origin of evil is traced alternately to natural and moral sources. As can be seen clearly in Plotinus, the tensions in the Platonic thesis are irresolvable. They jeopardize the goodness of the sensible world and render the union of soul and body problematic. See Plotinus's treatise "Descent of the Soul," *Enneads*, IV, 8. Plotinus's view fits nicely Ricoeur's "myth of the exiled soul," which expresses the "duality of the roots of existence." The discord in existence is chiefly seen in the conflict between body and soul. Naming the body constitutes a "purifying act of knowledge" that enables one to "perceive the self as soul" and hence to be liberated from the state of embodied conflict. See Ricoeur, *The Symbolism of Evil*, pp. 278–305.

51. . . . Deo et sua gratia supplente quod ad hoc perficiendum natura minus habebat.

52. . . . ex defectu principii superadditi principiis speciei.

53. See Romanus Cessario, O.P., *Christian Satisfaction in Aquinas: Toward a Personalist Understanding* (Washington, D.C.: University Press of America, 1982).

54. Et sic conveniens videtur ut universalis omnium causa illam creaturam in unitatem personae assumeret in qua magis communicat cum omnibus creaturis. . . . Homo etiam, cum sit creaturarum terminus, quasi omnes alias creaturas naturali generationis ordine praesupponens, convenienter primo rerum principio unitur, ut quadam circulatione perfectio rerum concludatur.

55. Si quis autem diligenter et pie incarnationis mysteria consideret, inveniet tantam sapientiae profunditatem quod omnem humanam cognitionem excedat, secundum illud Apostoli: Quod stultum est Dei, sapientia est hominibus (1 Cor. 1:25).

56. . . . neque de scientia neque de virtute praesumenti, daretur efficax auxilium contra peccatum per Christi incarnationem . . . per quam et instrueretur in dubiis, ne in cognitione deficeret; et roboraretur contra tentationum insultus, ne per infirmitatem deficeret.

57. . . . ad virtutem, per quam homo mortem fortiter sustinet, et ex caritate periculis mortis se obiicit.

58. Erant enim homines, propter superbiam, mundanae gloriae amatores. Ut igitur hominum animos ab amore mundanae gloriae in amorem divinae gloriae transmutaret, voluit mortem sustinere, non qualemcumque, sed abiectissimam.

59. . . . magna pars hominum, cultu angelorum, daemonum, et quarumcumque creaturarum praetermisso, spretis etiam voluptatibus carnis et corporalibus omnibus, ad solum Deum colendum se dedicaverunt, in quo solo beatitudinis complementum expectant.

60. MacIntyre, *After Virtue*, pp. 154–68, and *Three Rival Versions of Moral Enquiry*, pp. 82–126.

61. Milbank, *Beyond Secular Reason*, p. 360.

62. Auerbach, *Mimesis*, p. 23.

63. . . . sic et Deus congruenter alia sacramenta et praecepta ante incarnationem tradit, ad significandum futura: alia post incarnationem, ad exhibendum praesentia et rememorandum praeterita.

64. See Thomas R. Potvin, *The Theological Primacy of Christ According to St. Thomas and Its Scriptural Foundations*, Studia Friburgensia New Series 50 (Fribourg: University Press, 1973).

65. As John Milbank suggests, Christian trinitarian thought indicates that otherness need not entail conflict or exclude union (*Beyond Secular Reason*, p. 424). But he fails to note that certain philosophical teachings underlie the Christian articulation of distinction within unity. What frees the notion of otherness from dialectical conflict is at least in part Thomas's development and novel application of Aristotle's teaching that knowledge is not a confrontation but identity, actuality, and perfection. See Lonergan *Verbum*, p. 195.

66. Chenu, "Création et histoire," p. 394.

67. . . . quia Christus sua humanitate, secundum quam passus est et resurrexit, nobis et resurrectionem et vitam aeternam promeruit; sibi competit illud commune iudicium. . . . Christus in forma humanitatis iudicabit, quam omnes possint videre, tam boni quam mali. Visio autem divinitatis eius . . . a solis bonis poterit videri.

68. . . . animae torquebuntur, a naturali desiderio beatitudinis totaliter frustratae.

69. Sicut autem gloria in quam humana anima sublevatur, excedit naturalem virtutem caelestium spirituum . . . ; ita gloria resurgentium corporum excedit naturalem perfectionem caelestium corporum, ut sit maior claritas, impassibilitas firmior, agilitas facilior et dignitas naturae perfectior.

6. RECAPITULATION: THE *SUMMA CONTRA GENTILES* AS DIVINE COMEDY

1. In my thinking about comedy and tragedy, I have profited from conversations with Patrick Downey and from reading his dissertation, "Comedy and Tragedy and Their Central Importance to Philosophy and Theology" (Ph.D. diss., Boston College, 1993).

2. See Henry A. Kelly, *Ideas and Forms of Tragedy from Aristotle to the Middle Ages*, Cambridge Studies in Medieval Literature, 18 (Cambridge: Cambridge University Press, 1993).

3. Maritain, *Distinguer pour unir*, p. 15.

4. Milbank, *Beyond Secular Reason*, pp. 278–325.

5. Paul Ricoeur, *The Symbolism of Evil*, p. 219. René Girard, *Violence and the Sacred* (Baltimore: Johns Hopkins University Press, 1977), pp. 287–91.

6. Aristotle, *Metaphysics*, I, 2, and XII, 7.

7. Martha Nussbaum's influential work, *The Fragility of Goodness: Luck and Ethics in Greek Tragedy and Philosophy*, focuses upon the connection between contemporary discussions of moral luck and ethical dilemmas and Greek tragedy. She argues that fragility, contingency, and conflict are central to Aristotle's understanding of the moral life. Her view makes little sense of certain Aristotelian theses: his insistence on the truth value of moral reasoning, his description of the good life as a life of self-sufficiency, and his deliberate avoidance in the *Poetics* of tragedies that focus upon the incoherence written into the fabric of being.

8. Amelie Rorty writes, "The argument of the *Poetics* is intended to show that the best effects of tragic drama derive from its representational truthfulness rather than from ecstasy: that the turn of the plot depends on human agency rather than on demonic or divine forces. . . . It is a person's character (ethos), as determining his actions and choices, rather than any cosmic justice (dike)

or vengeance (nemesis) that determines his fate." See her "The Psychology of Aristotelian Tragedy," in *Essays on Aristotle's Poetics*, ed. A. Rorty (Princeton: Princeton University Press, 1992), p. 3.

9. Stephen A. White, in "Aristotle's Favorite Tragedies," (pp. 221–40), discusses the importance of the protagonist's "overcoming moral luck" in the tragedies praised by Aristotle.

10. Aristotle, *Nichomachean Ethics*, I. 6, I. 9, and I. 10.

11. Thomas's reference to poetry as *infima doctrina* at least concedes that it is a *doctrina*, a teaching (*Summa Theologiae*, I, 1, 9, objection 1). In the prologue to his commentary on the *Posterior Analytics*, he remarks that the goal of poetry is to "lead to virtue by a pleasing image."

12. Thomas More, *Dialogue of Comfort Against Tribulation*, chap. 13, quoted by Strauss in "On the Euthyphron," in *The Rebirth of Classical Political Rationalism*, p. 206.

13. Strauss, "On the Euthyphron," p. 206.

14. Girard, *Violence and the Sacred*, p. 287.

15. What, then, is the role of laughter in Christian narrative? As R. D. S. Jack points out, laughter arises from a recognition of the self-deceptive character of the life of fallen man (p. 163). The dominant medieval view accords well with Aquinas's understanding of sin: "vitium dicatur ex his quod est disposita contra id quod convenit suae naturae" (*Summa Theologiae*, I-II, 71, 2). "Malum . . . culpae committitur per recessum ab arte divinae sapientiae et ab ordine divinae bonitatis"; such a person is foolish and laughable (*ST*, III, 1, 1 ad 3). See also R. D. S. Jack, *Patterns of Divine Comedy*, (Suffolk: St. Edmundsbury Press, 1989), pp. 70–95, for an examination of the way medieval comedies incorporate laughter.

16. See Jack, *Patterns of Divine Comedy*, p. 138.

17. These arguments are pertinent to Nussbaum's critique of transcendence. See her "Transcending Humanity," in *Love's Knowledge*.

18. Given an understanding, such as that espoused by Strauss, of the relationship between the philosophical few and the ignorant many, there would be two human narratives, in fundamental opposition to one another. See Strauss, "The Problem of Socrates," p. 142.

19. I use the vague term "features" to avoid the claim that there is one "theory" of comedy to which all comedies must conform. I thus wish to distance my view from Frye's construction of a cosmic genre theory, unifying the whole of literature.

20. Northrop Frye, *Anatomy of Criticism* (Princeton: Princeton University Press, 1957), p. 213.

21. As Frye puts it, "comedy normally attains its happy ending through some mysterious and unexpected twist in the plot." See his *The Great Code: The Bible and Literature* (New York: Harcourt, Brace, Jovanovich, 1981), p. 156.

22. Ricoeur, *The Symbolism of Evil*, p. 231. Even though he separates the type of tragedy from the "Adamic myth," Ricoeur seems unable to escape the categories of tragedy. For a corrective, see Frye's *The Great Code*.

23. Northrop Frye, *Anatomy of Criticism: Four Essays*, p. 213.

24. Compare René Girard, *Things Hidden Since the Foundation of the World*, trans. S. Bann and M. Metteer (Stanford: Stanford University Press, 1987), p. 285. Girard sees the role of the Logos as disclosing the violence at the foundation of culture. Since the Logos is "foreign to any kind of violence . . . , it is forever expelled, an absent Logos that never has had any direct, determining influence over human cultures" (p. 271). Girard comes close to seeing the Logos as merely a negation of a negation; his denial that the Logos can inform culture would eliminate the possibility of a Christian narrative. The point of the Gospel is not merely to deconstruct the arbitrary and deceptive violence at the roots of fallen regimes, but to set up an alternative community, the Church. See the criticisms of Girard in Milbank's *Beyond Secular Reason*, pp. 392–98.

25. Jack, *Patterns of Divine Comedy*, p. 12.

26. Stanley Hauerwas, *Truthfulness and Tragedy* (Notre Dame: University of Notre Dame Press, 1977), p. 12.

27. Ricoeur, *Symbolism of Evil*, p. 324 and 328. Ricoeur fails to explore the role of comic narrative in the Judaeo-Christian scriptures and thus he can only speak of that narrative negatively, in terms of its eclipsing or undermining tragedy.

28. Northrop Frye, *T. S. Eliot: An Introduction* (Chicago: University of Chicago Press, 1963), p. 89.

29. Ibid., p. 90.

30. Sicut igitur sublimia possunt dici de homine illo ratione unionis, ut quod sit Deus, quod resuscitet mortuos . . . ; ita de Deo possunt dici humilia, ut quod sit natus de Virgine, passus, mortuus et sepultus.

31. *The Terrain of Comedy*, edited with an introduction by Louise Cowan (Dallas: Dallas Institute of Humanities and Culture, 1984), p. 15.

APPENDIX

1. Jordan, "The Protreptic Structure," p. 177. My discussion of the interpretation of the *Contra Gentiles* as a missionary work is mostly a summary of pp. 174–81 of Jordan's essay. Also see Robert Chazan, "The Barcelona 'Disputation' of 1263: Christian Missionizing and Jewish Response," *Speculum* 52 (1977), 824–42.

2. Jordan, "The Protreptic Structure," p. 182.

3. Leonard Boyle, *The Setting of the Summa Theologiae of St. Thomas* (Toronto: PIMS, 1982), p. 11.

4. Ibid., p. 16.

5. Raymundus Martinus, *Pugio Fidei adversus Mauros et Judaeos*, ed. Joseph de Voisin (Leipzig, 1587; reprinted Farnborough: Gregg, 1967), pp. 192–253.

6. Pierre Marc provides a comparison in the Introduction to *Contra Gentiles* I, pp. 62–65.

7. *Raymundiana seu Documenta*, p. 12.

8. Given the overlap between the *Contra Gentiles* and the *Pugio*, a debate arose over which work borrows from which. See Jordan's discussion of these debates in "The Protreptic Structure," p. 178, n. 20.

9. Kenny, *Aquinas on Mind*, p. 13.

10. Karl Barth, *Church Dogmatics*, trans. G. T. Thomson (Edinburgh: T. & T. Clark, 1936–1977), II, 1.

11. Bouyges, "Le plan du Contra Gentiles de S. Thomas."

12. See, for instance, F. van Steenberghen, *La Philosophie au XIII siècle* (Louvain-Paris, 1966), p. 323; 2d edition, 1991, p. 290, as well as Gauthier's comments, *Introduction* (1993), pp. 175–76. The view persists in what is otherwise an exemplary piece by Nicholas Wolterstorff, "The Migration of the Theistic Arguments: From Natural Theology to Evidentialist Apologetics," in *Rationality, Religious Belief, and Moral Commitment*, ed. R. Audi and W. Wainwright (Ithaca: Cornell University Press, 1986), p. 67.

13. Wolterstorff, "The Migration of Theistic Arguments," p. 79.

14. See Mark Jordan, *The Alleged Aristotelianism of Thomas Aquinas*, Gilson Lecture 15 (Toronto: PIMS, 1990), pp. 30–41, especially pp. 38–39.

15. Hans Frei, *The Eclipse of Biblical Narrative*, p. 365.

BIBLIOGRAPHY

ANCIENT AND MEDIEVAL AUTHORS

Thomas Aquinas. *Expositio super Dionysiam De divinis nominibus.* Turin and Rome: Marietti, 1950.

———. *Expositio super librum Boethii De Trinitate.* Leiden: Brill, 1955.

———. *In Aristotelis De Anima Commentarium,* ed. Angelus Pirotta. 4th ed. Turin and Rome: Marietti, 1965.

———. *In decem libros Ethicorum Aristotelis ad Nichomachum expositio,* ed. R. Spiazzi. Turin and Rome: Marietti, 1964.

———. *In octo libros Physicorum Aristotelis,* ed. P. M. Maggiolo. Turin and Rome: Marietti, 1965.

———. *Lectura super Johannem.* Rome: Marietti, 1952.

———. *Scriptum super libros Sententiarum,* ed. Mandonnet and Moos. Paris: Lethielleux, 1929–1933.

———. *Sententia super Metaphysicam.* Turin and Rome: Marietti, 1950.

———. *Sententia super Peri Hermeneias.* Turin and Rome: Marietti, 1955.

———. *Sententia super Posteriora Analytica.* Turin and Rome: Marietti, 1955.

———. *Summa Contra Gentiles,* ed. C. Pera, P. Marc, and P. Caramello. Turin: Marietti, 1961.

———. *Summa Contra Gentiles.* Book I, trans. A. Pegis; Book II, trans. J. F. Anderson; Book III, 2 vols., trans. V. J. Bourke; Book IV, trans. C. J. O'Neill. Notre Dame: University of Notre Dame Press, 1975.

———. *Summa Theologiae.* Turin: Marietti, 1948.

Aristotle. *Ethica Nichomachea,* ed. Bywater. Oxford: Clarendon Press, 1980.

———. *Metaphysics,* ed. Ross. Oxford: Clarendon Press, 1924.

———. *Physica,* ed. Ross. Oxford: Clarendon Press, 1950.

————. *Topica*. In *Organon Graece,* ed. Weitz, vol. 2. Leipzig, 1846, reprinted Aalen: Scientia, 1965.

Augustine. *De Doctrina Christiana,* ed. Martin. Corpus Christianorum Series Latina, vol. 32. Turnhout: Brepols, 1972.

Raymundus Martinus. *Pugio Fidei adversus Mauros et Judaeos,* ed. Joseph de Voisin. Leipzig, 1587; reprinted Farnborough: Gregg, 1967.

Raymond of Penafort. *Raymundiana seu Documenta quae pertinent ad S. Raymundi de Pennaforti vitam et scripta.* Monumenta ordinis Fr. Praed. historica, VI, 1, ed. Balme and Paban. Rome: 1898.

MODERN AUTHORS

Aertsen, Jan. *Nature and Creature: St. Thomas Aquinas's Way of Thought,* trans. H. D. Morton. Leiden: E. J. Brill, 1988.

Allard, Guy H. "Le 'Contra Gentiles' et le modèle rhétorique." *Laval Théologique et Philosophique* 30 (1974): 237–50.

Alston, William. "Divine and Human Action." In *Divine and Human Action,* ed. T. Morris, pp. 257–80. Ithaca: Cornell University Press, 1988.

————. "Functionalism and Theological Language." *American Philosophical Quarterly* 22 (1985): 221–30.

Arendt, Hannah. *The Human Condition.* Chicago: University of Chicago Press, 1958.

Auerbach, Erich. *Mimesis: The Representation of Reality in Western Literature,* trans. Willard R. Trask. Princeton: Princeton University Press, 1953.

Balthasar, N., and A. Simonet. "Le plan de la Somme contre les Gentiles de saint Thomas d'Aquin." *Revue néo-scolastique de philosophie* 32 (1930): 183–214.

Barnes, Jonathan. "Aristotle's Theory of Demonstration." *Phronesis* 14 (1969): 123–52.

————. "Proof and Syllogism." In *Aristotle on Science: The Posterior Analytics,* pp. 17–59. Padua: Editrice Antenore, 1981.

Barth, Karl. *Church Dogmatics,* trans. G. T. Thomson. Edinburgh: T. & T. Clark, 1936–1977.

Blanche, M. "Note." *Revue de Philosophie* 24 (1924): 444–49.

Blanchette, Olivia. *The Perfection of the Universe According to Aquinas: A Teleological Cosmology.* University Park: Pennsylvania State University, 1992.

Bouillard, Henri. *Conversion et grâce chez Thomas d'Aquin.* Paris: Aubier, 1944.

Bouyges, Maurice. "Le plan du Contra Gentiles de S. Thomas." *Archives de Philosophie* 3 (1925): 176–97.

Boyle, Leonard. *The Setting of the Summa Theologiae of St. Thomas.* Toronto: PIMS, 1982.

Brock, Stephen. "The 'ratio omnipotentiae' in Aquinas." *Acta Philosophica* 1 (1993): 17–42.

Broglie, Guy de. "De la place du surnaturel dans la philosophie de saint Thomas." *Recherches de science religieuse* 14 (1924): 193–246 and pp. 481–96; 15 (1925): 5–53.

Burnyeat, Miles. "Is an Aristotelian Philosophy of Mind Still Credible?" In *Essays on Aristotle's De Anima,* ed. A. Rorty and M. Nussbaum, pp. 1–26. Oxford: Clarendon Press, 1992.

Burrell, David. *Aquinas: God and Action.* Notre Dame: University of Notre Dame Press, 1979.

———. *Knowing the Unknowable God: Ibn-Sina, Maimonides, and Aquinas.* Notre Dame: University of Notre Dame Press, 1986.

Caputo, John. *Heidegger and Aquinas: An Essay on the Overcoming of Metaphysics.* New York: Fordham University Press, 1982.

Cessario, Romanus, O.P. *Christian Satisfaction in Aquinas: Toward a Personalist Understanding.* Washington, D.C.: University Press of America, 1982.

Châtillon, Jean. "Unitas, Aequalitas, Concordia vel Connexio." In *St. Thomas Aquinas 1274–1974: Commemorative Studies,* vol. 1, pp. 337–79. Toronto: PIMS, 1974.

Chazan, Robert. "The Barcelona 'Disputation' of 1263: Christian Missionizing and Jewish Response." *Speculum* 52 (1977): 824–42.

Chenu, M. D. *Introduction à l'étude de Saint Thomas d'Aquin.* Paris: J. Vrin, 1954.

———. *La théologie au douzième siècle.* Études Philosophie Médiévale, 3d ed. Paris: J. Vrin, 1976.

———. *La théologie comme science au XIII siècle.* 3d ed. Paris: J. Vrin, 1957.

———. "Création et histoire." In *St. Thomas Aquinas, 1274–1974: Commemorative Studies,* vol. 2, pp. 391–400. Toronto: PIMS, 1974.

Cleary, John. "On the Terminology 'Abstraction' in Aristotle." *Phronesis* 32 (1985): 13–45.

Corbin, M. *Le chemin de la théologie chez Thomas d'Aquin.* Paris: Beauchesne, 1972.

Corsini, E. *Il trattato "De Divinis nominibus" dello Pseudo-Dionigi e i commenti neoplatonici al Parmenide.* Turin, 1962.

Coulter, Gregory. "Aquinas on the Identity of Mind and Substantial Form." *Proceedings of the American Catholic Philosophical Association* 64 (1990): 161–79.

Cowan, Louise, ed. *The Terrain of Comedy.* Dallas: Dallas Institute of Humanities and Culture, 1984.

D'Andrea, Thomas. "Rethinking the Christian Philosophy Debate: An Old Puzzle and Some New Points of Orientation." *Acta Philosophica* 1 (1992): 191–214.

Deferrari et al. ed. *A Lexicon of St. Thomas Aquinas Based on the Summa Theologiae and Selected Passages of His Other Works.* Washington, D.C.: Catholic University of America Press, 1948.

Dewan, Lawrence, O.P. "St. Thomas, Aristotle, and Creation." *Dionysius* 15 (1991): 81–90.

Donnelly, Phillip J. "Discussions on the Supernatural Order." *Theological Studies* 9 (1948): 213–49.

Downey, Patrick. "Comedy and Tragedy and Their Central Importance for Philosophy and Theology." Ph.D. diss. Boston College, 1993.

Dunne, Joseph. *Back to the Rough Ground.* Notre Dame: University of Notre Dame Press, 1993.

Eco, Umberto. *The Aesthetics of Thomas Aquinas.* Cambridge: Harvard University Press, 1988; previously published as *Il problema estetico in Tomasso d'Aquino,* Milan: 1956 and 1970.

Fabro, Cornelio. *Participation et causalité selon St. Thomas D'Aquin,* pp. 381–97. Paris: Éditions Béatrice Nauwelaerts, 1961.

———. "The Intensive Hermeneutics of Thomistic Philosophy." *Review of Metaphysics* 27 (1974) 449–91.

———. "The Problem of Being and the Destiny of Man." *International Philosophical Quarterly* 1 (1961): 408–36.

———. "The Transcendentality of Ens-Esse and the Ground of Metaphysics." *International Philosophical Quarterly* 6 (1966): 389–427.

Feret, H. M. Review of N. Balthasar and A. Simonet. *Bulletin Thomiste.* 3 (1930–33): 105–12.

Finnis, John. *Natural Law and Natural Rights.* Oxford: Clarendon Press, 1980.

———. "Practical Reasoning, Human Goods, and the End of Man." *Proceedings of the American Catholic Philosophical Association* 58 (1987): 99–151.

Flint, Thomas. "Two Accounts of Providence." In *Divine and Human Action,* ed. Thomas Morris, pp. 147–81. Ithaca: Cornell University Press, 1988.

Fogelin, Robert J. "A Reading of Aquinas's Five Ways." *American Philosophical Quarterly* 27 (1990): 305–13.

Fortin, Ernest. Review of John Finnis's *Natural Law and Natural Rights. Review of Politics* 44 (1982): 590–612.

Frank, Daniel H. "The End of the Guide: Maimonides on the Best Life for Man." *Judaism* 34 (1985): 485–95.

Freddoso, Alfred J. "Medieval Aristotelianism and the Case Against Secondary Causation in Nature." In *Divine and Human Action,* ed. Thomas Morris, pp. 74–118. Ithaca: Cornell University Press, 1988.

———. "Logic, Ontology, and Ockham's Christology." *The New Scholasticism* 57 (1983): 293–330.

Frei, Hans. *The Eclipse of Biblical Narrative: A Study of Eighteenth and Nineteenth Century Hermeneutics.* New Haven: Yale University Press, 1974.

Frye, Northrop. *Anatomy of Criticism.* Princeton: Princeton University Press, 1957.

———. *The Great Code: The Bible and Literature.* New York: Harcourt, Brace, Jovanovich, 1981.

————. *T. S. Eliot: An Introduction.* Chicago: University of Chicago Press, 1963.

Funkenstein, Amos. *Theology and Scientific Imagination.* Princeton: Princeton University Press, 1986.

Garcia, Laura. "Divine Freedom and Creation." *Philosophical Quarterly* 42 (1992): 191–213.

Gardet, L. "La connaissance que Thomas d'Aquin put avoir du monde islamique." In *St. Thomas and the Problems of His Time,* ed. G. Verbeke and R. Verhelst, pp. 139–49. Louvain: Publications Universitaires, 1974.

Gauthier, R. A. *Introduction historique au tome I de l'edition bilingue de la Summa contra Gentiles,* pp. 7–123. Paris: P. Lethielleux, 1961.

————. *Introduction to Somme Contre les Gentiles,* Collection Philosophie Européenne dirigée par Henri Hude. Paris: Editions Universitaires, 1993.

————. *La morale d'Aristote.* Paris, 1958.

————. Préface to *Sententia libri de anima, Leonine edition.* Paris: J. Vrin, 1984.

Geach, Peter. "Omnipotence." In *Providence and Evil,* pp. 3–28. Cambridge: Cambridge University Press, 1977.

Geiger, Louis B. "L'homme, image de Dieu: À propos Summa Theologiae, Ia, 93, 4." *Rivista Filosofia Neo-Scolastica* 60 (1974): 511–32.

Gersh, Stephen. *From Iamblichus to Eriugena: An Investigation of the Prehistory and Evolution of the Pseudo-Dionysian Tradition.* Leiden: E. J. Brill, 1978.

Gilson, Étienne. *Being and Some Philosophers.* Toronto: PIMS, 1952.

————. *The Elements of Christian Philosophy.* Garden City: Doubleday, 1960.

————. *The Spirit of Medieval Philosophy,* trans. A. H. C. Downes. London: Sheed and Ward, 1936.

————. *Le Thomisme: Introduction à la philosophie de saint Thomas d'Aquin.* Paris: J. Vrin, 1944.

Girard, René. *Things Hidden Since the Foundation of the World,* trans. S. Bann and M. Metteer. Stanford: Stanford University Press, 1987.

————. *Violence and the Sacred.* Baltimore: Johns Hopkins University Press, 1977.

Gorce, M. M. "La lutte 'contre Gentiles' à Paris." In *Mélanges Mandonnet* I, pp. 230–43. Paris: J. Vrin, 1930.

Grégoire, H., and P. Orgeils. *Paganus: Étude de sémantique et d'histoire,* in *Mélanges Georges Smets.* Brussels, 1952.

Guindon, R. *Béatitude et théologie morale chez Saint Thomas d'Aquin.* Montreal: Editions de l'Université d'Ottawa, 1956.

Harre, R., and E. H. Madden. *Causal Powers: A Theory of Natural Necessity.* Oxford: Basil Blackwell, 1975.

Hauerwas, Stanley. *Truthfulness and Tragedy.* Notre Dame: University of Notre Dame Press, 1977.

Hayden, Dunstan. "Notes on Aristotelian Dialectic in Theological Method." *The Thomist* 20 (1957): 383–418.

Helm, Paul. *Eternal God*. Oxford: Clarendon, 1988.

Hudson, Deal W. "Contemporary Views of Happiness." In *The Great Ideas Today*, pp. 170–216. Chicago: Encyclopaedia Britannica, 1992.

Hughes, Christopher. *On a Complex Theory of a Simple God: An Investigation in Aquinas' Philosophical Theology*. Ithaca: Cornell University Press, 1989.

Irwin, Terence. *Aristotle's First Principles*. Oxford: Clarendon Press, 1988.

Jack, R. D. S. *Patterns of Divine Comedy*. Suffolk: St. Edmundsbury Press, 1989.

Johnson, Mark. "Did St. Thomas Attribute a Doctrine of Creation to Aristotle?" *New Scholasticism* 63 (1989): 129–55.

Jordan, Mark. *The Alleged Aristotelianism of Thomas Aquinas*. Gilson Lecture 15. Toronto: PIMS, 1992.

———. "The Evidence of the Transcendentals and the Place of Beauty in Thomas Aquinas." *International Philosophical Quarterly* 29 (1989): 393–406.

———. "The Names of God and the Being of Names." In *The Existence and Nature of God*, ed. Alfred Freddoso pp. 161–90. Notre Dame: University of Notre Dame Press, 1983.

———. "The Protreptic Structure of the Summa Contra Gentiles." *The Thomist* 50 (1986): 173–209.

Kelly, Henry. *Ideas and Forms of Tragedy from Aristotle to the Middle Ages*. Cambridge Studies in Medieval Literature, 18. Cambridge: Cambridge University Press, 1993.

Kenny, Anthony. *Aquinas on Mind*. London: Routledge, 1993.

———. *The Five Ways*. London: Routledge and Kegan Paul, 1969.

Klein, Jacob. *A Commentary on Plato's Meno*. Chapel Hill: University of North Carolina Press, 1965.

Koninck, Charles de. "Abstraction from Matter." *Laval Théologique et Philosophique* 13 (1957): 133–96, and 16 (1960): 53–69, 169–88.

Kovach, Francis J. *Die Aesthetik von Aquin*. Berlin: De Gruyter, 1961.

Kretzman, Norman, and Timothy O'Connor. Review of Christopher Hughes's *On a Complex Theory*. In *Faith and Philosophy* 9 (1992): 526–34.

Lachtermann, David. *Ethics of Geometry: A Genealogy of Modernity*. New York: Routledge, 1989.

Lafont, Ghislain. *Structures et méthode dans la Somme théologique de saint Thomas d'Aquin*. Paris: Desclée de Brouwer, 1961.

Laporta, Jorge. *La Destinée de la nature humaine selon Thomas d'Aquin*. Paris: J. Vrin, 1965.

Lesher, James. "The Meaning of NOUS in the Posterior Analytics." *Phronesis* 18 (1973): 44–68.

Lindbeck, G. "Participation and Existence in the Interpretation of St. Thomas Aquinas." *Franciscan Studies* 17 (1957): 1–22, 107–25.

Lonergan, Bernard. *Grace and Freedom: Operative Grace in the Thought of St. Thomas Aquinas*, ed. J. Patout Burns. New York: Herder and Herder, 1971.

————. *Verbum: Word and Idea in Aquinas,* ed. David Burrell. Notre Dame: University of Notre Dame Press, 1967.

Lubac, Henri de. *Surnaturel.* Paris: Aubier, 1946.

McInerny, Ralph. *Aquinas against the Averroists: On There Being Only One Intellect.* West Lafayette, Ind.: Purdue University Press, 1993.

————. *The Logic of Analogy: An Interpretation of St. Thomas.* The Hague: M. Nijhoff, 1961.

————. *The Question of Christian Ethics.* Washington, D.C.: Catholic University of America Press, 1993.

————. "Aquinas on Divine Omnipotence." In *L'Homme et sons univers au moyen âge. Actes du septième congrès international de philosophie médiévale,* ed. C. Wenin, pp. 440–44. Louvain-la-Neuve: Institut Supérieur de Philosophie, 1986.

MacIntyre, Alasdair. *After Virtue.* Notre Dame: University of Notre Dame Press, 1984.

————. *Three Rival Versions of Moral Enquiry.* Notre Dame: University of Notre Dame Press, 1990.

————. *Whose Justice? Which Rationality?* Notre Dame: University of Notre Dame Press, 1988.

Mackey, Louis. *Kierkegaard: A Kind of Poet.* Philadelphia: University of Pennsylvania Press, 1971.

————. "Entreatments of God: Reflections on Aquinas' Five Ways." In *Franciscan Studies* 37 (1977): 105–19.

Madigan, Arthur. "Varieties of Aristotelian Dialectic." Unpublished Essay.

Marc, Pierre. *Summa Contra Gentiles,* vol. 1. Turin: Marietti, 1967.

Marion, Jean-Luc. *L'idole et la distance: Cinq études.* Paris: Bernard Grasset, 1977.

Maritain, Jacques. *Distinguer pour unir ou les degrés du savoir.* Paris: Desclée de Brouwer, 1946.

Matthys, M. "Quid ratio naturalis doceat de possibilitate visionis beatae secundum S. Thomam in summa contra gentiles." *Divus Thomas* (Piacenza) 39 (1936): 201–28.

Maurer, Armand A. *About Beauty.* Houston: The Center for Thomistic Studies, 1983.

————. "St. Thomas on the Sacred Name 'Tetragrammaton'." *Mediaeval Studies* 34 (1972): 275–86.

Ménard, Etienne. *La tradition: Révélation, Ecriture, Eglise selon saint Thomas d'Aquin.* Studia 18. Paris: Desclée de Brouwer, 1964.

Merriell, D. Juvenal. *To the Image of the Trinity.* Toronto: PIMS, 1990.

Milbank, John. *Theology and Social Theory: Beyond Secular Reason.* Oxford: Basil Blackwell, 1990.

Modrak, Deborah. *Aristotle: The Power of Perception.* Chicago: University of Chicago Press, 1987.

————. "The Nous-Body Problem in Aristotle." *Review of Metaphysics* 44 (1991): 755–74.

Mohammed, Ovey N. *Averröes' Doctrine of Immortality.* Waterloo: Wilfred Laurier University Press, 1984.

Mondin, Battista. "Il principio 'omne agens simile sibi' e l'analogia dei nomi divini nel pensiero di S. Tomasso D'Aquino." *Divus Thomas* (Piacenza) 63 (1960): 336–48.

Morris, Thomas V. *The Logic of God Incarnate.* Ithaca: Cornell University Press, 1986.

Mulard, R. "Désir naturel de connaître et vision béatifique." *Revue des sciences philosophiques et théologiques* 14 (1925): 5–19.

Nussbaum, Martha. *Aristotle's De Motu Animalium: Text with Translation and Interpretive Essays.* Princeton: Princeton University Press, 1978.

————. *The Fragility of Goodness: Luck and Ethics in Greek Tragedy and Philosophy.* Cambridge: Cambridge University Press, 1986.

————. *Love's Knowledge.* Oxford: Oxford University Press, 1990.

————and H. Putnam. "Changing Aristotle's Mind." In *Essays on Aristotle's De Anima,* ed. A. Rorty and M. Nussbaum, pp. 27–56. Oxford: Clarendon Press, 1992.

Oeullet, Marc. "Paradox and/or Supernatural Existential." *Communio* 18 (1991): 259–80.

O'Rourke, Fran. *Pseudo-Dionysius and the Metaphysics of Aquinas.* Leiden: E. J. Brill, 1992.

Owen, G. E. L. "Tithenai ta phainomena." In *Aristote et les problèmes de méthode.* Louvain, 1961.

Owens, Joseph. *The Doctrine of Being in the Aristotelian Metaphysics.* 2d ed. Toronto: PIMS, 1963.

————. *St. Thomas Aquinas on the Existence of God: The Collected Papers of Joseph Owens,* ed. John R. Catan. Albany: SUNY Press, 1980.

————. "The Inseparability of the Soul from Existence." *New Scholasticism* 1987 (61): 249–70.

Péghaire, Julien. "L'axiome Bonum est diffusivum sui dans le néoplatonisme et le thomisme." *Revue de l'Université d'Ottawa* 1 (1932), Section Spéciale, pp. 5–30.

Pegis, Anton. *At the Origins of the Thomistic Notion of Man.* St. Augustine Lecture, 1963. New York: Macmillan, 1963.

————. "Nature and Spirit: Some Reflections on the Problem of the End of Man." *Proceedings of the American Catholic Philosophical Association* 23 (1949): 62–79.

————. "Penitus manet ignotum." *Mediaevil Studies* 27 (1965): 212–26.

————. "Qu'est-ce que la Summa contra Gentiles." In *L'Homme devant Dieu: Mélanges . . . de Lubac,* pp. 169–82. Paris: Aubier, 1964.

———. "St Thomas and the Nichomachean Ethics." *Medieval Studies* 25 (1963): 1–25.

———. "The Separated Soul and Its Nature in St. Thomas." In *St. Thomas Aquinas, 1274–1974: Commemorative Studies,* vol. 1: 131–59 Toronto: PIMS, 1974.

Pelikan, Jaroslav. "The Doctrine of the Filioque in Thomas Aquinas and Its Patristic Antecedents: An Analysis of Summa Theologiae, Part I, Question 36." In *St. Thomas Aquinas, 1274–1974: Commemorative Studies,* vol. 1: 315–36. Toronto: PIMS, 1974.

Pieper, Josef. *Happiness and Contemplation,* trans. Richard and Clara Winston. New York: Pantheon Books, 1958.

———. *Philosophia Negativa: Zwei Versuche über Thomas von Aquin.* Munich: Kösel-Verlag, 1953.

———. *The Silence of St. Thomas: Three Essays,* trans. J. Murray and D. O'Connor. New York: Pantheon Books, 1957.

Plantinga, Alvin. *Does God Have a Nature?* Milwaukee: Marquette University Press, 1980.

Potvin, Thomas R. *The Theological Primacy of Christ According to St. Thomas and Its Scriptural Foundations.* Studia Friburgensia, New Series 50. Fribourg: University Press, 1973.

Pritzl, Kurt. "Aristotle: Ways of Truth and Ways of Opinion." *Proceedings of the American Catholic Philosophical Association* 67 (1993): 241–52.

Richard, Robert L., S. J. *The Problem of an Apologetical Perspective in the Trinitarian Theology of St. Thomas Aquinas.* Rome: Gregorian University Press, 1963.

Ricoeur, Paul. *The Symbolism of Evil,* trans. E. Buchanan, New York: Harper, 1967.

Riet, Simone Van. "Le Somme contre les Gentils and la polémique islamo-chrétienne." In *St Thomas and the Problems of His Time,* ed. G. Verbeke and R. Verhelst, pp. 150–60. Louvain: Publications Universitaires, 1974.

Roques, René. *La Hiérarchie Céleste.* Paris: Éditions du Cerf, 1970.

Rorty, Amelie. "The Psychology of Aristotelian Tragedy." In *Essays on Aristotle's Poetics,* ed. by A. Rorty, pp. 1–22. London: Princeton University Press, 1992.

Ross, James. "Creation II." In *Divine and Human Action,* ed. Thomas Morris, pp. 115–40. Ithaca: Cornell University Press, 1988.

Sallis, John. *Being and Logos: The Way of the Platonic Dialogue* Atlantic Highlands, N. J.: Humanities Press International.

Salman, David. "Sur la lutte contra Gentiles de S. Thomas." *Divus Thomas* (Piacenza) 40 (1937): 488–509.

Smith, Gerard. "Philosophy and the Unity of Man's Ultimate End" *Proceedings of the American Catholic Philosophical Association* 27 (1953): 60–83.

Staley, Kevin. "Happiness: The Natural End of Man?" *The Thomist* 53 (1989): 215–34.

Steenberghen, F. van. *La Philosophie au XIII siècle*. Louvain-Paris, 1966; 2d edition, 1991.

Strauss, Leo. *Persecution and the Art of Writing*. Glencoe: The Free Press, 1952.

————. "How to Begin to Study Medieval Philosophy." In *The Rebirth of Classical Political Rationalism*, ed. Thomas L. Pangle, pp. 207–26. Chicago: University of Chicago Press, 1989.

————. "The Literary Character of the Guide for the Perplexed." In *Maimonides: A Collection of Critical Essays*, ed. J. A. Biuys, pp. 59–70. Notre Dame: University of Notre Dame Press, 1988.

————. "The Mutual Influence of Philosophy and Theology." *Independent Journal of Philosophy* 3 (1979): 111–18.

————. "On the Euthyphron." In *The Rebirth of Classical Political Rationalism*, ed. Thomas L. Pangle, pp. 187–206. Chicago: University of Chicago Press, 1989.

————. "The Problem of Socrates: Five Lectures." In *The Rebirth of Classical Political Rationalism*, ed. Thomas L. Pangle, pp. 103–83. Chicago: University of Chicago Press, 1989.

Stump, E., and N. Kretzman, "Absolute Simplicity." *Faith and Philosophy* 2 (1985): 353–82.

————. "Eternity, Awareness, and Action." *Faith and Philosophy* 9 (1992): 463–82.

Suermondt, Clément. *Tabulae Schematicae . . . Summae Theologiae et Summae contra Gentiles S. Thomae Aquinatis*. Rome, 1943; reprinted in *Opera Omnia*, ed. Leonine, vol. 16, Rome, 1948.

Sullivan, John E. *The Image of God: The Doctrine of St. Augustine and Its Influence*. Dubuque: Priory Press, 1963.

Tugwell, Simon. Introduction to *Early Dominicans: Selected Writings*, pp. 1–47. Classics of Western Spirituality. New York: Paulist Press, 1982.

Vagaggini, Cyprian. "Le hatise des rationes necessariae de saint Anselm dans la théologie des processions trinitaires de saint Thomas," trans. J. Evrad. In *Spicilegium Beccense. Congrès International du ix centenaire de l'arrivée d'Anselme au Bec*, pp. 103–39. Paris: J. Vrin, 1959.

Vogel, C. J. de. "'Ego sum qui sum' et sa signification pour une philosophie chrétienne." *Revue des Sciences Religieuses* 35 (1961): 346–53.

Wawrykow, Joseph. "'Merit' in the Theology of Thomas Aquinas." *Medieval Philosophy and Theology* 2 (1992): 97–116.

Weinandy, Thomas. Review of Thomas Morris's *The Logic of God Incarnate*. *The Thomist* 51 (1987): 367–72.

Weisheipl, James. *Friar Thomas D'Aquino: His Life, Thought, and Works*. Washington, D.C.: Catholic University of America Press, 1983.

White, Stephen. "Aristotle's Favorite Tragedies." In *Essays on Aristotle's Poetics*, ed. A. Rorty, pp. 221–40. London: Princeton University Press, 1992.

                                                          237

Wians, William. "Aristotle, Demonstration, and Teaching." *Ancient Philosophy* 9 (1989): 245–53.

Wippel, John. "Thomas Aquinas and the Problem of Christian Philosophy." Chapter 1 of *Metaphysical Themes in Thomas Aquinas,* pp. 1–33. Washington, D.C.: Catholic University of America Press, 1984.

Wolterstorff, Nicholas. "The Migration of the Theistic Arguments: From Natural Theology to Evidentialist Apologetics." In *Rationality, Religious Belief, and Moral Commitment,* ed. R. Audi and W. Wainwright, pp. 38–81. Ithaca: Cornell University Press, 1986.

Wood, Robert. "Image, Structure, and Content: On a Passage in Plato's Republic." *Review of Metaphysics* 40 (1987): 495–514.

INDEX OF NAMES

INDEX OF TOPICS